...MEN AT WORK

SECOND EDITION

Sociology for a New Century

A PINE FORGE PRESS SERIES

Edited by Charles Ragin, Wendy Griswold, and Walter W. Powell
Founding Editors: Charles Ragin, Wendy Griswold, Larry Griffin

Sociology for a New Century brings the best current scholarship to today's students in a series of short texts authored by leaders of a new generation of social scientists. Each book addresses its subject from a comparative, historical, and global perspective, and, in doing so, connects social science to the wider concerns of students seeking to make sense of our dramatically changing world.

SOCIOLOGY FOR A NEW CENTURY

WOMEN AND MEN AT WORK

SECOND EDITION

◆

IRENE PADAVIC
Florida State University

BARBARA RESKIN
Harvard University

PINE FORGE PRESS
An Imprint of Sage Publications, Inc.
Thousand Oaks • London • New Delhi

For information:

Pine Forge Press
An imprint of Sage Publications, Inc.
2455 Teller Road
Thousand Oaks, California 91320
E-mail: order@sagepub.com

Sage Publications Ltd.
6 Bonhill Street
London EC2A 4PU
United Kingdom

Sage Publications India Pvt. Ltd.
M-32 Market
Greater Kailash I
New Delhi 110 048 India

Printed in the United States of America

Library of Congress Cataloging-in-Publication Data

Padavic, Irene
    Women and men at work / By Irene Padavic and Barbara Reskin.—2nd ed.
    p. cm— (Sociology for a new century)
Includes bibliographical references (p.) and index.
    ISBN 978-0-7619-8710-9
    1. Sex discrimination in employment—United States.
    2. Women—Employment—United States. 3. Men—Employment—United States.
I. Padavic, Irene. II. Title. III. Series.
    HD6060.5.U5 R47 2002
    331.13'3'0973—dc21
    2002005212

10 9 8 7 6 5

Acquisitions Editor:	Jerry Westby
Editorial Assistant:	Vonessa Vondera
Production Editor:	Diana E. Axelsen
Typesetter/Designer:	C&M Digitals (P) Ltd., Chennai, India
Indexer:	Jee Young Kim and Linda Lee Eling
Cover Designer:	Sandra Ng

Contents

About the Authors

Irene Padavic is Associate Professor at Florida State University. Before becoming a professor, she worked in a variety of service-sector jobs: candy seller at a movie theater, waitperson, telephone solicitor, door-to-door promoter of real estate, paralegal, and marketing researcher. Her dissertation project provided experience in the industrial sector, where she worked as a coal handler in a power plant. Her research has been in the areas of gender and work, race differences in campus peer culture, economic restructuring, and changes in child care arrangements.

Barbara Reskin is Professor of Sociology at Harvard University and, when this book went to press, was president of the American Sociological Association. As a student, she supported herself in a series of female-dominated clerical jobs in such disparate settings as radio and TV stations, trucking firms, temp agencies, insurance companies, and universities. The fact that most jobs for women were boring, low paying, and dead-end encouraged her to get a Ph.D. Her research examines how workers' sex, race, and ethnicity affect their work opportunities. She is especially interested in strategies that minimize discrimination, the focus of her most recent book, *The Realities of Affirmative Action*.

For Randy and Robin
—Irene

For Joan, Lynn, and Naomi
—Barbara

Preface

A look at jobs advertised in an urban newspaper from the middle of the last century[1] provides a startling contrast to contemporary help wanted ads. Alongside reasonable requirements, employers frequently specified workers' sex, race, age, and other attributes that had no bearing on job performance.

Gender was so structured into jobs that employers and newspapers published separate listings for men and women. These sex-segregated want ads were standard until the 1970s, when members of the National Organization for Women threatened to sue the Equal Employment Opportunity Commission to force it to abide by the 1964 antidiscrimination law outlawing sex segregation.

Consider some job requirements from the "Help Wanted—Men" columns:

- Barber: Colored, experienced. Cavalry Detachment Barber Shop, Ft. Myer.

- Bartender: Middle-aged, sober.

- Driver: White, age 24–35. Must know city. Neat appearance. Good traffic record.

- Truck drivers and helpers: Must be experienced in handling furniture; must be willing to work and have good references.

The "Help Wanted—Women" section tended to be more specific regarding the kind of workers employers sought:

- Airline Hostesses for TransWorld Airlines: High school graduate, age 20 to 27, height 5'2" to 5'8", weight 100 to 135, attractive, unmarried. Apply in person.

- Cashier-Food Checker: White, middle-aged woman, honest, alert, intelligent. Experience in cashiering or food checking.

- File Clerk: White, attractive, typing required, PBX experience helpful.

- Fountain girl: White, for downtown drugstore; references.

- Secretary: Real estate office has opening for experienced secretary under 40.

The difference in the kinds of jobs men and women did can also be seen in the pay and working conditions that some ads specified. Most flagrant were pay differences. For example, an employment agency placed an identical listing for an "accountant-bookkeeper" in both sexes' columns, specifying a rate of $75 to $125 per week in the men's column and $65 to $100 a week in the women's. The work hours that ads listed for both sexes were typically 9 to 5, 5 days a week where employers were looking for white workers. In contrast, ads for female African American domestic workers described more extensive hours:

- G.H.W. [general house work]: Colored girl to live in; good with children. Age 18 to 30. Off Sun. and half day Thurs. $20 wk.

- Colored. Live In: modern home, private room and bath. Care of 1 child; must be able to iron men's shirts; other help. Wednesday and every other Sun. off. Salary depending on experience and willingness to assume other duties.

U.S. society has come a long way since the days of "colored barbers" and "white fountain girls." In 1964, Congress outlawed employment discrimination on the basis of race, color, national origin, religion, and sex, except in small firms.[2] As a result of this legislation, newspapers eventually got rid of sex-segregated classified ads and stopped mentioning race in them. And, little by little, some employers began hiring women in formerly all-male jobs.

Openly labeling jobs as men's or women's work—as was the practice 40 years ago—signals a highly segregated workforce and legitimizes assigning jobs based on workers' sex. But eliminating these labels does not ensure that jobs are available to anyone who is qualified. Even without the sex-segregated classified ads, most Americans can still readily distinguish "women's jobs" from "men's jobs," and millions of Americans still work in sex-segregated jobs. Among the jobs listed earlier, for example, secretary is still overwhelmingly female and truck driver overwhelmingly male. And jobs that are mostly male still pay more than jobs that are mostly female.

Comparing classified ads from the 1950s with contemporary help-wanted listings suggests that explicit sex inequality at work is not a constant. Its presence and extent vary tremendously, not only over time, but also across work settings. When hiring workers, some contemporary employers care about only work-related qualifications and treat female and male employees equally. Others do not. Examining the reasons for this variability in inequality is an important focus of this book. This focus—along with new data and updated scholarship—is the chief way that this edition differs from the previous one. We argue that the amount of sex inequality in a workplace depends on how employers organize work, the tasks involved, organizational leadership, and the existence of external pressures, among other factors. The chapters that follow illustrate the variation in sex inequality across places of work and review evidence about factors that are thought to heighten or reduce sex differentiation at work.

Chapter 1 examines what work is and discusses the three components of what we call "gendered work"—the sexual division of labor, the devaluation of women's work, and the construction of gender on the job—processes that we return to throughout the book. Chapter 2 provides a historical context for gendered work in the Western world. It analyzes the effects of industrialization and the evolution of the labor force. It also moves beyond a Western focus to examine the sexual division of labor in other geographic areas. Chapter 3 provides an overview of sex inequality in the workplace and introduces several general explanations for sex inequality that the following chapters assess.

Chapter 4 focuses on workers' segregation into different kinds of work on the basis of their sex, as well as their race and ethnicity. It also examines the causes of segregation and the mechanisms that affect its level. Chapter 5 looks at two expressions of *hierarchical* sex segregation in the workplace—differences in opportunities to move up and differences in the opportunity to exercise authority—and evaluates possible reasons for these differences. Chapter 6 focuses on the pay gap between the sexes, comparing men of color and all women to non-Hispanic white men in their average earnings, assessing trends in the earnings ratio for the sexes, evaluating explanations for the pay gap, and discussing strategies to reduce it. Chapter 7 examines work-family conflicts as well as the conflict that employed women and men face in trying to equitably distribute household tasks. It considers what government and employers can do and are doing to deal with the problems workers confront in combining paid and family work.

Notes

1. The August 23, 1956, Washington, D.C., *Evening Star*.
2. Subsequently Congress also outlawed age and disability discrimination.

Acknowledgments

This book is the product of the work of many people. We are indebted to the scholars whose ideas helped to shape our own and whom we cite in the pages that follow; to those students and colleagues who make our work fun; and to our friends who offered encouragement when we were ready to abandon this project, assume new identities, and leave town. That these groups are too large for us to thank by name does not diminish our indebtedness or gratitude. Among those who helped materially in our finishing this book are Suzanne Bianchi, Bill Bielby, Karin Brewster, Naomi Cassirer, Catalyst, Jan Combopiano, Marie Cowart, Julia Drisdell, Randy Earnest, Henry Eliassen, Robin Ely, Dorothy Friendly, Laura Geschwender, Lowell Hargens, Darlene Iskra, Jerry Jacobs, Matt Kaliner, staff of the Henry A. Murray Center, Jean Pyle, Radcliffe Institute for Advanced Study, John Reynolds, Steve Rutter, Liana Sayer, Annamette Sorensen, Jillaine Tyson, Vonessa Vondera, and Jerry Westby. Our greatest thanks go to Carrie Conaway, whose thoroughness and dedication in updating facts and figures was vital to our completing this revision.

1

Work and Gender

Underpinning all human activity is work. We spend most of our lives either preparing for work, working, or resting from work. Even when we are simply watching daytime talk shows, the evening news, or Monday night football on TV, we are enjoying the results of the labor of others. The workers who bring these television shows to millions of viewers include executives and administrators, personnel managers, advertising agents, writers and editors, producers and directors, newscasters and announcers, actors and musicians, production engineers, camera operators, electrical technicians, computer programmers, clerks and word processors, and maintenance workers. Fifty years ago, neither royalty nor oil barons could summon up the labor of so many thousands simply to entertain them.

Just as we take for granted the air we breathe, we take for granted the work that creates the world around us. This book aims to make that work visible so we can examine the work that women and men do and explore how workers, the workplace, and work are often permeated with gendered meanings.

What Work Is

Although people use the term *work* in many ways ("working on a relationship," "working on getting in shape"), in this book, its core meaning is "activities that produce a good or a service"—such as flipping burgers, designing software, testing silicon chips, or refueling military aircraft. We define **work** to include activities that produce goods and services for one's own use or in exchange for pay or support. This definition encompasses three kinds of work: **forced work,** which is performed under compulsion and provides little or no pay (for example, as slaves or prisoners); *paid* work (also called **market work**); and *unpaid work* (also called **nonmarket work**), which people perform for themselves and others.

Note: **Boldface** terms are defined in the Glossary/Index.

Forced work still exists. Although outright slavery is rare, debt-bondage and other slaverylike practices are widespread around the world, including in Europe and North America (International Labour Organization 2001). Women and children throughout the world, particularly recent immigrants and racial minorities, are especially vulnerable, and thousands are brought into the United States to work in the sex industry and in the domestic and cleaning industries (Domosh and Seager 2001:56; International Labour Organization 2001:5). Sweatshop conditions that we tend to associate with the developing world can be found also in the United States. In El Monte, California, for example, undocumented female Thai workers were locked inside factory walls topped with barbed wire, where they worked 17-hour days sewing women's and children's apparel for as little as 60 cents an hour (Domosh and Seager 2001:56). Men, too, are subjected to forced labor, as is the case for many prisoners, disproportionately African American, who work in prison industries and on Southern "chain gangs," where their labor is paid at rates far below minimum wage (Jones 1998:377).

An important form of nonmarket work in modern societies is domestic work—work that people do for themselves and members of their household. If you aren't convinced that unpaid work is really work, think of your experiences waxing a car, planning and cooking a meal that will impress your friends, buying gifts on a limited budget during exam week, taking care of a sick friend, or volunteering in the community.

The distinction between market and nonmarket work is a by-product of industrialization. For most of history, people did not see work as separate from the rest of their lives. Life was work, just as it was rest and recovery from work. The average person consumed what she or he produced, and few people were paid for their labor. Only with industrialization and the development of capitalism was work equated with paid activity. As people increasingly became engaged in this new form of work, the terms *unpaid work*, *nonmarket work*, and *domestic work* evolved to refer to much of the plain, old-fashioned, unpaid work that people have always done.

As more workers were drawn into paid jobs, however, people increasingly treated paid work as the only "real" work; the unpaid work that people did in their own homes became devalued or invisible.[1] Today, economists and statisticians who monitor the size and productivity of the workforce in industrialized countries reserve the term *work* for activities that people do for pay. American economists, for example, estimate the nation's gross national product in terms of the output of its paid workers. Defining work as paid production excludes much of the work done by people in developing countries as well as all of the work that women and men perform at home for their families (Mies 1998:ix).

This book examines the roles that women and men play in performing paid and unpaid work. We show that workers' sex profoundly affects their work lives, although the way that it does so sometimes depends on people's race, ethnicity, and class. We show, too, that the effects of sex on the kinds of work people do, the rewards it brings, and their family lives have varied throughout history and around the world. First, however, we must clarify the terms *sex* and *gender* and introduce the concepts of sex differentiation and gender differentiation.

Sex and Gender

Although many people use the terms *sex* and *gender* as synonyms, they have different meanings. We use the term **sex** for a classification based on human biology. Biological sex depends on a person's chromosomes and is expressed in reproductive organs and hormones. **Gender**, in contrast, refers to a classification that social actors construct that typically exaggerates the differences between females and males.

Sex Differentiation

All societies recognize the existence of different sexes, and all group people by their sex for some purposes. Classifying people into categories based on their sex is called **sex differentiation.** Because of the importance societies attach to sex, sex differentiation begins at birth when every new baby is assigned to one of two sexes on the basis of the appearance of the external genitalia. The term *the opposite sex* reveals how society construes males and females as not just different, but also as diametrically opposed. Sex differentiation, although it need not inevitably lead to sex inequality, is essential for a system of inequality. Distinguishing between females and males is necessary in order to treat the sexes differently. Thus, sex differentiation is usually part of a system of sex inequality—a **sex-gender hierarchy**—that generally favors males over females.

Gender Differentiation

The differences between women and men must seem to be large and consequential to justify unequal treatment of the sexes. **Gender differentiation** refers to the *social* processes that create and exaggerate biological differences (Reskin 1988; West and Zimmerman 1987). Gender differentiation also distinguishes activities, interests, and places as either male or female.

Together, sex differentiation and gender differentiation ensure that females differ from males in readily noticeable ways. Clothing fashions can accentuate and even create differences in the appearance of the sexes. For example, at times fashions have enhanced the breadth of men's shoulders or of women's hips or called attention to women's or men's sexual characteristics. After trousers were introduced in the nineteenth century, it was several years before men gave up the skintight breeches that "showed off [their] sexual parts" (Davidoff and Hall 1987:412). Shoe styles, too, have contributed to gender differentiation by exaggerating the difference in the sizes of women's and men's feet. In pre-Revolutionary China, upper-class Chinese women's feet were bound so they could wear tiny shoes; in the United States in the early 1960s, the only fashionable shoes that women could buy had narrow, pointed toes and three-inch heels.

Clothing for babies illustrates the creation of sex differences in appearance that have no natural basis. Disposable-diaper manufacturers, for example, market different designs for girls and boys. Until the beginning of the twentieth century, however, male and female infants were dressed alike—usually in white dresses. When Americans began to color code babies' clothing, they dressed boys in pink and girls in blue. Not until almost 1950 did the convention reverse, with blue becoming defined as masculine and pink as feminine (Kidwell and Steele 1989:24-27). Such shifts demonstrate that what is critical for maintaining and justifying unequal treatment between the sexes is not *how* cultures set the sexes apart but the fact that they do it at all.

The Social Construction of Gender

The process of transforming males and females—who are vastly more similar than different in biological terms—into two groups that differ noticeably in appearance is part of the **social construction of gender**. As anthropologist Gayle Rubin (1975:178) said, "A taboo against the sameness of men and women [divides] the sexes into two mutually exclusive categories [and] thereby *creates* gender." Rewards and punishments induce most people to go along with the social construction of gender and thus conform to cultural definitions of femininity and masculinity.

The Relationship Between Sex and Gender

A fable about a stranger who arrived at a village begging for food provides an analogy of the difference between sex and gender. When the villagers said they had no food at all, the stranger announced he had a magic stone with which he volunteered to make "stone soup." As the stone simmered in a pot of boiling water, the stranger told the villagers that the soup would be tastier if they could find just one onion to add to it. Someone admitted to having an onion, which was added to the pot. When the stranger said that the soup would be even better with a carrot, another villager produced a carrot. In this way, the stranger got the villagers to add potatoes, turnips, garlic, and even meat bones. The "stone soup" the stranger eventually dished out to the villagers was hearty and delicious. Although we do not want to push the analogy too far, sex resembles the stone and gender the soup. Like the stone, biological sex is the foundation on which societies construct gender. Like the soup, gender depends little on people's biological sex and mostly on how societies embellish it. And just as the stranger tricked the villagers into thinking that an ordinary stone was the essential ingredient in stone soup, cultures often deceive us into thinking that biological sex accounts for the differences between females' and males' behavior and life outcomes. In short, gender is a social construction that results from gender differentiation, not a biological inevitability.

In this book, we use the term *sex* when we refer to people's biological sex, and so we usually use it when comparing the ways organizations or societies treat females and males. We use that term to emphasize that people's sex influences how others act toward them. For example, we refer to *sex discrimination* and *sex segregation*. In contrast, we use the term *gender* to refer to differences between the sexes that are socially constructed.

A primary reason for the gendering of human activities is that it maintains males' advantages. Gender ideology and gendered organizations institutionalize the favored position of men as a group; in other words, organizations play a fundamental role in establishing a sex-gender hierarchy that favors men over women. Individual men, then, enjoy the benefits of being male without having to do anything to obtain those benefits. Most men are not even aware of the benefits they derive because of their sex. This is not surprising; almost all of us mistakenly attribute benefits we receive because of our ascribed characteristics (such as race, sex, or appearance) to our own efforts. But men's privileged position in organizations is not universal. Women have a stake in reducing gendering, and at various times and in different settings they have successfully organized to challenge it (see, for example, Schmitt and Martin 1999; Stombler and Padavic 1999).

Although sex is an important basis for differentiating people into categories, societies use other characteristics as well. Foremost are race and ethnicity; in many societies, religion, appearance, age, sexual orientation, and economic position are also important bases for sorting people into groups. Just as societies magnify the minor biological differences between males and females, they elaborate small differences between persons based on age, race, and ethnicity. Thus, ethnicity and age are also social constructions. The discussion of the history of work in Chapter 2, for example, shows that just over 100 years ago, families and employers treated children as small adults, who worked alongside their parents in fields and factories. Some societies still do not legally differentiate children from adults: Children can enter into marriage or be tried for murder. Today, however, Americans usually differentiate children, adolescents, and "senior citizens" from everyone else. Thus, childhood, adolescence, and "senior citizenship" have been socially constructed as special statuses. Some societies also engage in social differentiation on the basis of race and ethnicity. In the first half of the twentieth century, the designations of white and black were often matters of litigation (Haney-Lopez 1996). Patterns of immigration and world affairs have created a strong tradition of racial and ethnic differentiation in the United States, and people's race and ethnicity may influence their work lives. When we address the effects of such differentiation, remember that race and ethnicity may also have socially constructed meanings.

Gendered Work

To stress the fundamental role of gender differentiation in creating differences between men and women, some social scientists use **gender** as a verb. They call the process of gender differentiation *gendering* and speak of activities attached to one or the other sex as *gendered*. These terms signify outcomes that are socially constructed and usually give males advantages over females (Acker 1990:146; 1999; Britton 2000; Risman 1998). Institutions, including the institution of work, are shaped by assumptions about gender. This section focuses on three features of gendered work: (1) the assignment of tasks based on workers' sex, (2) the higher value placed on men's work than on women's work, and (3) employers' and workers' social constructions of gender on the job.

Societies produce and maintain gender differences—that is, they engage in gendering—in a variety of ways: through ideologies that support the gender *status quo*, through interactions among people, and through reward systems that encourage gender-appropriate behaviors and discourage gender-inappropriate ones. Thus, gender is a system of

"I see by your résumé that you're a woman."

social relations that is embedded in the way major institutions (including the workplace) are organized (Acker 1999; Britton 2000; Lorber 1992:748). This conception of gender encourages us to examine not only how social institutions create and maintain differences in their female and male members but also the conditions under which they effectively reduce gendering.

The Sexual Division of Labor

The assignment of different tasks to women and men—which is termed the **sexual division of labor**—is a fundamental feature of work. All societies delegate tasks in part on the basis of workers' sex, although which sex does exactly which tasks varies over time and across the countries of the world. Tasks that some societies view as "naturally" female or male are assigned to the other sex at other times or in other places. For example, whereas most tailors in the Middle East, North Africa, and India are male, this is a female occupation in more industrialized countries (Anker 1998:276). Hairdressers and barbers tend to be female in the member countries of the Organisation for Economic Co-operation and

Development (OECD), but not in India or China (Anker 1998:272-73). Although 85 percent of the world's maids and housekeepers are women, about half of the maids and housekeepers in Angola and India are male, as are one-third of those in Tunisia, Ghana, and Senegal and one-quarter of those in Egypt and Kuwait (Anker 1998:272).

Within the same country and the same general line of work, either sex may perform a particular job. Although women were twice as likely as men to work as food servers in the United States at the turn of the twenty-first century (U.S. Census Bureau 1998, 1999, 2000a), many restaurants—especially fancy ones—employed only waiters. Neither sex has a monopoly on the skills needed to serve food, but restaurants often enact a sexual division of labor in which one sex cooks and the other serves. Race, ethnicity, and age frequently figure into job assignments as well. For example, although most domestic laborers in the late nineteenth century were women, in California and Hawaii they were Asian men (Glenn 1996:122). Chapter 4 describes these divisions of labor in greater detail.

The division of labor between women and men varies over time, as the production of cloth illustrates. Up to the fourteenth or fifteenth century, producing silk was women's work, but during the sixteenth and seventeenth centuries it became an exclusively male task (Kowaleski and Bennett 1989). Over the succeeding centuries, at one time or another, textile manufacturers have hired women or men or sometimes both. Cloth production is not the only arena where the sexual division of labor has changed hands over time. In the world as a whole, women are more likely to be in "men's jobs" now than in the 1970s and 1980s (Anker 1998:412, 415). For example, in small countries that expanded textile exports because of the arrival of multinational corporations, the percentage of women doing jobs that men had formerly done has swelled over those two decades (in Mauritius the percent of females in such jobs climbed from 37 to 65 percent and in Fiji from 41 to 61 percent [Anker 1998:416]).

Changes in which sex performs a task usually occur slowly, however, because the existing sexual division of labor shapes social expectations about who should do certain types of jobs and because in many occupations turnover of an existing male workforce is slow.[2] Thus, in most of the world, the occupational categories that include production supervisors and general foremen, blacksmiths, toolmakers, bricklayers, carpenters, and other construction workers remain almost exclusively male (Anker 1998:274). Types of work become labeled in people's minds as belonging to one sex and being inappropriate for the other. In the African country of Gambia, for example, women have cultivated rice since the fourteenth century. During a desperate food shortage in the nineteenth century, the government tried to encourage men to help grow rice. The men refused, insisting that rice was "a woman's crop" (Carney and Watts 1991:641).

Under some conditions, however, the sexual division of labor is less rigid. Consider an example from U.S. history. In colonial America, survival required that everybody work. The sexual division of labor made men primarily responsible for growing food and women for manufacturing the products that their families needed. The sexes often cooperated, however, as in the family production of linen from flax plants. Boys pulled the flax and spread it out to dry. Then men threshed it to remove the seeds. After the stalks had been soaked, cleaned, and dried, men broke the flax with wooden daggers. Then women combed out the rough material and wound the flax around a distaff, from which they spun linen thread (and women got the nickname the "distaff sex"). Women repeatedly washed, bleached, and "belted" the thread with a branch against a stone before they wove it into fabric. When necessary, however, each sex did work usually done by the other (Earle 1896).

Women and children frequently do "men's jobs" when production pressures are high. In the Troyes section of France, at the turn of the nineteenth century, working the knitting frame was a decidedly masculine preserve. Yet women and older children operated the frame when a push was on to finish the week's production (Chenut 1996:87-88). When circumstances required assigning a person of the "wrong" sex to do a job in the family business, the work was sometimes hidden behind closed doors in order to avoid losing status (Davidoff and Hall 1998:242).

Nor did North American slave owners exhibit much regard for a conventional sexual division of labor. Enslaved African American women, men, and children were forced to work in factories, mills, and mines, as well as in fields. Although some tasks were assigned based on sex, women and children worked alongside men in processing iron, textiles, hemp, and tobacco; refining sugar; and lumbering. In fact, half the workers who dug South Carolina's Santee Canal were women. Female and male slaves together maintained railroad tracks. In iron mines and refineries, women lugged trams, loaded ore into crushers, and operated the furnaces and forges. Neither on plantations nor in factories did their sex spare enslaved women from grueling work (Jones 1998).

In sum, societies gender work by labeling activities as appropriate for one sex or the other. These labels influence the job assignments of women and men, and they influence employers' and workers' expectations of who ought to perform various jobs. Across societies and over time, however, no hard-and-fast rules dictate which sex should do a particular task, as long as men and women do different work.

The Devaluation of Women's Work

A sexual division of labor need not lead inevitably to inequality between the sexes. According to historians, although women and men in preindustrial Europe had different spheres, neither sphere was subordinate (Scott and Tilly 1975:44-45). In practice, however, sex differentiation fosters the tendency to devalue female activities and, hence, to sustain sex inequality.

The devaluation of women and their activities is deeply embedded in the major cultures and religions of the world. For example, the Judeo-Christian religion, a strong influence on Western culture, ascribed to female servants three-fifths the value of male servants (Leviticus 27:3-7). Although the extent to which women's work is devalued varies over time and across locales, it continues both because it is part of the ideology in many parts of the world and because it is in men's interest. Men, who more often than women occupy positions that set value on human activities, tend to accept male activities as the standard and see other activities as inferior—regardless of the importance of these activities for a society's survival (Lorber 1994:33-35).

The devaluation of women and their work is a key factor in the pay gap between the sexes. In the United States, for example, where most doctors are male, doctors are near the top of the income hierarchy; in Estonia, a country of the former Soviet Union where three-quarters of doctors are female, doctors' incomes are much closer to the average income (Barr and Boyle 2001:33). According to an 1825 British government report, spinning (a woman's job) contributed at least half the value to linen textiles, yet weavers (who were men) earned a minimum of 10 pence a day, compared to a spinner's three or four pence (Gray 1996:43). This calculation does not count the unpaid work that women put in as cultivators and preparers of the flax.

Generally, as Chapter 6 shows, the more heavily female an occupation, the less both female and male workers earn. Living in a culture that devalues female activities makes the practice seem natural. Consider 13-year-olds' afterschool jobs. A neighbor pays a boy $20 for 30 minutes' work shoveling snow and a girl $8 for an hour's baby-sitting (although these figures vary by geographic region). Why does the baby-sitter accept this pay gap? She may not realize how much less she earns per hour. But she has probably already absorbed her society's attitude that girls' jobs are worth less than boys'. Women are taught from childhood to have a reduced sense of entitlement; as a result, they expect less pay than men expect for the same level of performance, effort, or ability (Ridgeway and Correll 2000:117). In addition, men may grow up with an exaggerated sense of entitlement. In a series of experiments, college students assigned lower values to identical tasks when women did them and judged women's performance as inferior to men's, although the female students actually worked more quickly and accurately than the men did (Major 1989:108-10). Students who were told that women usually did the job thought it deserved less pay than those who had been told that men usually did it (Major and Forcey 1985).

In sum, cultural attitudes that devalue women are expressed in the lower value that many employers, workers, and societies place on the work that women usually do. This devaluation of women's work reduces women's pay relative to men's. In this and other ways (discussed further in Chapter 6), devaluation can help to preserve the sex-gender hierarchy.

The Construction of Gender on the Job

The construction of gender on the job is a by-product of the ways that employers organize work and workers produce goods and services. Employers and workers bring gender into the workplace through either conscious or unconscious sex stereotypes that may have little basis in reality and through policies and behaviors that assume that the sexes differ. Such gender differentiation plays a key role in sex inequality, and so it is prevalent to varying degrees in every social institution, including the institution of work.

Within the workplace, employers play a primary role in gendering (Acker 1990, 1999; Britton 2000). Employers often have a particular sex in mind when they create new jobs, set pay levels, and organize how work is to be done and under what conditions. For example, the machinery employees use will be designed quite differently if employers envision workers who average 5'11" and 175 pounds than if they envision workers averaging 5'4" and 130 pounds. Similarly, if employers have adult male workers in mind, they are more likely to assume that they will accept shift and overtime work. In contrast, employers who plan to hire women are more likely to organize jobs as part time and to create pay and benefit systems that encourage turnover.

When modern paid jobs evolved, most paid workers were male. As a result, the assumptions surrounding the creation of these jobs were gendered. The consequences of those assumptions have survived in many workplaces because of inertia in employers' personnel practices. This inertia stems from habit, the fact that people see change as more risky than doing business as usual, and ignorance of the impact of outmoded practices. Until the late 1960s, for example, many states barred employers from assigning women to jobs that could involve lifting more than 25 pounds. For years after the California Supreme Court struck down such "protective" laws as illegal under a 1964 federal antidiscrimination law, many employers continued to exclude women from such jobs. These employers did not consciously decide to disregard the court's decision; rather, they just conducted business as usual. Often it took an external event to prompt them to change their operating practices.

In addition, employers may introduce gender into the workplace through current practices. Sometimes employers use gender to control workers, to get more work out of them, or to sell products. When workers adhere to masculine gender-role norms requiring strength, endurance, and sacrifice, employers benefit. For example, when a male coal miner assigned to lift heavy steel rails remarked that it looked like a four-man job, his supervisor asked him, "Aren't you man enough?" (Yarrow 1987:9). Such gender norms can become self-enforcing, as when a meatpacker shrugged off a comment on his work-damaged hands, saying he was a man who earned his pay (Fink 1998:110).

Some employers emphasize workers' sex to divert workers' attention from bad working conditions or to prevent collective action (Tiano 1994:183). For example, global assembly lines that subject young women to long, dangerous work at low pay sometimes feature fashion shows and cosmetic sales on company property (Freeman 2000:185). A Caribbean firm offered in-house self-improvement programs on such topics as personal grooming, makeup, and prenatal care (Freeman 2000:188). Managers of a Hong Kong factory encouraged married women's orientation to family by granting women (but not men) paid one- or two-hour leaves to take care of family emergencies. For management, facilitating women's family orientations discouraged them from orienting to themselves as workers interested in higher wages or promotions (Lee 1997:130). By introducing programs and policies that orient young women to their appearance and to marriage and that orient married women to their families, companies reduce the likelihood that these women will protest working conditions.

Employers who turn a blind eye to sexual materials in the workplace also maintain gendered workplaces. A woman firefighter complained that, despite the supervisor's repeated warnings, a coworker still displayed pornographic pictures in his locker that were visible because he left the door open (Chetkovich 1997:76). A woman construction worker claimed: "There was a lot of pornography on the job, and when I would complain about it they would take it down and they would put up more" (Eisenberg 1998:72). Importantly, just as employers' actions and policies can introduce gender into the workplace, employers' policies can also curtail it. For example, employers' enforcement of sexual harassment polices has discouraged such practices in many workplaces.

Workers, too, construct gender at work. They may do so in order to forge bonds with other workers of the same sex, to express their gender identity, to attract or to exclude workers of the other sex, to get back at their employers, to control one another, and to entertain themselves.

Male and female workers sometimes differ in the ways they bring gender into the workplace. Many observers have commented on how all-male work groups affirm group members' masculinity by discussing such "male" concerns as sports and sex. Predominantly one-sex work groups may also engage in **gender displays,** which are language or rituals so characteristic of one sex that they mark the workplace as belonging to that sex. Male gender displays include sexual language and conversations about sex, as when military drill instructors call male recruits "girls, pussies, and wimps" (Barrett 1996). Blue-collar settings particularly encourage macho behavior. For example, men in dangerous settings such as offshore oil rigs often refuse safety helmets, and some men working around coal dust shun masks. Macho behavior also includes that by workers who use brute force rather than standard procedures to accomplish a task. Gender displays that signal the importance of bravado and muscle on the job imply that women don't belong (Eisenberg 1998; Weston 1990:146). White-collar workers, too, engage in such macho behavior. According to one study, male lawyers specializing in litigation likened themselves to "Rambo" in their single-minded pursuit and conquest of the "enemy." One said, "It's a male thing. . . . It's a competition. Men beating each other up, trying to show one another up. Only these aren't fistfights, they're verbal assaults." Men who lose were considered "weak," "impotent," or lacking "balls" (Pierce 1995:68). Such practices are not universal, however; employment practices and antidiscrimination laws can be effective in discouraging them.

Social interaction can also mark a workplace as off limits or open to the other sex, although gender is often a "ghost" in the background of interaction, rather than the focus of what is going on (Martin 2001; Ridgeway and Correll 2000). Sometimes, however, workers explicitly use gender to reinforce inequality. Male superiority can be asserted through words, as with the male judges who referred to women as "bitches, cats, and ball-busters" (Padavic and Orcutt 1997:694), or a lone woman electrician, who found "fucking lesbian electrician bitch" written on the bathroom wall (Eisenberg 1998:81). The only woman in a power-plant crew saw on a work room bulletin board a list headed "Twenty Reasons Why Beer Is Better Than Women" that sexualized and disparaged women ("You always know you're the first one to pop a beer"; "When a beer goes flat, you can throw it out"). The list reminded the woman that she was in male territory, where women were welcome primarily as sex objects (Padavic 1991).

Women also bring gender to the workplace. Sometimes they do this by swapping stories about their male partners and children or by celebrating marriages and births. Such stories can brag about husbands' successes; others can be contemptuous of men, for example, by describing men's incompetence at various tasks. Women meatpackers scorned their supervisor for his lack of stereotypically male attributes: "Oh, Clyde," Annie groaned in disgust, "Clyde can't even fix his own car" (Fink 1998:31). Women can also enact gender by defying conventional gender roles.[3] A sociologist observed this phenomenon in Mexico among female factory workers during the bus ride home from work. When a man boarded the bus, the women "chided and teased him. . . . They offered kisses and asked for a smile. They exchanged comments about his physical attributes and suggested a raffle to see who would keep him" (Fernandez-Kelly 1983:131-32). Both women and men workers also use gender to resist their employers. A company's policy of encouraging a family orientation among women workers backfired when the company asked workers to commute between Hong Kong and mainland China for training. Women who did not want to go argued that spending the night away from home violated their obligations as wives and mothers (Lee 1997:131). Likewise, male unionists have invoked notions of manly dignity to encourage other workers to join them in opposition to management.

In sum, employers and workers engage in gender differentiation at work by making sex salient when it is irrelevant and by acting on sex-stereotyped assumptions. Employers also gender work by sex-segregating jobs, by setting pay based on workers' sex, and by permitting the kinds of workers' practices discussed earlier. In other words, gender is constructed within places of work through organizational practices and interaction (Acker 1999; Ely and Meyerson 2000; Ridgeway and Smith-Lovin 1999). It is eroded by changes in these features.

Diversity in Gendered Work

How and how much work is gendered depends on the work site, the employer, and the characteristics of the workers. In some situations, workers' race has a greater effect than their sex does on jobs, pay, and day-to-day experiences. More commonly, sex, race, and other characteristics interact to shape workers' outcomes. At colleges and universities, for example, although most female workers do clerical work, white women are more likely to hold such jobs than women of color, who disproportionately hold custodial jobs. Meanwhile, being a white man increases a worker's chance of being an administrator or a professor; minority men more often hold blue-collar jobs. The chapters that follow show that sometimes the patterns are the same regardless of workers' race and ethnicity, and other times they differ. When race or ethnicity has been shown to make a difference in the effect of sex, we discuss it. Unfortunately, the available research on such differences is limited. Thus, without losing sight of this diversity, we focus on the importance of people's sex on their lives as workers.

Summary

Sex differentiation and gender differentiation are fundamental features of work. First and foremost, they operate through the sexual division of labor that assigns tasks to people partly on the basis of their sex and that labels certain tasks as "belonging to" or being appropriate for one sex or the other. Sex and gender differentiation also are expressed in the undervaluation of women's work or the overvaluation of men's work. These processes occur in the day-to-day interactions among workers and their bosses, as well as in the policies and practices of employers, governments, and families. Their result can make work a gendered institution, in which employers and workers often place undue emphasis on people's sex. It is important to recognize, however, that neither sex differentiation nor gender differentiation is universal or inevitable. Some employers hire both women and men for all jobs. In some places of work, neither sex introduces gender into the workplace to an appreciable degree. Instead, workers interact as individuals. This variability in the amount of sex differentiation across workplaces is not an accident. It results from how employers organize work, the tasks involved, organizational leadership, and the existence of external pressures. In the chapters that follow, we call attention to factors that exacerbate or reduce sex differentiation at work.

Notes

1. According to one estimate, women's unpaid household labor accounts for about one-third of the world's economic production (United Nations Population Fund 2000).
2. Jobs can change sex labels rapidly when men's labor is unavailable, as during wars or strikes, or an occupation changes in ways to become less attractive to men (Reskin and Roos 1990). But such changes are rarely permanent. In Japan during the twentieth century, for example, women worked underground as miners until a post-World War I recession led to laws sending women above-ground. They returned to the mines in response to the need for laborers during World War II, only to be forced out in 1947 after the war (Mathias 1993:101-105; Saso 1990:25-26).
3. Men in macho workplaces may be less able to draw on strategies that defy conventional gender roles because coworkers can punish men who are viewed as effeminate.

2

Gendered Work in Time and Place

Although every society assigns tasks on the basis of people's sex, the kinds of tasks that go to women and men have varied over time and around the world. This chapter traces the evolution of the Western sexual division of labor over the past 400 years. We first describe how Western preindustrial societies divided work between the sexes. We then show how industrialization, by commercializing work, created another sexual division of labor—paid employment for men and unpaid domestic work for women. Finally, we describe the sexual division of labor among Western and non-Western nations around the world.

The Sexual Division of Labor in Preindustrial Europe

In preindustrial Western societies, almost everyone worked. Most people devoted their lives to feeding and housing themselves. The rest—except for royalty and the nobility, who lived off others' labor—worked at making products or serving others. This section describes the work that women and men did in agriculture and manufacturing during this period.

Agricultural Work

Prior to industrialization, which began in the West in the eighteenth century, most people worked in agriculture, either as serfs who farmed land held by members of the nobility or, later, as peasants who owned small parcels of land (Hanawalt 1986). Among the serfs and peasants, men usually plowed and threshed, women weeded, and both sexes harvested. Girls and women took charge of raising domestic animals. Thus, they milked, churned butter, made cheese, and butchered animals. Women also made bread, beer, cloth, and clothing. Men built houses, hewed timber, harrowed, dug ditches, and cut hedges.

Consider a seventeenth-century Basque farm couple. The wife rose at dawn and lit the fire. Her husband and the hired men remained in bed while she made breakfast. After the men left for the fields, where they engaged in sowing, spading, plowing, and harvesting, the wife cleaned the house and prepared the noon meal, during which she remained standing, waiting on the men. In the afternoon, the wife joined her husband and the hired men in the fields until it was time for her to fix the evening meal. In the evening, the husband might repair tools or go to the village tavern. The wife spun by lamplight until around 11 P.M., when she would follow her husband to bed (Shorter 1975:67-72).

Before industrialization, the work of servants resembled that of peasants. Both sexes worked as servants, often for just their keep. An Englishwoman who began an apprenticeship as a servant when she was 9 years old described

> driving bullocks to [field] and fetching them in again; cleaning out their
> houses, and bedding them up; washing potatoes and boiling them for
> pigs; milking; in the field leading horses or bullocks to plough . . . ,
> digging potatoes, digging and pulling turnips . . . like a boy. I got up at
> five or six except on market mornings twice a week, and then at three.
> (Pinchbeck 1930:17-18)

Notice that in preindustrial agriculture, women's and men's tasks overlapped, although the sexual division of labor defined cooking, cleaning, and spinning as women's work. Although the jobs that women and men usually did were seen as equally valuable, preindustrial agriculture was hardly a paradise of sex equality. In 1823, an observer wrote of the Scottish Highlands that women were regarded as men's "drudges" rather than their companions:

> The husband turns up the land and sows it—the wife conveys the
> manure to it in a creel, tends the corn, reaps it, hoes the potatoes, digs
> them up, carries the whole home on her back, [and] when bearing the
> creel she also is engaged with spinning. (Quoted in Berg 1985:142)

Manufacturing Work

Even before industrialization, some people worked in manufacturing products—as craft workers in workhouses, workshops, or their own cottages. Men's and women's manufacturing work was organized under different systems of production, with men in guilds and women in workshops. And as a rule, although the sexes had similar levels of skills, men in manufacturing substantially outearned women and enjoyed more autonomy.

Women's Workshops. In medieval Europe, all-female workhouses existed in which female residents manufactured textiles.[1] These skilled workers dyed, wove, and embroidered fabric that they sewed into clothing for monks and nobles. In exchange for their labor, they received their board and room. Many were slaves of the nobility or the monasteries or the wives and children of slaves. Others were serfs or were imprisoned in the workhouses for crimes such as prostitution.[2]

Although these women's workshops died out before industrialization, their legacy as women's work lives on. The textile factories that sprang up in the early years of industrialization relied almost exclusively on female workers, and in most of the world, textile manufacturing is still considered women's work.

Artisans. A more enduring preindustrial system of production was the guild system, in which **artisans** (craft workers) produced a variety of products from scratch. **Guilds**—associations of tradespeople or craft workers organized to protect their members' interests—oversaw most production that occurred outside the home, from silverware, iron tools, and wheels to fabric, bread, and beer. Like the textile workers in the women's workshops, artisans were skilled workers who produced fine products. However, unlike the workshop workers, almost all artisans were men, and they earned an income from the products they made and sold.

The guilds—the precursors of modern unions—controlled the apprenticeship systems through which artisans learned their craft. Given their goal of restricting competition, guilds closed apprenticeships to a variety of people, including most women. The wives of master craft workers worked alongside their husbands, and in the early Middle Ages, guilds sometimes allowed widows to continue their late husbands' work. Gradually, however, guilds restricted wives' and widows' rights to pursue their husbands' trade, and eventually the status of master craft worker was off-limits to women (Howell 1986). The monopoly of artisanal work that men enjoyed in the preindustrial period continues today in men's virtual monopoly of the skilled trades, as Chapter 4 shows.

Cottage Industry. Before industrialization shifted production to factories, peasants—mostly women and children—manufactured some goods at home through a system of **cottage industry.** Cottage workers might spin wool, make lace, weave cloth, or attach shirt collars, for which they were paid on a piecework basis (by the amount of work completed, called a **piece rate**). Their earnings were often the household's only cash income.

Peasant women, whose first priority was work for their own families, made time for cottage industry by laboring every available minute. A historian described seventeenth-century British women cottage workers: They "knitted as they walked the village streets, they knitted in the dark because they were too poor to have a light; they knitted for dear life" (Berg 1985:103). As cottage workers, then, women and children participated in the earliest labor force.

The Industrial Revolution

For many centuries, people survived by doing agricultural and pre-industrial manufacturing work. Then, in the eighteenth century, capitalism transformed how Western Europeans produced and distributed goods and services. Family production was replaced by market production in which capitalists paid workers wages to produce goods in factories and mines. As paid workers, people manufactured products that were sold by middlemen. This **Industrial Revolution,** which lasted over 200 years in the Western world, is still under way in developing countries.

The Emergence of the Labor Force

In moving the production of goods from home to factory, industrialization created a new institution: a **labor force,** comprised of people who work for pay or actively seek paid work. In England, where industrialization's major changes occurred in the last half of the eighteenth century and the early nineteenth century, thousands of peasants who were forced off the land made their way to cities in search of jobs. These peasants were the first recruits into the modern industrial labor force.

The creation of the labor force split working people into three groups: wage workers and **unemployed** persons who sought paid jobs (the labor force), and the **nonemployed.** Of course, a class of nonemployed people was not new; throughout history, privileged classes have been exempt from productive work. However, at this juncture, the new category of the non-employed were not the "idle rich," but rather a growing group of unpaid workers who cooked and cleaned for family members, raised children, cared for sick relatives, and provided social and emotional support to family, friends, and community. This distinction between paid work in the labor market and unpaid domestic work by the "nonemployed" has had important consequences for gender inequality, because for the past 200 years, men have been more likely than women to belong to the labor force, and women have been more likely than men to be unpaid workers.

Industrialization and the Sexual Division of Labor

Industrialization created two new distinctions between men's and women's work roles. The first assigned men to paid work and women to the unpaid work of running a household. Based on this distinction, employers organized work and set pay on the assumption that workers were men. The twentieth-century union movement's push for a family wage was based on a second assumption: that men support women and children. This division of paid and unpaid work according to sex is the subject of the rest of this chapter. The second new division of labor among people who worked in the labor force segregated women and men into different jobs. This division is the subject of Chapter 4.

The Sexual Division of Paid and Unpaid Work

Throughout the nineteenth century, the labor force became increasingly male. Early in the period, as cottage industries gave way to small textile factories, many employers continued to hire women and children because they worked for lower wages and were more available for hire than men in some areas (Valenze 1995). However, as employment became urbanized, women's **labor force participation** fell, and the labor force became **masculinized**. For example, in 1840, women and children made up about 40 percent of the industrial workforce in the United States; by 1870, three out of four industrial workers were male (Baxandall, Gordon, and Reverby 1976:83); and by 1890, only 17 percent of women worked for pay outside the home (Goldin 1990).

The number of people seeking jobs during this period often exceeded the number of jobs. The result was hordes of **unemployed** people desperate for work. Employers took advantage of the situation by cutting pay. Early unions viewed women and children as a threat to men's jobs and wages, so they set out to drive children and women out of all factory and mining jobs (Pinchbeck 1930). Unions found allies in middle-class reformers, who sought laws to protect children and women from dangerous or immoral working conditions.[3] Pressure from unions and reformers led nineteenth-century lawmakers in Europe and the United States to pass **protective labor laws** banning exploitative employment practices.

Protective labor laws prohibited the employment of children and women for more than a specific number of hours a day, from lifting more than specified weights, from working at night, and from holding certain jobs. Although they protected some women from brutal working conditions, at the same time these laws denied many women high-paying factory jobs. Gendered assumptions gave women but not men protection from hazardous work and gave men but not women the right to weigh the risks against the rewards in deciding how to earn a living. Laws limiting the number of hours women could work were common in the United States and Britain. Other laws actually required employers to segregate specific lines of work by denying some jobs to women—such as practicing law, tending bar, delivering telegrams, and working as street-car conductors. Except during the two world wars, the U.S. government followed this protectionist policy until 1964. In putting many lines of work off-limits to women, protective labor laws contributed to the masculinization of the labor force and reinforced the assumption that it was men's responsibility to support their families.

Despite protective labor laws, the movement to bar women from all factory jobs failed. Need drove many women to work for pay, and employers sought women for low-paying factory jobs (Pinchbeck 1930). Because employers could pay women less than men, textile mill owners actively recruited unmarried female workers, promising parents to keep their daughters from the "vices and crimes" of idleness (Lerner 1979:189). Most families welcomed their daughters' income (Dublin 1993). In sum, although thousands of women remained in the labor force, the labor force became increasingly male throughout the nineteenth century.

The Ideology of Separate Spheres

The preceding account of the masculinization of labor force omits a crucial qualification: It was married, not single, women who were least likely to be employed. Comparing married and single women's labor force participation at the turn of the twentieth century tells the story: only 6 percent of married women were in the labor force, compared to 40 percent of single women over age 10 (Folbre 1991:465).

Why was labor force participation among married women so low? A major factor was the **ideology of separate spheres.** This ideology, which was born among the English upper-middle classes, called for the separation of family life from paid work. It held that a woman's proper place was in the home and not in the workplace, and its corollary was that a man's natural sphere was *not* in the home; instead, it was in the world of commerce—or, at any rate, at his job (Davidoff and Hall 1987:364-67; Skolnick 1991:30-31).

This ideology of separate spheres encouraged men to work away from home and women to confine productive activities to the household. Reinforcing these beliefs were stereotypes of men as strong, aggressive, and competitive and of women as frail, virtuous, and nurturing—images that depicted men as naturally suited to the highly competitive nineteenth-century workplace and women as too delicate for the world of commerce.

Respectable married women had two responsibilities: creating a haven to which their husbands could retreat from the world of work and demonstrating through their own nonemployment their husbands' ability to support their families. An employed wife was a sign of her husband's failure (Westover 1986:67). As a British woman who worked as a tailor near the turn of the twentieth century recalled,

> I never went out to work after I was married. There wasn't many who did. They used to cry shame on them in them days when they were married if they went to work. They used to say your husband should keep you.

Similarly, a woman who worked at a Midwestern meatpacking plant in the mid-twentieth century said that her husband was ridiculed because of her job and that "if you worked in a packinghouse, you were a slut and that's all there is to it" (Fink 1998:102).

Wives' employment brought shame not only on their husbands but also on themselves. An upper-class Englishwoman commentator pointed out in 1839 that

> gentlemen may employ their hours of business in almost any degrading occupation and, if they but have the means of supporting a respectable establishment at home, may be gentlemen still; while, if a lady but touch any article, no matter how delicate, in the way of trade, she loses caste, and ceases to be a lady. (Ellis in Davidoff and Hall 1998:287)

Notions of women's frailty and their role as ornaments reinforced the sexual division of labor. The small waists that middle-class women achieved through tightly laced corsets both symbolized and ensured their incapacity to do productive work.

The ideology of separate spheres forced men as well as women into narrow roles. For middle-class men, the ideology demanded the dogged pursuit of economic success. Just as a woman's respectability rested on performing domestic roles and not doing paid work, a man's rested on how well he performed his market roles: Masculinity was measured "by the size of a man's paycheck" (Gould 1974). Upholding his end of the breadwinner-homemaker bargain meant for many men "sacrific[ing] himself on the altar of family responsibility" (Kimmel 2000:176). Men's obligation to provide family support has sometimes entailed migrating to find work (Amott and Matthaei 1996). As a Filipino working in Saudi Arabia said, "There is only one thing we talk about at night in the barracks. . . . How we want to go home to our families, after earning big money. Nobody goes to Saudi out of choice. You sacrifice for the [economic improvement] of your family" (Margold 1995:287). Thus, the ideology of separate spheres restricted both women and men, yet it nevertheless bestowed the social rewards of prestige and power in the public sphere on some men, but not women (Clark 1995:263).

Even the Great Depression of the 1930s, which brought record unemployment among American men, failed to draw large numbers of married women into the labor force. Families sent their children to work before mothers would take jobs outside the home. For their part, employers (including the government) were reluctant to hire married women while men were out of work. In fact, section 213 of the Federal Economy Act of 1932 led to the layoffs of many women whose husbands also worked for the federal government and set the precedent for similar policies at state and local levels (Blackwelder 1997:97).

The ideology of separate spheres has contributed to the gendering of modern work in several ways. First, although it assigned men the obligation to support their families, it also provided them with a way to win social approval. Women, too, gained obligations, but their relegation to the home put them outside the system of pay for labor and hence the opportunity for social rewards. Second, social values that encouraged employers to ban women from many jobs legitimized sex discrimination. Third, employers could justify low pay for women because men presumably supported them, and women's economic dependence on men solidified men's authority in the family.

The Sexual Division of Labor Among the Poor and Working Class

The ideology of separate spheres was beyond the reach of many married women, particularly poor and working-class women, who were often immigrants or minorities. Comparing the labor force participation rates of married women from different race and ethnic groups is instructive. In 1920, for example, only 7 percent of married European American women were in the labor force, compared to 18 percent of married Asian American women and one-third of married African American women. Although these rates trail those of their unmarried counterparts, it is clear that labor force participation was more of a necessity for women of color than for white women.[4]

In reserving paid jobs for men, the ideology of separate spheres espe-cially hurt working-class wives, whose families could not get by on one worker's paycheck. As a result, many working-class women sought ways to earn money at home, such as doing piecework or taking in laundry, sewing, or boarders. These alternatives usually meant lower pay and longer hours than working away from the home (Westover 1986).

Minority women also were frequently unable to achieve the separate spheres ideal. In the sharecropping system that followed Emancipation, African American women labored in the fields alongside husbands and children. In the late nineteenth century and early twentieth century, many sharecroppers moved North, where both the women and the men sought paid jobs. Similarly, in the early decades of the twentieth century, when the United States recruited Mexicans for temporary agricultural jobs, Mexican women did backbreaking work alongside their husbands on huge "factory farms" in the Southwest (Amott and Matthaei 1996).

As these examples indicate, even during the heyday of the ideology of separate spheres, thousands of women worked for pay—minority women of all ages, young single women, widows, and married women whose husbands had deserted their families or did not earn enough to support them. Employers in the market for cheap labor did not care whether women were married. Married immigrant women and former slaves were particularly likely to be employed. They labored in sweatshops, factories, offices, schools, and other families' homes, and some did piecework in their homes. For these women, staying out of the labor force would have meant starvation for themselves and their families.

In sum, the sexual division of labor that assigned men to the labor force and women to the home encouraged employers to structure jobs on the assumptions that all permanent workers were men and that all men had stay-at-home wives. These assumptions both freed most male workers from domestic responsibilities and consigned them to 12- to 14-hour workdays. They also bolstered the belief that domestic work was women's responsibility, even for women who were employed outside the home. The chapters that follow trace the consequences of these gendered assumptions and employment practices, which lingered long after economic and social forces had begun to erode sex differences in labor force participation.

The Convergence in Women's and Men's Labor Force Participation

The legacy of the ideology that married women should not work outside the home has continued into modern times. Not until the 1970s did married women's likelihood of paid employment catch up with that of single and divorced women. Moreover, although society now expects married women to participate in the labor force (indeed, welfare reform mandates it for poor women), it continues to define domestic work as women's sphere (see Chapter 7). Nevertheless, the gap between men's and women's labor force participation rates has narrowed considerably, as Exhibit 2.1 shows. In 1890, 84 percent of men over the age of 14 were in the labor force, compared to only 18 percent of similar women. If the Census Bureau had counted farm wives on the same basis as it counted farmers and if it had counted women who ran boardinghouses, women's labor force participation rate for 1890 would have been about 28 percent (Goldin 1990:44-45). Over the next hundred years, women's participation in the labor force climbed steadily while men's labor force participation fell slightly. By the end of the twentieth century, almost 74 percent of men and 60 percent of women were in the labor force (U.S. Census Bureau 1998, 1999, 2000a). Experts project that women's and men's labor force participation will continue to converge (Fullerton 1999).

EXHIBIT 2.1

Trends in U.S. Labor Force Participation Rates by Sex, 1890-2000

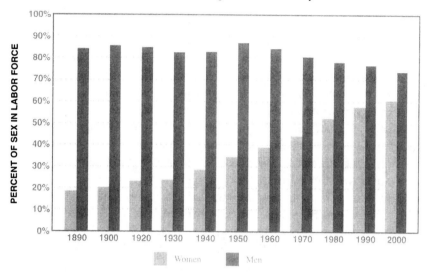

Source: U.S. Census Bureau 1975; U.S. Women's Bureau 1993:1; authors' calculations from the March 1998, 1999, and 2000 Current Population Surveys.
Note: Figures for 2000 are averages of 1998, 1999, and 2000 Current Population Survey data.

Although the labor force participation of women of all racial and ethnic groups has increased, race and ethnicity nevertheless are linked to women's and men's labor force participation rates. By the end of the twentieth century, black women's rate slightly surpassed white women's: 60 percent of white women and 64 percent of African American women were in the labor force. Hispanic women were less likely to be in the labor force—at 56 percent. Among men, the pattern differs: 79 percent of Hispanic men, 74 percent of white men, and 66 percent of black men were employed or seeking work by the end of the twentieth century (U.S. Census Bureau 1998, 1999, 2000a).

The differences in labor force participation among these racial and ethnic groups reflect both employers' demands for workers of particular sexes, races, and ethnicities and the economic circumstances of their families that either encourage or discourage employment. Black women have always been employed in great numbers, both because employers sought workers for low-wage, low-status jobs and because discrimination against black men heightened black women's need to work for pay.

American Indian women's participation is lower than black and white women's because they are concentrated in the Southwest, where fewer jobs are available (Amott and Matthaei 1996). Puerto Rican women's labor force participation is lower than white women's because they have finished fewer years of school, on average, which limits the jobs for which they are qualified, and because they are more likely to be single parents, which has impeded labor force participation in the past (Corcoran, Heflin, and Reyes 1999:135). Mexican American women are less likely than European American women to have had enough schooling and to be sufficiently fluent in English to qualify for some jobs, and they are geographically concentrated in Texas and California, where labor markets are tight (Corcoran et al. 1999:124). The long-run trend is toward convergence in labor force participation among female racial and ethnic groups. Among men, however, the differences in labor force participation among black, white, and Hispanic men have been increasing. Hispanic men, as a whole, are slightly more likely than Anglo men to participate in the labor force, largely because of their concentration in the Southwest, which offers them agricultural employment that does not require high levels of education (Harrison and Bennett 1995). African American men's rates fall short of those of white and Hispanic men due to their lower levels of education, the spatial mismatch between their places of residence (inner cities) and locations of jobs (suburbs), deindustrialization (which disproportionately eliminated jobs in which they were concentrated), and a higher disability rate.

Summary

The shift of production from homes during industrialization in Western societies transformed men into wage laborers who left home each day for jobs in factories, shops, and offices. These jobs expanded men's economic roles in their families: They became both the producers of the commodities their families needed or wanted and the earners who could pay for these products. The decline of domestic production, in turn, robbed women of the role of breadwinning, and left them with the invisible and socially devalued tasks of housekeeping and child rearing. Thus, in the wake of industrialization, women found themselves with limited options. Because social norms and job discrimination curtailed their participation in the labor force, women's path to economic security and respectability was through a husband and domestic work, whereas unpaid home work denied women the esteem that society grants those who are economically productive. Men accrued the social and economic benefits accorded to the performance of "real" work away from the home.

The Sexual Division of Labor Around the World

Although countries differ widely in the degree to which they conform to a sexual division of labor, they share some similarities. First, no country counts as "employed" those people who do unpaid work in their own homes. The large numbers of people—disproportionately women—performing unpaid care work in their homes are excluded from statistics, even though such domestic labor is crucial to sustaining the labor supply (Elson 2000:23, 28).[5] Second, women's participation in the labor force has been increasing in most countries since the 1970s (United Nations 1999, 2000), and they make up about 40 percent of the world's paid workers (World Bank 2000). Much of this growth has been in the informal sector of the economy where income, benefits, and job security are precarious (Elson 2000; United Nations Population Fund 2000). Third, worldwide, women's work is less valued than men's, which is reflected in the lower pay of those who are employed and the lower prestige and power of those who do unpaid domestic work (Chen 2000; R. Smith 1999).

Sex Differences in Economic Activity Rates

Exhibits 2.2 and 2.3 present data on the economically active population age 15 and over at the end of the twentieth century. International data on employed women and men need to be interpreted with caution. Census takers' and respondents' perceptions about what makes up economic activity, along with women's greater tendency to work at tasks that are invisible or difficult to measure (such as informal work and subsistence production), can lead to underestimates of women's economic activity rates (United Nations Population Fund 2000: technical notes to Table 5d).[6] Moreover, because the data have no upper age limit, they underestimate both sexes' economic activity rates in regions where early retirement is popular, such as Europe and Scandinavia. Nevertheless, we can draw some conclusions about the sexual division of labor worldwide.

Women's participation in economic activity is lowest in Muslim societies that strictly segregate the sexes. In Saudi Arabia and Pakistan, for example, four-fifths of men are in the labor force, compared to less than one-fifth of women. Only 8 percent of women were economically active in the Occupied Palestinian Territories, compared to 68 percent of men, and

EXHIBIT 2.2
Economic Activity Rates for Women, 1995-1997

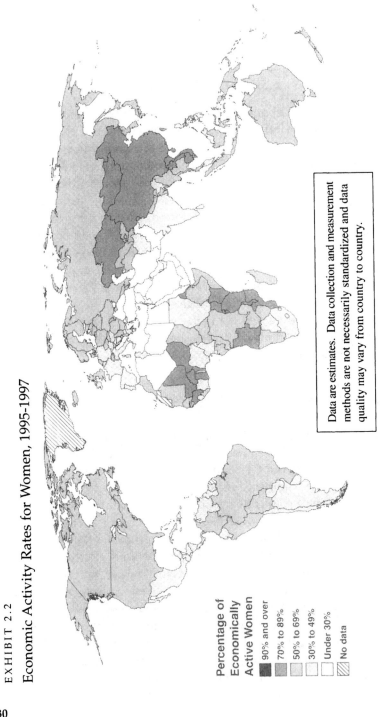

Percentage of
Economically
Active Women

■ 90% and over
▨ 70% to 89%
▨ 50% to 69%
☐ 30% to 49%
☐ Under 30%
☐ No data

Data are estimates. Data collection and measurement methods are not necessarily standardized and data quality may vary from country to country.

Source: United Nations 2000, table 5.D.

EXHIBIT 2.3

Economic Activity Rates for Men, 1995-1997

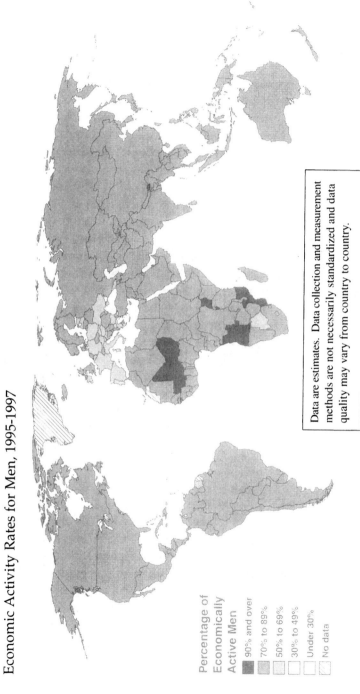

Percentage of
Economically
Active Men

90% and over
70% to 89%
50% to 69%
30% to 49%
Under 30%
No data

Data are estimates. Data collection and measurement methods are not necessarily standardized and data quality may vary from country to country.

Source: United Nations 2000, table 5.D.

only 17 percent in Iraq, compared to men's rate of 75. In developing countries that are not Muslim, such as Mexico and Brazil, men's rates of economic activity greatly exceed women's because of cultural conventions regarding who should work outside the home. In Mexico, for example, women's rate is 39 percent, compared to men's rate of 84 percent, and in Brazil women's economic activity rate is 51 percent, compared to men's rate of 82 percent.

The African countries of Tanzania, Mozambique, and Burundi have the highest recorded rates of female and male labor force participation— 83 percent for women and over 90 percent for men. China also reports a very high rate of female labor force participation (74 percent, compared to men's rate of 86 percent), reflecting the Marxist ideology that all able-bodied adults have both a right and an obligation to work.

Western European women's rates are lower than those in other developed countries, largely due to public policies encouraging women's domestic roles. Women's rate in Western Europe averages 49 percent, compared to 53 percent in Eastern Europe (men's rate in both regions is about 70 percent). In the United States and Canada, women's rates are around 60 percent, compared to about 75 percent for men. The sex gap in labor force participation is smaller than this in Scandinavian countries, such as Sweden (where women's rate is 65 percent and men's is 72) and Norway (where women's rate is 68 percent and men's is 78 percent), in part because public policies help women to combine paid and family work by providing paid parental leaves and prorated benefits for part-time jobs. We see in these patterns the influence of economic development, social policies, and cultural norms.

Informal Sector

In the industrialized world, employment typically involves a formal relationship between an employer and employee. In the developing world, however, much employment is in the **informal sector.** This sector is made up of small enterprises, the workers that these enterprises employ regularly, and casual workers with no fixed employment (Elson 2000:25). It includes both paid and many unpaid workers, especially people who work in family businesses and farms. Still other informal economy workers are self-employed or employ others, including small shop owners and street vendors. Such workers perform a range of tasks, such as writing letters for a fee, wrapping candy, collecting and recycling trash, street vending, and sex work. Neither labor regulations nor labor unions cover workers in the informal sector, so they rarely have health insurance or job security. Compared to the formal economy, the pay is low and the working conditions are poor (Pyle 1999:82).

Thousands of women and men work in the informal sector. According to one estimate, including agricultural workers, three-quarters of all workers in Africa and Asia and almost one-half in Latin America are in this sector.[7] Although regions vary widely in women's share of jobs in the informal sector, in much of the developing world, women are more likely than men to work in this sector (Elson 2000; United Nations 2000).

Globalization

The past two decades have witnessed a dramatic increase in **globalization,** the process by which owners of capital rapidly move money, goods, and jobs around the world in response to changing economic conditions. Several factors have fostered globalization: the actions of powerful institutions, such as multinational corporations and lending organizations such as the World Bank and the International Monetary Fund, the removal of state controls on trade and investment, and the spread of new information and communication technologies (Elson 2000:29; Pyle 1999). Because much of the macroeconomic policy that guides globalization assumes a male breadwinner who supports a wife and children as his dependents, the effects of globalization are gendered (Sen 2000; United Nations 1999).

Export-led development—producing goods and services for export rather than for domestic consumption—has become an increasingly important strategy for developing nations since the 1960s. This strategy has been responsible for large increases in female employment in certain sectors, particularly production jobs (Joekes and Weston 1994). Women's lower wages are an inducement to employers to hire them; for example, South Korean women earned only 58 percent of men's wages in 1994 (Kim and Kim 1995). Stereotypes of women as "nimble-fingered," compliant, and tolerant of repetitive work also account for employers' preference for women in many of these jobs (Domosh and Seager 2001:52; Pyle 1999:90).[8] Data on the ratio of male to female workers in export production are hard to come by (Pyle 1999), but women make up over 80 percent of workers in factories in export-processing zones in Mexico, Taiwan, Sri Lanka, Malaysia, and the Philippines and over 70 percent in South Korea and Guatemala (Domosh and Seager 2001:49).

Multinational corporations (MNCs) have become major employers in the past 20 years. Their export-oriented employment is responsible for 20 percent of the manufacturing jobs in several Asian, African, and Latin American countries (Joekes and Weston 1994). In sectors in which the highest business cost is wages rather than equipment, employers prefer women because they can pay them less than men. For this reason, these corporations employ mostly men in the heavy-industry sector (e.g., petrochemicals and automobiles) and mostly women in the consumer-goods sector (e.g., electronics, shoes) and the service sector, such as claims processing and airline reservations (Pyle 1999:90).

Although MNCs sometimes offer better pay and working conditions than local employers, MNC workers of both sexes are subject to long hours, mandatory overtime, unhealthy working conditions, and frequent work speedups (Pyle 1999:91; 2001). The severity of conditions depends in part on how long a nation has been involved in export-led growth, however, with those countries involved for longer periods having some-what higher wages and better working conditions due to workers' efforts (Pyle 1999:91). Yet, efforts to organize workers can backfire; the short-term result can be police repression, and the long-term result is often MNC flight to other countries where workers are more tractable (Pyle 2001).

For educated women with professional skills or access to capital, globalization has created better-paying opportunities and more auto-nomy (Elson 2000; Pyle 1999:84). Its effects on men and women who lack skills, particularly in developing countries, are mixed (Pyle 1999:102). Highly educated men in computer-related fields have done well in the global economy, but lower-skilled men tend to be confined to jobs in construction or mining that are dangerous and insecure. The impact of globalization on workers depends partly on how a nation is integrated into the global economy. Because international competition often means that the goods can be made more cheaply elsewhere in the world, globali-zation can draw workers into the labor force, only to leave them unem-ployed when the MNCs move. For example, in some places globalization advantages one group of women workers at the expense of another, as happened when companies moved production from the Caribbean to Mexico in the wake of the North American Free Trade Agreement (Joekes and Weston 1994).

Globalization has spurred international migration. Although men are the larger group of adult migrants, women's share has been increas-ing more rapidly in recent years (Elson 2000:31). Many Asian women, for example, emigrate temporarily as domestic workers or "entertainers" (Oishi 2001; Pyle 2001). Asian countries differ in whether they encourage (or allow) women to migrate for such jobs. Some countries have a stake in supporting such migration because it improves the balance of trade; others prohibit it to protect women's virtue.

In conclusion, the most powerful institutional actors in the global economy—multinational corporations and international trade organizations—do not hold gender equity as a goal. Organizations that do hold this goal—the United Nations, the International Labor Organization, and many nongovernmental organizations—have less institutional power than MNCs and trade organizations (Pyle 1999:98). Thus, little basis for women's equal integration into the new economy has been laid. Moreover, because the international financial system has no structures for dealing with the insecurities and risks that globalization creates, these risks tend to be borne by the workers at the bottom levels of the global economy, where women are concentrated. Thus, although both women and men face job loss when recessions and economic crises hit, women are more vulnerable (Pyle 1999:102).

Summary

This chapter has examined one major way that industrialization changed the sexual division of labor: It concentrated men in paid work away from the home and women in nonpaid domestic work in the home. In the Western world, this division of labor was most extreme during the nineteenth century. Its consequences persist today in gendered assumptions about men's and women's work and in the devaluation of women's work in both Western and non-Western societies. Chapter 4 examines a second form that sexual division of labor took under industrialization— the segregation of employed women and men in different kinds of work.

Notes

1. When Japan was industrializing at the end of the nineteenth century, it had similar all-female workshops (Kondo 1990:269-70).
2. Some historians believe that the owners treated the women's workshops as brothels (Herlihy 1990:85).
3. Eighteenth- and nineteenth-century British mine and factory owners openly exploited workers. Boys and girls as young as age 6 and women in their 60s labored in coal pits and in copper and lead mines. According to a mining supervisor, they worked "up to their knees in water." A commissioner described girls and women as "chained, belted, harnessed like dogs . . . crawling on hands and knees . . . dragging their heavy loads over soft slushy floors" (Pinchbeck 1930:248-49). Factory and mining work was dangerous for adults, too. For example, men who ran "spinning mules" in textile factories had to lift 160-pound frames every three seconds for 12 hours a day (Cohen 1985).

4. The labor force participation rate for unmarried European American women was 45 percent, 39 percent for Asian American women, and 59 percent for African American women (Amott and Matthaei 1996, Table 9.2).

5. The domestic burden has grown in many countries where economic restructuring has led to cuts in government services that had been provided in the public sphere. Government cutbacks mean that these services must be picked up in the domestic sphere (Pyle 1999:85; United Nations Population Fund 2000).

6. According to the United Nations Population Fund (2000: technical notes to Table 5d), the "economically active" population includes "all employed and unemployed persons, including those seeking work for the first time, employers operating unincorporated enterprises, persons working on their own account, employees, contributing family workers, members of producers' cooperatives, and members of the armed forces." Included also are such nonmonetary activities as producing foodstuffs, fetching water, and collecting firewood for personal consumption along with constructing, repairing, and renovating an owner-occupied dwelling.

7. Excluding agricultural workers, up to one-half of the urban labor force in Africa and Asia and one-quarter in Latin America and the Caribbean can be found in this sector (Elson 2000:25).

8. Although many employers once sought this package of attributes only in young unmarried women, in many countries they increasingly are turning to married women.

3

An Overview of Sex Inequality at Work

This chapter first summarizes women's and men's unequal status in the contemporary American workplace. Then it introduces several general explanations that may account for sex inequality at work.

Sex Inequality in the Contemporary American Workplace

The workplace is often a context for sex inequality in our society. First, insofar as employers concentrate women and men in different workplaces and assign different duties to them, the workplace maintains sex differentiation. Second, because jobs are the primary way that most adults acquire income and social standing, sex differentiation in jobs leads to unequal earnings, authority, and social status for women and men. Finally, interaction at work may subject women to subtle and not-so-subtle expressions of inequality—from paternalism to sexual harassment and from invisibility to ostracism; it may also subject men to long work hours and to unsafe work practices.

Sex inequality at work takes three primary forms.

Sex Segregation. Chapter 1 showed that throughout history, societies have imposed a sexual division of labor in which women and men perform different tasks. Another term for this sexual division of labor is **sex segregation,** the concentration of men and women in different kinds of work. America's workplaces tend to be sex segregated, like those in the rest of the world. The modal pattern is for men to work with other men and for women to work with other women. It is the unusual worker who has a coworker of the other sex who does the same job, for the same employer, in the same location, and on the same shift (Carrington and Troske 1994; Nelson and Bridges 1999; Petersen and Morgan 1995). Of course, other ascribed characteristics of workers besides their sex affect what jobs they get. Workplaces also are segregated by race, ethnicity, and age. African American women are concentrated in different jobs than Mexican American women, for example, who in turn are underrepresented in jobs in which European American women predominate. European American men, Latinos, and Asian American men tend to be concentrated in different jobs. Importantly, the jobs in which minority and majority women and men are concentrated not only are different, they are also unequal.

Sex Differences in Promotions and Authority. Across the board, men do not have a promotion advantage over women. There are subgroups and work contexts in which each sex has an advantage, however. Men still dominate the top levels in the organizations that employ them and monopolize the highest ranks in most occupations and professions. Even in predominantly female lines of work, such as nursing, the higher the position, the more likely the jobholder is to be male (Williams 1995). Many women who achieve jobs in midlevel ranks find top-level positions beyond their reach. This phenomenon is known as the **glass ceiling:** an invisible ceiling prevents some workers from advancing. This is not to say that all the bad jobs are staffed by women and all the good jobs by men. Both sexes are distributed across the range of good and bad jobs. But when you look at the tails of the occupational distribution, you will find more men in really good jobs and more women in really bad ones (Kalleberg, Reskin, and Hudson 2000, Table 4). Moreover, women supervise fewer subordinates than men and are less likely to control financial resources. Even female managers—whose numbers have grown dramatically—are less likely than male managers to make decisions, especially decisions that are vital for their employer (Jacobs 1992; Reskin and Ross 1992).

Sex Differences in Earnings. In the United States and around the world, men outearn women. At the turn of the twenty-first century, for example, U.S. women who worked full time, year-round, averaged a little over 72 percent of what similar men earned (U.S. Census Bureau 1998, 1999, 2000a). Put differently, for every dollar paid to a woman who worked full time, year-round, a man earned $1.39. What's more, men are more likely than women to have health insurance and other benefits. The consequences of these disparities in earnings and benefits follow workers into old age; among retired persons, women have lower incomes and higher rates of poverty than men. In 1997, elderly unmarried women had average incomes of $11,161 a year compared to $14,769 for elderly unmarried men and \$29,278 for elderly married couples (National Economic Council Interagency Working Group on Social Security 1998). As a result, among the elderly, 13 percent of women were in poverty, compared to 7 percent of men.

The three chapters that follow look more closely at how and why gender is linked to advantages and disadvantages on these three dimensions. Now we provide overviews of the reasons social scientists offer for these types of sex inequality.

Explanations for Sex Inequality in the Workplace

Sex inequality persists in many places of work in part because it is embedded in the ideology of many societies and because the beneficiaries in systems of inequality have a stake in maintaining social arrangements that give them an advantage. But before considering these general approaches to understanding widespread sex inequality, it is important to remember that we can explain only phenomena that vary. If sex inequality at work were universally high, we would have no way to find out its causes. We could only guess. Because the degree of sex inequality varies across places of work within the United States and other countries, researchers can determine what factors are associated with higher and lower levels of inequality and, hence, explain it.

Although the discussion that follows focuses on Western cultural beliefs about gender and work, bear in mind that Western beliefs are by no means universal. As you saw in Chapter 1, men's work in one culture may be women's work in another. Cultural values can also change, either in response to outside influences or in response to pressure from within a society. Regarding the former, anthropologists, geographers, and historians have documented how the introduction of Western notions about the sexual division of labor into non-Western societies has undermined women's traditional economic roles. In India, for example, the transformations brought about by the "green revolution" (the introduction of high-yield seeds, chemical fertilizers, and pesticides) displaced women's labor because the large-scale mechanized agriculture it inspired falls in men's traditional realm (Dunlop and Velkoff 1999). Thus, whereas previously 20 women would have been employed hand milling rice, now one man is employed to operate the milling machine (Ramamurthy 1996:473). Similarly, although water-related tasks had been in women's domain in Zaire, when Western relief workers arrived in the wake of the Rwandan refugee crisis in 1994 to train locals to install plumbing, they trained men, not women (Enloe 2000). A sense of urgency overrode any desire on relief workers' part to take time to challenge the traditional sex-stereotyped assumptions that technical tasks are men's domain. As for cultural change from within, the Taliban government, which held power in Afghanistan between 1996 and 2001, banned women from holding any public jobs, even though Afghani women had been active in the labor force for decades. Such changes are rarely generated solely from within a culture, however. In the case of Afghanistan, the rise of the Islamic fundamentalist Taliban government can be attributed partly to earlier actions of the U.S.S.R. and the United States, as well as the regional powers of Saudi Arabia and Pakistan (Burns and Levine 1996).

In this section, we begin by discussing some general factors that have historically maintained high levels of sex inequality at work. We then consider what we can conclude about the factors associated with higher or lower levels of sex inequality across work settings.

Gender Ideology and Inequality at Work

All systems of inequality are supported by an ideology that justifies differential rewards and opportunities. **Gender ideology** is a set of widely shared assumptions about the way the sexes are and what the relations between them are and ought to be. The content of the gender ideology shapes both norms about how people are expected to behave and sex stereotypes. A nineteenth-century poem by Alfred Lord Tennyson illustrates the assumptions present in gender ideology around the world:

> *Man for the field and women for the hearth:*
> *Man for the sword and for the needle she:*
> *Man with the head and woman with the heart:*
> *Man to command and woman to obey;*
> *All else confusion.*

The first assumption the poem expresses is that women and men innately differ in fundamental ways and hence are naturally suited for different roles in life. The ideological claim, however, is not simply that the sexes differ, but that men and women are opposites. What one sex is, the other is not. For example, the second line in Tennyson's poem, which says that men are governed by reason ("the head") and women by emotion ("the heart"), attributes to the two sexes opposing ways of dealing with life.

As Chapter 1 argues, gender difference is not left to chance; societies go to great lengths to ensure that the sexes differ in appearance, talents, interests, and so forth. One way to produce difference is by separating the sexes ("man for the fields, woman for the hearth"), as in the ideology of separate spheres. In many developing countries, this ideology limits women's employment options. In fundamentalist communities in the United States and abroad, employment patterns differ dramatically from those in Western urban communities. Physical segregation keeps women close to home and out of the paid labor force. In some fundamentalist communities, women without male relatives who can support them are forced to find ways to earn income without incurring the public shame of employment. In some rural Muslim communities, women work at home, weaving, embroidering, or hand-rolling cigarettes for very low wages (Wilkinson-Weber 1999:69, 197). Occasionally, however, women work outside the home, particularly in the occupations of teaching and medicine where they serve a female clientele (Smith 1994:321). In the contemporary Western world, where women are firmly established in the workforce, the most dramatic expressions of the ideology of separate spheres are in customarily male industries (e.g., construction, mining, railroads) and in the unequal division of housework.

As Chapter 2 shows, one way that societies achieved gender difference after the Industrial Revolution was a sexual division of labor that assigned men to paid jobs and women to domestic work in their own homes. This sexual division of labor supported the ideological assumption that only paid work is "real work," which implies that women do not do real work. This assumption supports gender inequality at work in several ways. First, employers organized jobs on the assumption that workers had a woman at home who took care of them when they were away from work, fed them, washed their clothes, gave them emotional support, helped their careers, and dealt with family problems.

Second, the assumption implies that employed women are temporary workers who will quit when they are needed at home or can afford to stay home. Hence, employers do not need to accommodate women's needs as primary family caregivers. Third, it assumes that employed women are not committed to their careers. Hence, employers do not need to provide promotion opportunities for women and should not assign them to positions where turnover might be a problem.

The assumption that men work for pay and women do not implies that employers must pay men enough to support themselves and their dependents and provide for a retirement income, but that they do not need to pay women enough to support themselves in the present, much less after retirement. From these assumptions three corollaries follow:

- Men, as the "real" breadwinners, deserve priority for high-paying jobs.

- Because women are the "real" domestic workers, men don't need to know how to do housework and are entitled to leisure when they are not working for pay.

- As "real" workers, men, but not women, invest in acquiring skills. From this, it follows that men's jobs are more skilled than women's, which in turn implies that men's jobs merit higher pay than women's jobs.

The second gender-linked ideological assumption in Tennyson's poem is that men are naturally superior to women. This assumption legitimates sex inequality across all spheres of activity. In the workplace, it justifies men's monopoly of top-level jobs and decision-making posts. According to Barbara Bergmann (1986:114-16), many employers adhere to an informal segregation code that keeps women from supervising men and that reserves the training slots leading to higher-level jobs for men. Men may rule over women and junior men, women rule over women, but women rarely rule over men.

A corollary of this assumption of male superiority is **paternalism,** the notion that women, like children, are inferior creatures whom men must take care of (Jackman 1994). For example, an article directed to male supervisors of women who worked in the transportation industry during World War II instructs them to: "Give every girl an adequate number of rest periods during the day. . . . Be tactful when issuing instructions or making criticisms. . . . Be reasonably considerate about using strong language around women" (Sanders 1943:257).

Sex Stereotypes. **Sex stereotypes**—socially shared beliefs that link various traits, attributes, and skills with one sex or the other—are part of gender ideology. Common sex stereotypes assume that men are naturally more rational, aggressive, and stronger, and that women are more emotional, passive, and nurturant. For example, 60 percent of Americans believe that women are naturally better suited than men are to caring for children (Davis, Smith, and Marsden 2000).

Sex stereotypes often operate in tandem with race stereotypes. Thus, some employers stereotype black women as single mothers. This leads them to see black women as more in need of jobs than black men (whom they stereotype as not having families) and, hence, makes them more desirable workers than black men. At the same time, this stereotype leads employers to assume that black women would have problems arranging child care, which would cause them to miss work (Browne and Kennelly 1999).

Stereotypes are "overlearned," which means that they are habitual and automatic. As a result, they influence our perceptions and behaviors without our awareness. According to social psychological research, we all engage in unconscious as well as conscious stereotyping, and we do so automatically to process the flood of complex information that the world presents to us. This means that we stereotype people independently of whether we like or dislike the group to which they belong (Bodenhausen and Macrae 1996). If a newscaster reports a complaint that a police officer used excessive force, who do you imagine wielding the nightstick? Very likely, an adult police*man*. (Some of us may even doubt that a police-woman is capable of such aggressiveness.) Automatic stereotyping explained an embarrassing experience for an elevator operator at the House of Representatives who told a newly elected African American congresswoman that she could not use an elevator reserved for members of the House; he had assumed that congressional representatives were not black and female. Importantly, stereotypes about who should do what kind of work affect everyone in a society: prospective workers, customers, and the people who hire workers, assign them to jobs, and set their pay.

Sex Labeling of Jobs. Sex stereotypes, in conjunction with stereotypes about the characteristics that various jobs require, lead jobs to be labeled as either men's or women's work (Oppenheimer 1968). For example, Western cultures stereotype men as assertive and competitive. These notions, along with the assumptions that assertive salespeople sell more cars and that combative lawyers win more cases, imply that men will naturally outdo women at selling cars or arguing cases in court. Both sex stereotypes and job stereotypes are often off the mark. Insurance companies, for example, have learned not only that a soft sell is often more effective than a hard sell, but also that women are perfectly capable of delivering a hard sell when it is called for. Nonetheless, you will see in the following chapters that sex and job stereotypes contribute to various forms of sex inequality at work.

We tend to take for granted the governing ideologies with which we grow up, and hence we rarely question them. Their invisibility makes these assumptions especially powerful in shaping our behavior. For example, if it never occurs to a branch manager that a female clerk might accept a promotion to night manager, he will not offer her the promotion. The manager's assumptions about sex differences in women and men workers' desire for promotion, need for a raise, willingness to work nights, or family responsibilities prevent him from even considering offering the promotion to a woman. Unless external circumstances prompt us to examine the assumptions our ideologies make, they will support gender inequality at work.

Men's Efforts to Preserve Their Advantages in the Workplace

A second explanation for sex inequality emphasizes the idea that privileged or **dominant groups** try to preserve the advantages their group enjoys (Blauner 1972; Collins 1974; Goode 1982). Monarchs rarely give up their kingdoms, and corporate executives rarely voluntarily step down to less-powerful positions; on the contrary, powerful groups are bent on retaining and even expanding their power and privileges. They do so in a variety of ways, including denying **subordinate groups** the opportunity to acquire the skills needed to advance and segregating them into different spheres.

Men and women do not differ when it comes to the impulse to retain their advantages. They do differ in their social positions, however, and women usually lack the power or the incentive to exclude men from "women's" jobs. When women occupy powerful structural positions, they exercise power to exclude others. For example, history offers accounts of white women resisting the entry of women of color into their domain (Glenn 1996:139; Milkman 1987).

Why do some men see women as threats to their advantaged position? First, we stress that all men do not regard women as threats; many welcome women's employment gains. Nevertheless, some men fear that women might take jobs away from them, outperform them on the job, or lead employers to cut a job's pay. Furthermore, if women can perform "macho" jobs such as coal mining, police work, truck driving, and construction, these jobs lose their capacity to confirm male workers' masculinity. Some men also fear that having female coworkers will lower the prestige of their work. A male law professor reportedly rejected a female applicant for a faculty position, insisting: "This is a law school, not a goddamn nursing school!" Finally, men may worry that women's equality at work will undermine men's privileges in other realms: If women earned as much as men and had as much authority at work, they could insist on greater equality in the family, the community, and national political life. In view of all the benefits that men, especially white men, enjoy because of their sex, it is not surprising that some men take action to preserve their advantaged status.

Like other groups concerned about competition from lower-paid workers, the first line of defense of some male workers has been to try to exclude women. As we saw, guilds typically barred women from apprenticeships. More recently, states refused to license women to practice law and women could not get jobs as police officers, among dozens of examples of organized exclusion. One effective exclusionary strategy has been to prevent women from acquiring the necessary qualifications for what are considered customarily male jobs. Some unions, for example, have barred women from apprenticeship programs, and before 1970, professional schools admitted few women.

When entry barriers begin to give way, some workers try to drive out outsiders by making them miserable on the job. For example, when the U.S. Department of the Treasury hired its first women in 1870, men blew smoke and spat tobacco juice at them and yelled catcalls (Baker 1977:86). A hundred years later, women entering customarily male blue-collar jobs received similar treatment. A woman described how, on her first day on the job at a construction site, the foreman said, "I never worked with no fucking woman and I ain't never going to. I will run you off of this job before this week is over" (Eisenberg 1998:132). Another strategy to drive out female pioneers is to prevent them from doing the job properly by denying them information, giving them the wrong tools, or sabotaging their work (Eisenberg 1998). Even if most men are neutral or welcoming, a few can create a hostile environment (Bergmann and Darity 1981).

When barriers to training or entry disappear—either because there are enough jobs so that women don't pose a threat or because an employer no longer tolerates such barriers—sex inequality declines. This has occurred in several occupations in the United States in the last three decades of the twentieth century (Reskin and Roos 1990).

Employers' Actions

The amount of sex inequality at work depends largely on the actions of employers, because it is employers who hire workers, assign them to jobs, decide whom to promote, and set pay. Employers have contributed

Source: © Clay Bennett, *The Christian Science Monitor*; used by permission.

to sex inequality primarily by concentrating women in some jobs and excluding them from others. In contrast, some have undermined inequality by assigning jobs without regard for workers' sex. To understand how employers' hiring practices produce sex inequality, consider the three ways that employers locate prospective workers. Some choose from a pool of applicants, some use formal intermediaries such as employment agencies, and still others rely on referrals by their employees. This third method—workers' referrals—is most common because it is free and efficient at screening out unacceptable job candidates. However, recruiting new employees through workers' referrals tends to perpetuate inequality. First, people's social networks tend to comprise others of the same sex, ethnicity, and race (Braddock and McPartland 1987; Lin 2000). Second, sex stereotypes, fear of competition, and concern with coworkers' and bosses' reactions prevent workers from recommending someone of the "wrong" sex or race. For example, a worker whose sister-in-law is looking for work may hesitate to nominate her for a job in his all-male department because his coworkers may be mad, his boss will hold him responsible if she doesn't measure up, or she may blame him if the boss or workers give her a hard time.

Employers also contribute to levels of sex inequality through job assignments. Who ends up in what job is almost entirely up to employers and managers, whose biases or stereotypes can lead them to assign women and men to different jobs or whose hiring practices may fill jobs without regard to workers' sex. A sex discrimination lawsuit against Lucky Stores, a West Coast grocery chain, illustrates how stereotypes and managerial discretion excluded women from some jobs. At the trial, a Lucky's executive testified that his experience managing a store 30 years earlier had convinced him that "men preferred working on the floor to working at the cash register . . . and that women preferred working at the cash register" (*Stender et al. v. Lucky* 1992). The qualifications that employers require also influence whom they assign to what jobs. Some organizations require experiences that, although unnecessary to do the job, are more common among men. Requiring production experience for a management job, for example, may unnecessarily restrict the number of women in the pool of job candidates. Recently Home Depot was sued for sex discrimination, in part because it steered job applicants with previous cash register experience into jobs as cashiers. Because women were more likely to have such experience, they rarely got jobs on the sales floor. When Home Depot altered this and other practices, sex segregation declined.

Why might employers treat female and male workers differently? They may do so because of either conscious or unconscious biases toward women or because they believe it will be more profitable in the long run.

Discrimination. **Discrimination** is treating people unequally because of personal characteristics that are not related to their performance.[1] Few would claim that a local park is discriminating by refusing to hire a 9-year-old girl as a lifeguard. Presumably, age is relevant to ensuring the safety of a pool full of swimmers (and the park wouldn't hire a 9-year-old boy either). In contrast, refusing to hire a 19-year-old because she is female while hiring 19-year-old males is sex discrimination, because sex is irrelevant to the ability to perform the job.

Around the world and for most of the history of the United States, employers have openly discriminated on the basis of sex, as well as on the basis of race, ethnicity, national origin, age, appearance, and sexual orientation. Employers have refused to hire women and other social minorities, segregated them into jobs different from those held by white men, denied them promotions, and paid them lower wages. Until quite recently, employers discriminated without a second thought. In the mid-nineteenth century, the publisher of the *New York Herald*, for example, stormed into the newspaper's office one day and bellowed, "Who are these females? Fire them all!" (Robertson 1992:46). In 1977, when the *New York Times* was sued for sex discrimination, its publisher asked why a private company "can't have men around if it wants to?" (Robertson 1992:186). Although such discrimination seems outrageous today, until 35 years ago, it was both legal and commonplace. It took the civil rights movement of the early 1960s to persuade Americans that race discrimination is unfair and to spur Congress and state legislatures to outlaw employment discrimination based on sex as well as race and national origin.

Congress outlawed employment discrimination on the basis of race, national origin, religion, sex, age, and disability by passing Title 7 of the 1964 Civil Rights Act and its amendments. The law made it illegal for employers with at least 15 full-time workers to treat workers differently based on the characteristics listed earlier in hiring, job assignment, discharge, compensation, and other terms, conditions, or privileges of employment. Most states also passed laws against discrimination in employment.

The agency charged with enforcing the law, the Equal Employment Opportunity Commission (EEOC), has been underbudgeted for much of its history, however, so the burden of enforcement has fallen largely on the victims of discrimination (Reskin 2001). Nonetheless, cases against a few large employers have expanded all workers' legal rights to jobs, irrespective of their sex or race. With some of these firms, the EEOC negotiated consent decrees that led the employers to restructure their personnel practices. Others in the same industry have voluntarily followed suit. Despite progress, antidiscrimination enforcement agencies and the courts still receive thousands of legitimate complaints of employment discrimination. For example, investigators for the federal Office of Federal Contract Compliance Programs (OFCCP) found that Dart, Inc., gave male applicants tests of mechanical aptitude for well-paying, semiskilled jobs while it gave female applicants tests of manual dexterity for low-paying, unskilled jobs (Reskin 1998). The world's largest home-improvement retailer, Home Depot, agreed to pay over $85 million to settle sex discrimination lawsuits claiming that it had passed over women for sales and management positions and confined them to low-paying jobs (Roush 1997), and in 1999 the Kohler Corporation agreed to pay almost $1 million for hiring practices that kept women out of nontraditional blue-collar jobs. In the 1990s, the

Equal Employment Opportunity Commission received more than 24,000 complaints of sex discrimination per year (U.S. Equal Employment Opportunity Commission 1999), and over one-third of 2,000 Americans surveyed said that they had personally faced discrimination in the job market (NBC News/*Wall Street Journal* 2000). A small proportion of these complaints allege "reverse discrimination," as Chapter 4 shows; most complaints are from women and minorities (Burstein 1991:518).

Sexual harassment is a form of discrimination under Title 7.[2] The Equal Employment Opportunity Commission and the courts have recognized two types of illegal sexual harassment. One is *quid pro quo*, in which a supervisor demands sexual acts from a worker as a job condition or promises work-related benefits in exchange for sexual acts. The other is "hostile work environment," in which a pattern of sexual intimidation, touching, verbal abuse, or displays of offensive literature make a worker so uncomfortable that it is difficult for her or him to do the job.

Sexual harassment is endemic in the workplace: The EEOC reported almost 16,000 complaints in 2000 (U.S. Equal Employment Opportunity Commission 2001a), although most complaints go unreported. It contributes to sex differences in workplace outcomes. First, women are more likely to be harassed than men (only one EEOC complaint in seven was from a man), and the vast majority complained of treatment by men. Second, compared to men who have been harassed, women who have been harassed are nine times more likely to quit a job, five times more likely to transfer, and three times more likely to lose a job (National Council for Research on Women 1995).

The courts have held employers liable for both types, ruling that employers are responsible for their employees' on-the-job actions if the employer has been informed of the problem. Sexual harassment can be expensive. Not counting the toll on productivity, monetary damages can be high; in 2000, the EEOC collected $55 million from employers for sexual harassment violations of Title 7. Successful lawsuits cost employers additional millions. For example, the EEOC estimated that Mitsubishi Motors Manufacturing will pay 350 current and former employees $300,000 each (the maximum allowed under a federal cap) plus $9.5 million to settle a private sexual harassment lawsuit.

Statistical Discrimination. Another reason some employers discriminate against women is the belief that employing women will reduce profits because they are less productive or more costly to employ. The idea that women may be more expensive employees stems from the assumption that motherhood will cause women to miss more work than men or will lead to higher turnover rates. The practice of treating individuals on the basis of beliefs about the group to which they belong is called **statistical discrimination.** Although employers may legally refuse to hire or promote an individual who cannot do the job, it is illegal to treat an individual differently solely because she or he belongs to a sex, race, or national-origin group that is, on average, less productive or more costly to employ. Moreover, workers' productivity, absenteeism, and turnover are largely a function of production processes and job qualities. Statistical discrimination is illegal under U.S. antidiscrimination laws.

Customers' and Male Workers' Attitudes. Some employers discriminate against men or women out of deference to the prejudices of their customers or workers. Until the early 1970s, for example, airlines refused to hire male flight attendants because they claimed their passengers preferred females. Then the Supreme Court let stand a lower court ruling that customers' discriminatory preferences do not justify sex discrimination (*Diaz v. Pan American* 1971), opening the occupation of flight attendant to men (and eventually to older people). Nonetheless, many employers still defer to customers' discriminatory preferences (Trentham and Larwood 1998). A study of female security workers found that most security firm clients don't care, but the few who expressed a preference wanted men (Erickson, Albanese, and Drakulic 2000:314). Client or customer preferences can combine gender and race/ethnicity, as was the case among employers who told a temporary agency not to send any "Maria's" or Kim's"—by which they meant Latinas or Asian women (Rogers 2000). This study of temporary agencies found a widespread desire for workers from certain sex and racial/ethnic groups, although clients expressed it through the use of code words, as when they requested "articulate" or "front office" applicants, by which they meant "white." Although some temporary agencies refused such requests, many honored even the most egregious ones, particularly if they came from a major client.

Sex Differences in Workers' Preferences and Productivity

Up to now, we have focused on how the actions of employers and male workers contribute to sex inequality in the workplace. Now we turn to explanations that emphasize the differences between female and male workers. Some social scientists and employers argue that women choose customarily female jobs, do not want promotions, and willingly accept lower wages because, unlike men, they are not primarily oriented to career success.

Why should women willingly settle for fewer opportunities and rewards than men? Why should men work harder or aspire to greater occupational heights? The main explanations that social scientists have proposed boil down to the claim that women's primary orientation is to their families, not their jobs, and that the reverse is true for men.

Human-Capital Theory. Mainstream economic theory assumes that labor markets operate in a nondiscriminatory fashion, rewarding workers for their productivity. Thus, if women are worse off than men, it is because they are less productive workers. This assumption cannot be tested, however, because measuring productivity is impossible for many jobs. So researchers examine characteristics that they assume affect productivity— the skills, experience, and commitment that workers bring to their jobs. Economists refer to workers' skills and experience as their **human capital.** Theoretically, according to economists, through education, training, and experience, male workers invest in their human capital, and these investments enhance their productivity. Human-capital theory assumes that women's orientation to their families inhibits their investment in education, training, and experience and thus makes women less productive than men (Blau, Ferber, and Winkler 1998; Polachek 1981).

The amount of schooling people have is indeed important for whether they are in the labor force, the jobs they hold, their authority, and their earnings. But sex differences in years of education are not very consequential for explaining most forms of sex inequality in the workplace. Although male and female workers similarly average a little more than 12 years of education, men are both less likely than women to finish high school and more likely to go beyond the master's degree (Bianchi 1995). In addition, male and female college students tend to major in different subjects, and this difference contributes to the pay gap between women and men (Jacobs 1996a:175). Although the sexes are about equally likely to obtain bachelor's degrees in business, women are overrepresented in the humanities, education, and foreign languages (Eisenhart 1996:232; Morgan 1999). Men are overrepresented in engineering, where they received 82 percent of bachelor's degrees (Morgan 1999), and in computer science, where they received 83 percent of such degrees (Camp, Miller, and Davies 2000). In general, about 30 percent of women or men would have to change majors for the sexes to be identically distributed across majors (Jacobs 1995). Thus, educational differences contribute considerably to sex inequality in science and engineering occupations, but such occupations represent about 3 percent of jobs (Wilkinson 1998). For most other occupations, educational differences play a minor role in sex inequality.

Job training is a different story. Women and men tend to receive different kinds of training because the most important source of training occurs on the job, and women and men do different jobs. In addition, women's jobs are less likely than men's jobs to provide on-the-job training (Kilbourne, England, Farkas, Beron, and Weir 1994). Women are more likely than men to obtain training on their own (Amirault 1992). Employers often expect workers in traditionally female occupations, such as nursing and cosmetology, to obtain and pay for their own training before they start work. People also acquire training in the public school system and in community colleges. In the past, much of the job training that public schools provided was sex segregated, channeling males and females into different courses. In fact, the federal law that established vocational education specified job training for males and home economics for females. Another source of training is apprenticeship programs, most of which are run by unions in conjunction with the U.S. Department of Labor. Like their ancestors, the medieval guilds, these training programs often exclude women (Eisenberg 1998). In fact, the occupations that the U.S. Census Bureau lists as having formal apprenticeship programs are virtually all male (U.S. Census Bureau 1998, 1999, 2000a). These differences in job training contribute to women's lower workplace status.

Experience, the third proxy for human capital, presents a more complicated picture. Women average less work experience than men, although the difference has been narrowing. In the mid-1980s experts predicted that the average 18-year-old woman would be in the labor force about 29 years, 9.4 years less than the average 18-year-old male (Smith 1985).[3] Women are also less likely than men to be continuously employed (Wilson and Wu 1993, table 5). The chapters that follow address the effects of experience on the assignment of women and men to different jobs, on women's and men's chances of promotion, and on the earnings gap.

Before leaving this subject, we note that some people question the assumption that more educated or experienced workers are more productive. Of course, many factors affect workers' productivity apart from the training and experience they bring to the job. For example, productivity is strongly influenced by the way employers organize work and the commitment that workers bring to their job.

In sum, the human-capital theory that sex inequality at work arises from women's lower human capital could better explain inequality 30 years ago, when it was first proposed, than it can today. Now that most women plan on paid employment for most of their lives, their investments in education and experience increasingly resemble men's. Nonetheless, Chapters 4 through 6 show that human-capital differences between the sexes still account for some of the sex inequality in today's workplace.

Gender-Role Socialization. Human-capital theory does not try to explain its assumption that women are oriented primarily to their families rather than their careers. Gender-role socialization theories address that issue. **Gender-role socialization** is the process by which social institutions—including families, peers, schools, workplaces, and the media—inculcate a society's expectations of acceptable dress, speech, personality, leisure activities, and aspirations for each sex (Kimmel 2000:122; Stockard 1999:224).

Gender-role socialization might contribute to unequal workplace outcomes in several ways. First, it might lead women to be oriented more to their families and men more to their jobs. Traditionally, girls tended to be socialized to want to have babies, cook, and do domestic work, whereas boys were socialized to earn a living and to place other family obligations below work ones. Insofar as such differences in socialization persist, then it might be the case that the different socialization of females and males incline them to pursue those jobs that society has deemed acceptable for their sex. Also, socialization may contribute to a tendency for men and women to hold different values that affect their work lives, such as how important it is to have authority on the job or to make lots of money. Finally, men's gender-role socialization may encourage them to expect a sexual division of labor at work that reserves for them certain jobs, an inside track on promotions, a position of authority, and higher pay for their work, as well as a sexual division of labor at home that relieves them of most day-to-day domestic work. Because men are usually the workplace decision makers, some men are in a position to enforce these expectations.

Can the concept of gender-role socialization help explain workplace inequality? Some sociologists and economists argue that socialization orients women (but not men) to home and family, so women choose jobs that are easy to combine with their duties to their families. A different path to the same result is the idea that family demands hamper women's ability to compete with men for jobs and promotions. Similarly, traditional socialization for men is consistent with their pursuit of jobs in which they can achieve economic success. Women's responsibility for most of the domestic work and child rearing and most men's avoidance of these tasks also are consistent with this explanation for men's advantaged position at work. Are such traditional socialization experiences and attitudes typical today? A recent survey of over a quarter million first-year students at four-year colleges showed that 73 percent of both women and men listed "raising a family" as an essential objective for themselves; men were only slightly more likely than women to list as an essential goal "being very well off financially" (American Council on Education and UCLA Higher Education Research Institute 2001).

Other research casts further doubt on the idea that sex inequality reflects the sexes' different orientations to their families and jobs. Importantly, women's job commitment is no lower than men's (Aven, Parker, and McEvoy 1993; Marsden, Kalleberg, and Cook 1993). Moreover, the kind of job a worker holds affects career commitment more than does the worker's sex (Bielby and Bielby 2002; Marsden et al. 1993), and the same factors—working conditions, autonomy on the job, and promotional opportunities—increase men's and women's commitment (Cassirer and Reskin 2000). In fact, women report devoting more effort to their jobs than men do in jobs with similar amounts of autonomy (Bielby and Bielby 1988). Studies based on national data found little or no effects of family commitments on women's work effort (Bielby et al. 1995; Marsden et al. 1993). Of course, sex differences in attachment to family roles can contribute to men's higher rates of labor force participation and their greater numbers of hours worked per week and weeks worked per year, which in turn bolsters their earnings advantage.

Although popular discourse assumes that childhood socialization permanently shapes adult outlook, it is not very important for explaining women's and men's concentration in different jobs, their different rates of promotion, and their different average earnings. People are subject to social influences throughout the course of their lives, not just during childhood. Many workplace outcomes attributed to childhood socialization probably reflect the result of lifelong processes of **social control**—the ongoing rewards and punishments people experience in response to their behavior. Imagine a couple with two children. When the wife's employer sends her for a week of management training, her husband is glad for an excuse to spend more time with the kids. But when he tells his boss that he can't work overtime because he has to pick up the children from day care, the boss disapproves. The next year, when his wife proposes another trip, he balks. His reaction is not a result of the subtle messages he may have absorbed as a child; rather, it is more closely related to present-day rewards (enjoying his kids, pleasing his wife) and punishments (having his boss question his commitment). His wife's case illustrates the same point. When she was 19 years old, she may have thought that she would work for a few years after marriage and then quit to raise her children, returning to work after the children were older. But the reward of being selected for management training and the potential punishment of scraping by on one income are likely to trump these adolescent assumptions.

Summary

Sex inequality in the workplace is manifest in several ways: The sexes are concentrated in different jobs; women are often confined to lower-ranking positions than men and are less likely to exercise authority; women earn less than men; men work longer hours; and predominantly male jobs are more likely to expose workers to physical hazards. Social scientists have advanced several explanations for these disparities: cultural factors, sex stereotypes, the preservation of male advantage, and discrimination by employers. Also contributing to unequal outcomes are differences in men's and women's training and experience. Bear in mind, however, that our goal is to explain why the level of sex inequality varies across work settings, across groups, across countries, and over time. To answer these questions, social scientists must see if variation in causal factors is linked systematically to variation in levels of sex inequality. In the next three chapters, we return to the general explanatory factors presented in this chapter, paying special attention to evidence that variation in these factors is associated with variation in sex differences in workplace opportunities and rewards.

Notes

1. Sociologist Robert Merton (1972:20) proposed a similar definition: Discrimination consists of treating functionally irrelevant characteristics as if they were relevant.
2. The EEOC and the courts also have held that harassment based on race and on disability are discriminatory under Title 7.
3. These are the most recently available projections.

4

Sex Segregation in the Workplace

When the British Foreign Office hired its first female employees in the last half of the nineteenth century, it hid them in an attic to prevent any contact with male workers. On payday, the hallways were cleared of men before the women were sent running down to the first floor to pick up their wages (Cohn 1985:129). However bizarre such rigid separation of the sexes may seem today, some countries remain as strict. In some Muslim countries, female sales clerks work only in shops catering to women clientele, and female factory workers are employed only in factories where the whole workforce is female. Some garment factories in Bangladesh, for example, employ women on one floor and men on another to ensure that no interaction occurs between them (Anker 1998:26).

Contrasting these examples with the United States in the first decade of the twenty-first century, where women and men sometimes work side by side, you might conclude that Western societies have eliminated sex segregation at work. In this chapter, we show that although the form and extent of segregation vary, American women and men are still often concentrated in different kinds of work. We use the theories introduced in Chapter 3 to explain why levels of segregation vary across times, places, and work settings.

Sex segregation in the workplace refers to the different distributions of men and women across different occupations, jobs, and places of work. Sometimes and in some places, as in the preceding examples, sex segregation separates the sexes physically: Women and men do the same (or different) tasks in different settings. For instance, a bank may employ female managers at its suburban branches and employ male managers downtown, or a security firm may hire female guards for day shifts and men for night shifts. The concept of sex segregation also applies to situations in which the sexes share the same place of work but do different jobs, as in a research laboratory where female technicians work alongside male scientists or in an office shared by female clerks and male managers.

Notice that this second form of segregation is identical to the concept of the sexual division of labor, which we discussed in Chapter 1.

Consequences of Sex Segregation

Why does it matter that women and men do different jobs? Sex segregation matters for the same reason that the U.S. Supreme Court outlawed public school segregation in 1954: Among socially unequal groups, separate is not equal. Separating groups into different places or different roles facilitates unequal treatment. In addition, it implies that treating groups differently is appropriate. Because people's jobs place them in the status system, provide income, and confer prestige, segregating the sexes into different jobs contributes to women's lower pay and authority—at work, in their families, and in the larger society.

The most immediate consequence of sex segregation is that it lowers women's earnings relative to men. This happens in two ways. First, women tend to be overrepresented in lower-paying jobs and men in higher-paying ones. Second, occupations that are predominantly female tend to pay less to both male and female incumbents than predominantly male occupations pay.

Another consequence is that once jobs and equipment are designed with a certain sex in mind, segregation tends to perpetuate itself. For example, segregation can prevent women from acquiring the skills that would help them move into better and less-segregated jobs. While male artisans in a Japanese confectionery factory taught younger men the art of flower decorations, young women's low-level production jobs kept them too busy to learn the skill, so they continued to be excluded from flower-decorating jobs (Kondo 1990). Equipment design offers another example of the self-perpetuating nature of segregation. Until recently, almost all airline pilots were men, and cockpits were designed accordingly. As a result, women experience more difficulty than men in reaching all the controls (Williams 2000:77). The cabs of long-haul trucks can present similar problems. Segregation thus presents a "catch-22": equipment designs that exclude women mean that women are unlikely to be in such jobs, so equipment designers continue to design equipment that fits only men, thereby perpetuating segregation.

The consequences of segregation at work have ramifications for women's position in society more broadly. For example, the most common path into Congress is through the practice of law. The set of mechanisms that results in women working as legal secretaries, paralegals, or even legal-aid lawyers and that prevents them from becoming senior partners in major law firms has limited the number of women lawmakers who might devise legislation to ease women's workplace difficulties. In this way and many others, sex segregation in the workplace plays a fundamental role in maintaining sex inequality in modern societies.

Although lines of work reserved for men tend to be better than those to which women are consigned, the sex typing of work does not invariably advantage men. First, much of the job growth around the world has tended to favor service occupations, which are generally female-dominated, rather than production ones, which are more often male. Men's underrepresentation in service work can thus hurt their chances of employment (Anker 1998:403). Second, many occupations reserved for men have health drawbacks. In the United States, employers are more likely to hire men for hazardous jobs, such as truck driver, logger, and construction worker (England 1996:68), with the result that 93 percent of occupational deaths are men's (U.S. Bureau of Labor Statistics 1999a, Table A-6). Trucking, which is almost all male (95 percent) and the most common occupation for black and Hispanic men and third most common for white men, is far from ideal work. Because the total hourly pay is low, two-thirds of drivers admitted to regularly violating the law that requires an 8-hour break after driving 10 hours. The average driver worked over 65 hours a week, even though the legal limit is 60, and a third of drivers admitted to having dozed or fallen asleep at the wheel in the previous month (Belzer 2000:163). Clearly, not all men—or even all white, Anglo, native-born men—end up in prestigious, high-paying jobs. Nonetheless, sex segregation generally favors men by reducing competition for "their" jobs.

Sex segregation is also a source of labor market inefficiency worldwide: Excluding workers from occupations contributes to rigidity in labor markets, wastes human resources, and makes it harder for economies to respond to changes in global conditions.

Finally, society as a whole pays a price when employers use workers' sex—or any other irrelevant characteristics, such as race, age, or sexual orientation—to segregate them into jobs that fail to take full advantage of their abilities. When the United States was the only economic superpower, it could get away with wasting the talents of most of its female and minority citizens. Those days are over. Today, no country can afford to bury intelligent, energetic, talented workers of any color or sex in jobs filing insurance claims, emptying wastebaskets, or serving French fries.

A History of Sex Segregation in the United States

Sex Segregation in the Seventeenth and Eighteenth Centuries

Segregation between female and male paid workers in the United States had its roots in the unpaid work of the first immigrants. Among the colonists, 9 out of 10 people worked at agriculture (Ryan 1983:27), growing food and producing goods mostly for their own families. Their sexual division of labor resembled that of European peasants and farmers. Most men did agricultural work, while women managed the household and manufactured most of the items the household consumed. Women also earned an income by selling or bartering homemade products such as soap and lace and by providing such services as spinning or caring for the sick. However, the work of the sexes often overlapped, with either sex doing what needed to be done.

During the eighteenth century, commerce thrived in the growing country. Many families operated small businesses as shopkeepers, butchers, shoemakers, apothecaries, printers, coopers, silversmiths, innkeepers, jailers, and so on. But for women, widowhood was the only path to independent entrepreneurship in these lines of work (Ryan 1983:24).

At the same time, thousands of women and men worked without pay as slaves or indentured servants. Male slaves usually did field work; females worked both in the fields and indoors. But the precise sexual division of labor among enslaved people depended on slave owners and on geographic location. For example, slaves on South Carolina rice plantations performed a wide variety of jobs because plantations were run as self-contained villages: Twenty-five percent of men and 8 percent of women worked in specialized tasks such as boatman, blacksmith, cobbler, laundress, seamstress, and animal raiser (Jones 1998:194-95). In contrast, the demand for labor in the Cotton Belt states of Mississippi, Alabama, and Louisiana meant that the vast majority of slaves were field hands, regardless of their sex (Jones 1998:195).

In sum, during the seventeenth and eighteenth centuries, a line divided women's work from men's work among both slaves and free people, but this line was not strictly drawn.

Sex Segregation in the Nineteenth Century

During the nineteenth century, although most Americans still worked as farmers, industrialization expanded the kinds of jobs each sex did. Some domestic tasks that women had done, such as cloth making, moved to factories but remained "women's work." When others commercialized, they became men's work—for example, preparing the dead for burial.

Men heavily outnumbered women in the labor force as a whole (see Exhibit 2.1) and in most occupations, so most jobs were defined as men's work, including several that we think of as women's work today. For example, the few clerical workers that businesses employed in the nineteenth century were male. In 1870, for instance, only 3 percent of office clerks, stenographers, typists, bookkeepers, cashiers, and accountants were women (Davies 1982, table 1).

Women monopolized a few occupations, especially those whose low pay and poor working conditions did not attract men, such as **domestic service**. The Civil War expanded women's access to factory jobs and such jobs as nurse and teacher (Hooks 1947:10), but most employed women worked in domestic service, farming, and textiles, while most employed men worked as farmers, laborers, and carpenters (Ruggles and Sobek et al. 1997).

By the end of the nineteenth century, Americans' ethnicity, as well as their race and sex, affected the jobs they did. As immigration increased, national origin became another characteristic that employers considered in choosing workers. Native-born white men worked in factories or as craft workers, clerks, entrepreneurs, or professionals. Chinese men worked as migrant farm workers, miners, and railroad builders (Amott and Matthaei 1996:196). Puerto Rican immigrant men worked in garment manufacturing, cigar-making, hotel and restaurant jobs, and laundries. The most common job for single female immigrants—especially Irish, Scandinavian, and German women—was domestic service. Women who had come from Ireland were also frequently employed in the textile mills, where they replaced the New England farm girls the mills had recruited. Jewish immigrant women were concentrated in sewing and the other "needle trades" (Hogan 1996:42). Thus, although a few native-born white women were employed as nurses or teachers, most employed women toiled 12 hours a day for subsistence wages in factories, mills, or sweatshops or as servants. Employed men, particularly immigrants and racial minorities, also typically worked under arduous conditions for low pay, but not as low as women's earnings.

Thus, at the dawning of the twentieth century, sex segregation in the workplace was firmly established. Some occupations that women had pursued 50 years earlier at home for their families or in commerce as small-scale entrepreneurs had become men's work. New occupations created by industrialization were quickly sex-labeled as women's or men's work.

Sex Segregation in the Twentieth Century

The twentieth century brought new opportunities for women. World War I (1914-1918)—like the Civil War and World War II—drew men out of the labor force and into the military. The war also halted the flow of immigrants. The resulting labor shortage gave women and African American civilian men access to jobs that white men had previously filled. Although military work was men's work, white men and African American men had different experiences. African American men were relegated to positions of servitude as stevedores and menial laborers. Forbidden commissions, only 11 percent saw combat (Jones 1998:320-21).

After the war, employers rehired returning soldiers, pushing African American men and women of all races back into jobs as laborers and domestic servants. Despite the optimism of a 1919 Women's Bureau poster titled "New Jobs for Women"—which featured female machinists, streetcar conductors, elevator operators, "traffic cops," and mail carriers[1]—women retained few customarily male jobs after the war ended in 1918.

The bureaucratization of work in the early twentieth century altered the sexual division of labor, eventually giving rise to millions of clerical jobs that became labeled as women's work and a sizable number of management jobs that were initially labeled as men's. The growth and bureaucratization of firms required armies of clerks, and employers were drawn to women because they could pay them low wages and because women's preference for clerical labor over factory jobs provided a ready labor supply. By 1930, 95 percent of all typists and stenographers were female (Hooks 1947:75). Employers reserved management positions for men, thus establishing a pattern that persisted until 1990. Men's office jobs as managers, accountants, bookkeepers, and cashiers were often on job ladders, whereas job ladders were rare for predominantly female clerical workers. In fact, instead of rewarding experience by promoting women, many employers ensured turnover, thus keeping wages low, by insisting that they quit when they married.

Immediately prior to World War II, men outnumbered women by at least three to one in four-fifths of the 451 occupations. In more than half of the occupations, men outnumbered women by more than nine to one. In contrast, women outnumbered men nine to one in only 10 occupations: housekeeper; dressmaker; laundress; trained nurse; practical nurse; attendant to physicians or dentists; telephone operator; stenographer, typist, and secretary; servant; and boardinghouse keeper (Hooks 1947: 30). A few predominantly male and predominantly female occupations (e.g., housekeeper, laundress, servant) were available to people of color, but the lion's share was reserved for whites.

World War II (1941-1945) again disrupted sex and race segregation. Labor shortages impelled industries to turn to women and minority men for customarily white-male jobs. African American civilian men gained access to unionized craft jobs, and labor shortages in manufacturing and clerical jobs gave African American women alternatives to domestic work. A shortage of agricultural labor led the government to bring Mexican nationals to the United States on temporary work permits to do farm labor.[2] This program paved the way for Mexicans' continuing concentration in agricultural work.

The war years opened the doors to jobs that custom had closed to women: from working as streetcar conductors to practicing medicine, from building cargo planes to flying them. In order to attract women to the customarily male jobs, employers likened blue-collar jobs to women's homemaking activities. One slogan assured women, "If you can run a sewing machine, you can operate a rivet gun." With this strategy, employers implicitly acknowledged women's ability to do them in times of peace as well.

When the war ended, however, employers laid off women from customarily male jobs (Milkman 1987:102-103). The Air Force grounded its female pilots without providing any veterans' benefits, and civilian employers laid off female welders, machinists, and electricians. Many women dreaded returning to traditionally female, low-paid clerical, service, sales, and factory jobs, and for African American women, to domestic service. But few had any choice. World War II had little long-run effect on levels of sex segregation. Virtually no women worked in auto assembly jobs at the General Motors plant in Linden, New Jersey, for two decades after the war, for example (Milkman 1997:28), even though thousands of women worked at this plant and others like it during the war.

The 1960s brought the first federal regulations attacking sex segregation. Title 7 of the 1964 Civil Rights Act made it illegal for employers or unions to discriminate on the basis of sex. The law specifically addressed segregation, making it illegal to "limit, segregate, or classify . . . employees in any way which would deprive or tend to deprive any individual of employment opportunities or otherwise adversely affect his status as an employee, because of such individual's race, color, religion, sex, or national origin." The regulatory agencies did not take seriously the prohibition of sex segregation until the 1970s, however, so the level of sex segregation remained essentially the same in 1970 as in 1960. The 1970s brought an unprecedented 7-point drop in the index of occupational sex segregation. This decline had several causes. The growth of already integrated occupations and the shrinkage of heavily segregated occupations helped. But the 1970s also witnessed women's entry into traditionally male jobs. Thousands of women became bank managers, bartenders, public relations specialists, book editors, pharmacists, insurance adjusters, bus drivers, and typesetters, occupations that had been mostly male. Women's entry into customarily male occupations has usually been precipitated by a shortage of male workers because men have gone off to war, found greener pastures at home, or the occupation has outgrown the male labor supply (Reskin and Roos 1990). Women made more modest gains in many other customarily male occupations and professions.

Although women in formerly male occupations outearn women who remain in customarily female occupations, within the formerly male occupations, many women are concentrated in lower-paying specialties. For example, male bakers work in production baking, whereas female bakers work in grocery store bakeries. Thus, declines in occupational-level segregation in the 1970s and 1980s sometimes left job-level segregation intact.

Sex Segregation in the Contemporary United States

A casual look at the world around us—especially the world that television, movies, and magazines depict—suggests that women and men are finally integrated at work. Certainly they were less segregated at the end of the twentieth century than at any time in the country's history. But integration has been an uphill battle, and we're not there yet. For example, although women make up slightly over half the country's bus drivers and bartenders, they hold fewer than 3 percent of the nation's construction jobs and just 5 percent of repair jobs. Women are 14 percent of police officers, a proportion that was unimaginable 20 years ago; but among firefighters, men still outnumber women 20 to 1. Almost two-thirds of retail sales workers are female; but within that broad category, women make up over 75 percent of apparel salespersons and only 22 percent of hardware and building supply salespersons (U.S. Census Bureau 1998, 1999, 2000a).

In reviewing the amount of segregation at the beginning of the twenty-first century, we need to distinguish different levels at which segregation occurs. Common distinctions are made between occupational-level segregation, job-level segregation, and establishment-level segregation. **Occupations** are collections of jobs that involve similar activities across establishments. For example, a produce clerk belongs to the occupation of "stock handlers and baggers"; a health-insurance claims adjuster belongs to the occupation "insurance examiners, adjusters, and investigators"; a school custodian belongs to the occupation "janitors and cleaners." **Jobs** are specific positions in specific establishments in which workers perform specific activities. Here are some examples of jobs: produce clerk at the Big Bear Grocery in Columbus, Ohio; health-insurance claims adjuster at the Prudential Insurance Company in Topeka, Kansas; custodian at the Bryn Mawr elementary school in Seattle, Washington. **Establishments** are facilities that produce goods or services, such as factories, offices, or stores. Examples include the Centerville Station of the U.S. Postal Service in Tallahassee, Florida; the Borders Bookstore on Liberty Street in Ann Arbor, Michigan; and the Radio Shack at Central Square in Cambridge, Massachusetts.

Occupational-Level Sex Segregation. The U.S. Census Bureau distinguishes over 500 different occupations. Every 10 years, the U.S. census collects information about workers' occupations that lets us estimate women's and men's segregation into different occupations. At the turn of the twenty-first century, many women still worked in primarily female occupations. Of the approximately 66 million women in the labor force, 30 percent worked in just 10 of the 503 detailed occupations (see Exhibit 4.1). Secretary topped the list. If we add related office occupations (for example, general office clerk, typist), these "administrative support" occupations employed about one woman in four. Other predominantly female lines of work that employed millions of women include retail sales (4.7 million women); food preparation (3.8 million); school teaching (4.3 million); nursing (3.2 million); and cashiering and bookkeeping (4.2 million).[3] Despite World War II, the women's liberation movement, antidiscrimination laws, and affirmative action, the most common occupations for women at the turn of the twenty-first century were almost identical to those that employed the most women in 1940.

Men were also concentrated in a handful of occupations, but only two occupational categories appear on both sexes' top 10 list—"salaried manager, administrator, not elsewhere classified" and "salaried sales supervisor or proprietor"—and these include diverse jobs, so the women and men in them may do very different kinds of work.

In most occupations, men substantially outnumber women. For example, approximately 865,134 men and 6,761 women repaired vehicles; 1,410,125 men and 22,694 women worked as carpenters; and 299,483 men and 38,905 women sold motor vehicles and boats (U.S. Census Bureau

EXHIBIT 4.1

Top 10 Occupations for Each Sex, 2000

	Number
WOMEN	
Total labor force	*65,983,000*
Secretaries	2,984,000
Managers & administrators, n.e.c.*	2,518,000
Cashiers	2,490,000
Supervisors and proprietors, sales occupations	2,042,000
Registered nurses	1,974,000
Teachers, elementary	1,844,000
Nursing aides, orderlies, and attendants	1,833,000
Bookkeepers, accounting and auditing clerks	1,736,000
Waiters and waitresses	1,165,000
Receptionists	1,090,000
MEN	
Total labor force	*74,627,000*
Managers and administrators, n.e.c.*	5,487,000
Supervisors and proprietors, sales occupations	3,054,000
Truck drivers	2,958,000
Janitors and cleaners	1,614,000
Carpenters	1,410,000
Cooks	1,300,000
Computer systems analysts and scientists	1,166,000
Sales representatives, mining, manufacturing, and wholesale	1,164,000
Laborers, except construction	1,058,000
Supervisors, production occupations	960,000

Source: Authors' calculations from March 1998, 1999, and 2000 Current Population Surveys.
Note: Figures are averages of 1998, 1999, and 2000 Current Population Survey data.
*The U.S. Census Bureau uses the abbreviation *n.e.c.* to denote miscellaneous occupations that are "not elsewhere classified."

1998, 1999, 2000a). In a much smaller number of occupations, women substantially outnumbered men. For example, approximately 2,984,073 women and 46,259 men worked as secretaries; 1,090,050 women and 41,804 men worked as receptionists; and 2,489,827 women and 740,143 men were cashiers.

Although comparing the numbers of women and men across particular occupations signals sex segregation in the workplace, it does not tell us how much segregation exists. For a single summary of the extent of sex segregation, we use the **index of occupational segregation,** which represents the proportion of female (or male) workers who would have to change to an occupation in which their sex is underrepresented for the sexes to be evenly distributed across occupations and, hence, fully integrated. The index would equal zero if men and women were perfectly integrated; it would equal 100 if every occupation employed only men or only women. At the turn of the twenty-first century, the index of occupational segregation was 52.1. Thus, 52.1 percent of the female labor force, or almost 39 million American women, would have to shift to disproportionately male occupations to achieve occupational-level integration (U.S. Census Bureau 1998, 1999, 2000a).

Job-Level Sex Segregation. Considerable sex segregation exists within occupations, however, because men and women within the same occupational category perform different jobs. At Deloitte & Touche, for example, women accountants were assigned to clients in the nonprofit, health care, and retail sectors; they rarely were assigned to mergers and acquisitions, "male" areas (Sturm 2001:138). Similarly, although women are about as likely as men to be in the occupational category of writers, only about a quarter of screenwriters are female (Bielby and Bielby 1996).

Multiply these differences within a handful of occupations by 500 occupations, and you can see that data on people's occupations underestimate the amount of sex segregation in the workplace. To calculate the amount of job segregation in the United States, we would need to know what job every man and woman holds. But obtaining information on the exact tasks of the approximately 75 million employed men and 66 million employed women—along with information about who employs them to do these tasks—is impossible.

Establishment-Level Segregation. A third component of sex segregation is the differing distributions of women and men who pursue the same occupations across different establishments (Nelson and Bridges 1999; Petersen and Morgan 1995). For example, female state prison guards tend to work in female prisons and male guards in male prisons (Britton 2003). The greater tendency for male than female servers to work at pricey restaurants (where tips are higher) is another example (Neumark 1996; Rab 2001). Estimates of the amount of establishment segregation are available for a few occupations or industries. For instance, about two-thirds of textile, apparel, and finishing machine operators would have to switch to different establishments for women and men to be integrated (Carrington and Troske 1998).

Race and Sex Segregation. In the United States, employers are more likely to use workers' sex than any other personal characteristic in assigning them to jobs. However, they also take into account workers' race, ethnicity, age, and other irrelevant characteristics. Black women's work history illustrates the combined effects of both sex and race segregation (Jones 1998). When the hope of better jobs and schools drew African American men and women to the North in the late nineteenth and early twentieth centuries, employers refused to hire African American women for clerical and sales jobs, and most had to settle for jobs as domestic servants, who were at their employers' beck and call 24 hours a day (Jones 1998). The few available factory jobs—often in the steel, automobile, garment, and meat-processing industries—were physically punishing and paid rock-bottom wages. Not until Congress outlawed race discrimination in 1964 did many employers begin to hire African American women for clerical jobs, and today's firms still tend to segregate women of color from white women. In clerical work, for instance, minority women are overrepresented in low-paid occupations, such as file clerk, social welfare assistant, and insurance examiner (King 1993:18).

Like black women, black men were also confined primarily to service jobs in the past, where they worked as doormen, elevator operators, railroad porters and conductors, waiters, and janitors. Employers that hired both whites and African Americans often segregated them from each other and from workers of the other sex (Jones 1985:182). For example, during the 1930s Philco employed a few black men as laborers, but only in the shipping room. As a result, many whites did not realize that Philco employed any African Americans (Cooper 1991:326). Even the demand for labor during World War II could not always overcome institutionalized prejudice against putting black men in "white men's jobs": Almost half of U.S. steel mills refused to hire any African Americans during the war, and those that did confined them to unskilled jobs (Jones 1998:347). Nevertheless, many black male custodians were able to rise to machinist and assembly-line worker positions in this period, and some retained these jobs after the war (Jones 1998:346).

Employers have also historically segregated Asian and Hispanic women into different lines of work from men of their own ethnic background and from white Anglo women. In the canning factories of 50 years ago, for example, employers put Mexican American women to work chopping vegetables and gave Anglo women the easier job of packing cans (Amott and Matthaei 1996:77). Chinese American women were predominantly employed in factories as garment and cannery workers in

EXHIBIT 4.2

Top Occupations for Blacks, Hispanics, and Whites, by Sex, 2000

BLACK WOMEN	Number	BLACK MEN	Number
Total labor force	*8,247,000*	*Total labor force*	*6,990,000*
Nurse's aide, orderly	606,000	Truck driver	448,000
Cashier	422,000	Janitor, cleaner	307,000
Secretary	234,000	Salaried manager, administrator n.e.c.	196,000
Teacher, elementary school	214,000	Cook	181,000
Registered nurse	188,000	Salaried sales supervisor, proprietor	165,000
Cook	183,000	Laborer, except construction	162,000
Janitor, cleaner	166,000	Guard	151,000
Salaried manager, administrator, n.e.c.*	159,000	Misc. machine operator, n.e.c.	136,000
HISPANIC WOMEN		HISPANIC MEN	
Total labor force	*5,912,000*	*Total labor force*	*8,446,000*
Cashier	299,000	Truck driver	369,000
Secretary	214,000	Cook	345,000
Nurse's aide, orderly	193,000	Janitor, cleaner	301,000
Private household cleaner, servant	193,000	Farm worker	293,000
Janitor, cleaner	182,000	Gardener, groundskeeper	271,000
Cook	160,000	Salaried manager, administrator, n.e.c.	253,000
Maids, "housemen"	157,000	Construction laborer	237,000
Salaried manager, administrator, n.e.c.	136,000	Salaried sales supervisor, proprietor	216,000
WHITE WOMEN		WHITE MEN	
Total labor force	*48,872,000*	*Total labor force*	*55,827,000*
Secretary	2,441,000	Salaried manager, administrator, n.e.c.	4,848,000
Salaried manager, administrator, n.e.c.	2,139,000	Salaried sales supervisor, proprietor	2,517,000
Salaried sales supervisor, proprietor	1,691,000	Truck driver	2,070,000
Cashier	1,635,000	Carpenter	1,120,000
Registered nurse	1,612,000	Sales rep., mining, mfg., and wholesale	1,043,000
Teacher, elementary school	1,493,000	Janitor, cleaner	955,000
Bookkeeper	1,451,000	Computer systems analyst	887,000
Nurse's aide, orderly	967,000	Supervisor, production occupations	763,000

Source: Authors' calculations from the March 1998, 1999, and 2000 Current Population Surveys.
Note: Figures for 2000 are averages of 1998, 1999, and 2000 Current Population Survey data. Blacks and whites include people of Hispanic origin.
*The U.S. Census Bureau uses the abbreviation, *n.e.c.** to denote miscellaneous occupations that are "not elsewhere classified."

the early years of the twentieth century, although by 1930 many had found work as teachers, particularly in Hawaii, where discrimination was less severe than on the mainland (Amott and Matthaei 1996:208).

Today, there remains a great deal of occupational sex segregation and a moderate amount of occupational race segregation among workers of the same sex.[4] As Exhibit 4.2 shows, in the years 1998 to 2000, of the eight occupations employing the most men from broad racial-ethnic groups, only four also employed large numbers of women: a miscellaneous category of managers and administrators that the Census does not classify elsewhere, salaried sales supervisors and proprietors, cooks, and janitors and cleaners. The large number of managerial occupations in the United States and the broad range in their attractiveness ensures that this category appears on all groups' top eight lists. Beyond this similarity, the lists illustrate the race and sex segregation of jobs. Note, for example, that despite the hundreds of thousands of secretaries and truck drivers, each appears on the lists of only one sex.

In sum, sex segregation occurs across establishments, jobs, and occupations, and it varies by race and ethnicity. Most importantly, it is extensive. Consider the experience of a recent college graduate, who wrote us about the law firm where she worked in the spring of 2002:

> It's a big firm (about 125 attorneys) and while that group is fairly
> diverse, the rest of the firm has surprised me with amazingly rigid
> segregation. All the secretaries, around a hundred of them, are female.
> Only two are black; all the rest are white. Even the temps (like me) are all
> female. I found this especially surprising since I know the temp agency
> has males they could send here. All the people who work in the copy
> department (about six of them) are black; all but one is female. All the
> people who work in the mailroom (about eight of them) are white males.
> All the people who work in the fax department (about eight people,
> again) are middle-aged white women. All the people who work in the
> lobby (about 10 people), checking IDs and signing in guests are black.
> (Charity Shumway, personal communication, 2002)

Thus, although sex segregation has declined over the past two generations (in contrast to the past, the law firm employs female as well as male attorneys), most of the other jobs remained segregated by both sex and race.

Cross-National Differences in Sex Segregation

According to a report from the International Labour Organization drawing on data from the last two decades of the twentieth century, occupational sex segregation is "extensive in every region, at all economic development levels, in all political systems, and in diverse religious, social and cultural environments" (Anker 1998:403). Half of all workers worldwide pursue occupations that are at least 80 percent one sex. And the best jobs generally go to men. For example, whereas women were about 42 percent of salespersons and shop assistants worldwide, they were only 18 percent of sales supervisors and buyers. Worldwide, women tend to be limited to fewer occupations than men: Three-quarters are crowded into just seven occupations (nurses, secretaries/typists, housekeepers, bookkeepers and cashiers, building caretakers and cleaners, caregivers, and sewers and tailors; Anker 1998:411).[5] Most of these occupations appear to conform to stereotypes of women as caring, patient, nimble-fingered, skilled at household tasks, and docile. Yet in some countries and regions, men hold jobs that are traditionally female in the West. For example, half of the nurses in Senegal and Tunisia and one-third in Bahrain and Mauritius are male (Anker 1998:264).

Although regions differ in the extent of sex segregation, countries within the same region tend to be similar, attesting to the importance of social and cultural factors for levels of sex segregation. The Middle East and North Africa have the highest levels of occupational segregation, and countries in the Asia/Pacific region have the lowest. The former Communist countries of Eastern Europe had levels that resembled those in the member countries of the Organisation for Economic Co-operation and Development (OECD). Among the OECD countries, North America had the lowest levels of segregation, and the Scandinavian countries had the highest. Almost half of women in Scandinavia are in female-dominated occupations, compared to one-third in the North American countries. Public policies in the Scandinavian countries, although advocating equality for women and men, encourage mothers to work part time, and part-time workers tend to be concentrated in predominantly female occupations.

Trends in Sex Segregation

As we showed earlier, the sex type of many lines of work has been stable for centuries. In occupations that have endured from preindustrial times, the sexual division of labor hung on throughout the twentieth century, reflecting the importance that societies attach to gender. However, which sex does what task has varied over time. In this section, we first consider how types of work have shifted between the sexes over the centuries. Then we examine trends in the amount of occupational sex segregation in the United States.

Shifts in Sex-Typed Jobs

Even when paid work was highly segregated by sex, some tasks have switched back and forth between the sexes over time. This was the case in the production of cloth, for example, as we showed in Chapter 1. It was first produced by women in the workshops of the Middle Ages, then its commercial production transferred to male artisans in guilds in the sixteenth century, and then, by the 1840s, back to women working in cottage industries or in factories (Pinchbeck 1930:315). For the past century, textile production has remained one of the top occupations for American women.

A few other once-male occupations have undergone **feminization**, in which an occupation switches from mostly male to mostly female. For example, having recruited the first telephone operators from the boys who delivered telegrams, AT&T replaced them with young women after customers complained about the boys' rudeness and pranks. Only after the Equal Employment Opportunity Commission charged AT&T with sex discrimination in 1970 did AT&T again hire male operators. Thirty years later, however, 85 percent of telephone operators were still female.

Through the first several decades of the twentieth century, most bank tellers were men, but during World Wars I and II, banks hired women to replace the men who had entered military service. Between World War II and the end of the century, as men found more promising jobs elsewhere, women's share of bank teller jobs climbed from 45 percent to almost 90 percent.

Such reversals in which sex performs an occupation are rare. When they do occur, they almost always involve women replacing men as the majority (Reskin and Roos 1990). Men rarely take over predominantly female work. An exception occurred, however, after Title 9 required universities to equalize resources, including coaching salaries, for women's and men's sports. As a result of the increased attractiveness of coaching jobs, men began displacing women, and 10 years later, men coached half of women's collegiate programs (up from 10 percent before passage; Alfano 1985). Predominantly female jobs pay less than male jobs and are generally less desirable. Because men as a group have more choices, few have to settle for customarily female jobs. But men whose race, ethnicity, or nativity reduce their options are more likely to work in predominantly female jobs.

Twentieth-Century Trends in Occupational Sex Segregation

Between 1900 and 1970, occupational segregation was quite stable, with the index of occupational sex segregation hovering between 65 and 69.

EXHIBIT 4.3

Indexes of Occupational Sex and Race Segregation, 1900-2000

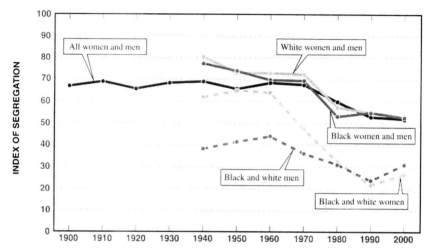

Sources: Gross 1968, table 2; Jacobs 1989, table 2; King 1992, chart 1; authors' calculations from the March 1998, 1999, and 2000 Current Population Surveys.
Note: Figures for 2000 are averages of 1998, 1999, and 2000 Current Population Survey data.

During these 70 years, women's share of the labor force grew dramatically, and employers reorganized work and introduced new technologies, causing the disappearance of some occupations (e.g., ice man) and the emergence of others (e.g., programmer). However, many employers continued to assign men and women to different occupations.

Exhibit 4.3 tracks the change in occupational sex segregation during the twentieth century. For the post-1940 period, this figure also presents separate estimates of sex segregation among African Americans and whites. Although levels of sex segregation in these two groups are similar, race segregation still confines African Americans of both sexes to different and usually less-desirable occupations than those that same-sex whites hold.

This exhibit shows several other important trends. First, throughout the twentieth century, sex has been more important than race in allocating workers to occupations. During the past 60 years, occupational segregation between African Americans and whites has declined more than women's segregation from men. Notice that the two lines in Exhibit 4.3 that denote sex segregation lie above the two lines that represent racial segregation. Between 1940 and the turn of the century, the index of race segregation among women dropped from 65.4 to 26.8; the race segregation index for men declined from 44.4 to 31.2 (computed from King 1992; U.S. Census Bureau 1998, 1999, 2000a). Because African Americans make up a much smaller share of the labor force than women, integrating blacks into occupations dominated by same-sex whites is easier than integrating tens of millions of women into mostly male occupations. Second, until 1960, black and white women were more segregated based on their race than were black and white men—largely because of African American women's heavy concentration in domestic service. Third, by 1980, racial segregation had declined sharply, especially among women. Fourth, declining sex segregation of occupations in the 1970s and 1980s stalled in the 1990s. At the turn of the twentieth-first century, the sex segregation index was about 52, compared to 53 in 1990, but 62 in 1980.

In sum, during the 1970s and 1980s, social, legal, and economic pressures prompted some employers to change their personnel practices and encouraged women and a smaller number of men to pursue sex-atypical lines of work. As a result, there is more variation in which workers are assigned to which jobs and lower overall levels of segregation. Men whose fathers were truck drivers, janitors, and letter carriers work as librarians, teachers, and flight attendants. Women whose mothers were teachers, typists, waitresses, and homemakers work as veterinarians, sales managers, bus drivers, and physicians. Thirty years ago, a popular riddle told of a boy who was injured in a car crash. His father rushed him to the hospital, where he was taken directly into the operating room. There the surgeon took one look at the boy and said, "I can't operate on him; he's my son." The riddle—Who was the surgeon?—baffled people in the early 1970s. No one asks this riddle now. Its demise signals the entry of large numbers of women into medicine and other formerly all-male occupations.

Nevertheless, most women and men remain segregated into different occupations and jobs. For every woman who worked as a doctor between 1998 and 2000, for example, 83 women held clerical jobs, 15 operated factory machines, 14 were sales clerks, 10 worked as nurses' aides, and 6 served food. At the beginning of the twenty-first century, segregation continues to separate millions of working women and men into different and unequal jobs.

Explanations and Remedies for Sex Segregation

The cultural universality of the sexual division of labor has led some people to conclude that the sexes are naturally suited to different kinds of

"Let's face it: you and this organization have never been a good fit."

work. For all but a couple of jobs, however, social factors, rather than biology, dictate what tasks employers assign to each sex. As we have seen, levels of segregation have varied over time, across countries, and across different industries and firms within our society. This variation allows researchers to test explanations for segregation. Because variation in the actions of employers and workers may account for variation in levels of sex segregation, explanations for segregation examine the factors that influence an employer's job-assignment practices and the factors that determine a worker's pursuit of particular lines of work.

Employers' Actions

Employers usually have final say over who does what jobs.[6] If all employers in a particular time or place use segregative personnel practices, levels of sex segregation will be high. At times or in places where more employers implement gender-neutral practices, levels of segregation are lower. Thus, how employers or their agents assign workers to jobs is important in explaining how extensively the sexes are segregated into different jobs.

Why should the sex, race, and ethnicity of prospective workers influence the personnel decisions of **gatekeepers**—bosses, managers, and supervisors who have the authority to restrict access to jobs? The processes that might influence employers' preferences fall into three categories. The first includes gatekeepers' beliefs about who ought to do particular jobs and their propensity to stereotype the sexes as having different characteristics, skills, and circumstances. The second includes whether gatekeepers believe that employing one sex or the other in particular jobs will be more economically advantageous. The third category includes gatekeepers' personal likes and dislikes—a preference for others of their own sex or a distaste for workers of the other sex. These processes are often institutionalized in personnel practices, which in turn directly influence the amount of sex segregation.

Sex Labeling of Occupations and Jobs. The ubiquity of the sexual division of labor means that many occupations are associated in people's minds with one sex or the other. These occupational **sex labels** that link some occupations (e.g., nurse) with women and others (e.g., plumber) with men influence the preferences of employers as well as workers (Oppenheimer 1968). Consider, for example, Hollywood studios' preference for male screenwriters for some film genres. According to a talent agent: "When we get a call for a writer, they'll say, 'Who do you have who can write an action-adventure piece?' If I suggest a woman, well, they laugh at me" (Bielby and Bielby 1996:266).

Not all occupations have sex labels. Some, such as accountant, are gender neutral in most people's minds because they are aware of both female and male accountants. Others, such as "Irish-moss bleacher" are gender neutral because few of us have any idea what Irish-moss bleachers do. The more jobs in an economy that people view as "belonging" to one sex or the other, the higher the level of sex segregation.

Whether we label occupations as female or male depends on what we see around us. The passage of antidiscrimination laws and regulations in the mid-1960s and the reemergence of feminism a few years later helped to weaken sex segregation by challenging the sex labeling of occupations. By the mid-1970s, the Equal Employment Opportunity Commission had banned sex- and race-segregated help-wanted ads, and terms such as "girl Friday" disappeared from the language (Graham 1990).

The integration of occupations can change language as well as occupations' sex labels. A case in point is "flight attendant." When airlines reserved this job for women, they construed it as a job for nubile, attractive young women. In fact, National Airlines advertised with full-page ads depicting an attractive and sexy young woman saying, "I'm Cheryl [or another female name]; fly me!"[7] and Continental Airlines' ad campaign asserted, "We really move our tails for you!" After the Supreme Court ruled that airlines' refusal to employ men as flight attendants was illegal (*Diaz v. Pan American World Airways, Inc.* 1971), airlines increasingly employed male flight attendants and the term *stewardess* began to disappear. The efforts of government bureaucracies and others to create gender-neutral language have also encouraged gender-neutral job titles ("letter carrier" rather than "mailman," "firefighter" rather than "fireman," and "server" or "waitperson" rather than "waitress" and "waiter").

Sex Stereotypes. Sex stereotypes also shape employers' and employees' views of prospective workers, so the prevalence of sex stereotyping contributes to sex segregation. Employers' (and workers') stereotypes— mental images of a social group that link personal attributes with group membership—can influence job assignments, promotions, and termi- nations (Reskin 2000). For example, although company managers assigned both female and male white-collar workers to blue-collar jobs during a power-plant strike, plant supervisors' sex stereotypes led them to reassign most women from customarily male jobs (e.g., operator) to customarily female jobs, such as plant cleaner (Padavic and Reskin 1990).

The sex stereotypes of some members of the population are particularly influential because of the positions they hold. For instance, sex stereo- typing by legislators, judges, and other policymakers contributed to high levels of sex segregation. Stereotypes of women as weak and corruptible justified "protective" labor laws that barred women from jobs such as tending bar or delivering telegrams and limited their access to other jobs by prescribing special treatment at work (e.g., maximum hours, a daybed in the restroom). In a notorious 1873 decision, the Supreme Court upheld an Illinois statute denying women the right to practice law because

> [t]he natural and proper timidity and delicacy which belongs to the
> female sex evidently unfits it for many of the occupations of civil life.
> The constitution of the family organization which is founded in the
> divine ordinance, as well as in the nature of things, indicates the domestic
> sphere as that which properly belongs to the domain and functions of
> womanhood. The harmony of interests . . . which belong . . . to the family
> institution is repugnant to the idea of a woman adopting a distinct and
> independent career from that of her husband. (*Bradwell v. Illinois* 1873)

More recently, the Job Corps, a major antipoverty job-training pro- gram of the 1960s, trained young African American men in the skilled trades and young African American women in homemaking, thereby opening better jobs to men, but not women (Quadagno and Fobes 1995). Of course, legislatures, the courts, and other policymakers can also work against stereotypes about appropriate jobs for women and men. In 1989, the Supreme Court sent a clear message to employers that sex stereotyping is not permissible when it found Price Waterhouse guilty of sex discrimination for using sex stereotypes in evaluating Ann Hopkins for partnership (see Chapter 5 for details).

Little systematic research exists on the impact of sex labels and sex stereotyping on levels of segregation. However, according to a recent study, law firms whose hiring criteria included stereotypically female traits, such as getting along well with others, tended to employ more women as associates than firms whose stated hiring criteria included stereotypically male traits, such as aggressiveness (Gorman 2001).

Stereotyping fosters sex segregation because employers automatically resort to their stereotypes when they lack relevant information about individuals, because stereotypes can affect employers' evaluations of workers, and because stereotypes can distort our recollections of others' behavior and our predictions of their future behavior. Employers' personnel practices can prevent stereotypes from having these segregative effects (Reskin 2000). Accurate "individuating" information can prevent stereotyping, so organizations with personnel practices that provide full information about job candidates should be less segregated than other organizations (Bielby 2000; Heilman 1995). The use of written job descriptions, complete and relevant information about job candidates, and clear standards of evaluation can prevent stereotypes from influencing employers' decisions (Bielby 2000; Reskin 2002).

Economic-Based Preferences. Employers' desire to maximize productivity or to minimize employment costs affects which workers they employ in jobs. Employers who believe that workers' sex affects productivity or the cost of doing business often take sex into account in filling positions. The clearest example of this, which has been dubbed statistical discrimination, refers to employers' preference for an *individual* woman or man based on traits that they believe are characteristic of women or men in general. Imagine that an employer knows that his male managers are more likely than female managers to have health problems that require hospitalization. In order to keep his insurance rates down, he selects the female applicant instead of the male applicant, without any information about either applicant's health. Regardless of whether or not this strategy would save the employer money in the long run, over time its consequence is segregative, and the practice is illegal under Title 7 of the 1964 Civil Rights Act.

Employers may favor one sex for certain jobs because they fear how current incumbents or customers will react to a nontraditional worker (Bergmann and Darity 1981). Unhappy workers could create headaches for management and might even reduce production. Concerns about customers' negative response to sex-atypical workers (the excuse Pan American Airlines offered for denying men jobs as flight attendants) are similarly segregative. A Canadian study of private security workers found that employers preferred to send male guards to dangerous sites—such as solitary patrols at warehouses—and preferred to send women to sites where other women worked, such as hospitals, even though the latter sites turned out to be the most dangerous for guards, who have to restrain violent patients (Erickson, Albanese, and Drakulic 2000:305, 308). U.S. law does not permit either customers' or coworkers' preferences as justifications for employers taking sex into account in making job assignments.

Preference for Members of One's Own Group. Some gatekeepers feel more comfortable with workers of their own sex; others actively dislike workers of the other sex (at least as employees). The incidence of such likes and dislikes varies across employers and over time, of course. When they are common and employers are free to act on them, they raise segregation levels (Reskin 2002).

A large body of social psychological research indicates that people tend to prefer others from their own group (Brewer and Brown 1998). Employers who desire people who will "fit in" may express this in-group preference in hiring or job assignments. Although in-group preference— or cronyism—probably plays an important role in job segregation, we do not have much concrete evidence of its impact.

We do know the kinds of personnel practices that permit or discourage in-group favoritism from increasing sex segregation (Reskin 2002). For example, when candidates' qualifications were ambiguous, experimental subjects tended to select people of their own sex and race. Similarly, when evaluative criteria were clear, subjects were more likely to ignore candidates' race and sex in making choices (Salancik and Pfeffer 1978). The more discretion gatekeepers have in personnel decisions, the more likely in-group preference will play a segregative role. Consider a practice at Microsoft Corporation that led to a discrimination lawsuit. Managers' evaluations of subordinates were based largely on a "lifeboat" criterion: Whom would managers want with them if they were stuck in a lifeboat? This system opened the door to in-group favoritism, and because most managers at Microsoft are white men, it allegedly operated in their favor (Abelson 2001:A12).

Hostility Toward Members of the Other Sex. Some gatekeepers exclude persons of the other sex for a simple reason—aversion to their presence at the work site. Although there are surely employers who dislike male workers, the examples of hostility we found were directed toward women, and we suspect that this is far more common. A witness's testimony in a sex discrimination case illustrates misogynistic exclusion: The supervisor, on turning down the plaintiff for a job, said, "Fucking women; I hate having fucking women in the office" (*Heim v. State of Utah* 1993).

In 1964, Congress acted to eliminate exactly this type of discrimination: intentional discrimination based on out-group hostility.[8] Pervasive racial discrimination in employment prompted the law, and legislators had race discrimination in mind when they passed Title 7 of the 1964 Civil Rights Act (see Chapter 3). In including sex discrimination, they provided a mechanism for workers to challenge intentionally sex-segregated jobs. Complaints and lawsuits under Title 7 have helped to reduce segregation in some firms by opening jobs to sex-atypical workers. For example, a class-action lawsuit against Home Depot led it to redesign its personnel practices to ensure women's access to formerly all-male sales jobs (Sturm 2001). The extent of the impact of Title 7 has varied, however, depending on the priorities of the President and Congress. Thus, the enforcement of discrimination and affirmative action regulations has been a hit-or-miss proposition. This variation in enforcement allows us to discern the impact of antidiscrimination and affirmative action regulations on sex segregation. The 1970s featured both enforcement of these regulations and an unprecedented decline in the index of segregation.

Affirmative action regulations can also discourage sex segregation. In 1967 President Johnson amended an executive order requiring federal contractors not to discriminate based on race to include sex discrimination. The amended order also required contractors to take positive steps (i.e., **affirmative action**) to ensure that they would not discriminate. Affirmative action refers to policies and procedures designed to prevent discrimination before it occurs. Typically, it involves modifying personnel practices to ensure that minorities and women (the "protected groups" to whom the regulations apply) have job access that is equal to white men's. The executive orders direct contractors to set goals (but not quotas) for integrating minorities and women into their workforce and to develop mechanisms to achieve those goals.

Many employers have discovered that affirmative action is good business. It helps employers recruit talented employees, and it serves as a defense against discrimination suits. Most employers who have incorporated affirmative action into their personnel practices see no reason to return to the old system. For example, in response to the question of whether the Air Force would consider abolishing its policy of integrating basic training, the branch's top sergeant replied flatly: "Our gender-integrated approach to basic training works" (Ricks 1998). It is impossible to determine exactly how much federal affirmative action requirements have reduced segregation, but without doubt, they have expanded women's access to nontraditional jobs when they have been enforced (Reskin 1998).

To the extent that government regulations make a difference, they do so primarily by motivating employers to modify segregative employment practices (Tomaskovic-Devey and Skaggs 1999). We now examine several personnel practices that affect levels of segregation.

Recruitment Practices. One practice that affects the level of sex segregation is how employers recruit workers. Employers vary in how they recruit workers, with most recruiting through referrals from current workers (i.e., word-of-mouth recruiting; Marsden and Gorman 2001; Miller and Rosenbaum 1997:513). This practice helps to maintain the sex and race composition of an employer's workforce because, more often than not, members of workers' networks are their same sex and race (Lin 2000). So employers' use of informal networks to fill jobs in which white men are concentrated reproduces the demographic composition of those jobs.

Even in professional jobs in which one would expect employers to seek the most-qualified workers, word-of-mouth recruiting occurs, and its effects are predictably segregative. For example, over half of law faculty who were hired between 1986 and 1990 found their jobs through networks, with better jobs especially likely to be filled through networks. Men were more likely than women to find their jobs this way, presumably because most law faculty members are male, so men were more likely than women to obtain the most desirable law school posts (Reskin, Hargens, and Merritt 2001).

In contrast, **open recruitment** techniques publicly announce job openings so outsiders can learn about sex-atypical jobs. These techniques include posting job openings and advertising them in places that are widely accessible (in other words, not in the men's locker room) and using employment services that do not cater to narrowly defined groups. One study found that using state-run employment agencies and community groups increased the representation of black men and, to a lesser degree, Latinos (Moss and Tilly 2001). The result should be the same for other excluded groups, including women. A study of over 500 employers found that open recruitment methods increased women's share of management jobs, whereas the use of informal recruitment methods increased men's share (Reskin and McBrier 2000).

More generally, employment practices that reduce individual decision makers' discretion help to prevent stereotyping, statistical discrimination, in-group favoritism, and out-group hostility from affecting personnel decisions (Bielby 2000; Reskin 2000). Bureaucratic personnel practices (job postings, written job descriptions and evaluation criteria, written records for job candidates) tend to curtail managerial discretion, thereby fostering sex integration (Heilman 1995:12).

Accountability for employment decisions also fosters integration by checking the effects of gatekeepers' likes and dislikes and stereotyping. Consider an experimental study in which students were asked for recommendations regarding who should be hired as teaching assistants. When the students knew that the decision-making process would be kept secret, they tended to recommend candidates of their own sex and race. When the decision-making process was public, candidates' race and sex were less likely to affect students' choices (Salancik and Pfeffer 1978).

In the same way, organizations that hold decision makers responsible for implementing policies designed to ensure workplace equality will be less segregated (Bielby 2000:124). Having a top leader who is committed to equal employment opportunity is crucial (Thomas and Ely 1996), but it is not enough. Good intentions are often watered down at lower levels, due to the actions of supervisors or workers. For example, a utility company whose chief executive was committed to sex equality assigned both women and men white-collar workers to traditionally male jobs during a strike at a power plant. Plant supervisors reassigned most of the women to jobs cleaning the plants, however, denying women exposure to traditionally male-skilled jobs (Padavic and Reskin 1990). Conversely, knowing that senior people are paying attention can lead lower-level supervisors to try to meet expectations (Sessa 1992). For example, one supervisor forbade bad language from the male crew out of fear that it would drive off the women workers. One of his workers said: "I think that pressure came directly from the office. . . . We want to keep these women"

(Eisenberg 1998:70). Supervisors who know they are responsible for ensuring fair practices on the job will curtail actions on the part of coworkers that are intended to drive women out.

Informing decision makers ahead of time that that they will be held accountable for their judgments also tends to make them less likely to rely on stereotypes (Tetlock 1992). For accountability to make a difference, decision makers must know that departing from prescribed procedures will have negative consequences for them (Sturm 2001:157).

More effective in reducing segregation is using gender-conscious practices that treat the sex of underrepresented workers as a plus factor in selecting among qualified candidates for a position. Gender-conscious employment practices include identifying and mentoring women who are potential candidates for management, targeting recruitment efforts toward traditionally female pools, and giving preference among fully qualified candidates to women for positions in which they are underrepresented.

Outdated Assumptions. How employers conceptualize and structure jobs can either hinder or expedite a group's entry into jobs in which they are underrepresented. Formulating job requirements on the assumption that men do some jobs and women do others makes integration difficult to achieve. Such employers may not necessarily intend to exclude women, but their assumptions can have that effect. Employers often require qualifications, set work schedules, and structure tasks and time use based on the background and circumstances of the workers they employed when they created jobs.

Regarding qualifications, if male veterans initially filled the job, military experience might become a tacit job requirement. If most early incumbents had a master's degree in business, the employer might require an MBA. If one sex is more likely to have these required credentials, the other sex would continue to be excluded, even if the credentials are not necessary to perform the job. In contrast, linking required qualifications to actual job duties can encourage integration. Until the 1970s, for example, large banks required that managers have MBA degrees, although many clerical workers could learn much of what they needed to know to be managers. After the federal government warned banks to eliminate discriminatory practices, some let women substitute experience for an MBA degree. This change opened bank management positions to thousands of women (Reskin and Hartmann 1986). Just as the demand for workers in the expanding technology jobs of the 1990s led many high-tech companies to recruit people with nonstandard qualifications and experience, so too could employers reconsider the formal requirements and focus instead on the skills needed.

Equipment designed on the assumption that it will be used by larger bodies can present a structural barrier to smaller people's ability to perform a job. Equipment designed for averaged-size white men may exclude the average woman as well as some Asian or Latino men. Installing new equipment can be expensive, but redesign of equipment occurs on a regular basis anyway, as companies replace worn-out or obsolete equipment (Williams 2000:109). New equipment that meets the specifications for average male *and* female workers would open more jobs to women. Another investment that would make many blue-collar jobs more available for women is mechanical lifting devices that make brawn less important (Eisenberg 1998:130; Williams 2000). Jobs, too, can be redesigned so that they accommodate a greater proportion of the labor force. Jobs in which a worker must be able to lift 125 pounds, even if required to do so only once a day, could be changed so that one forklift driver could be assigned all such tasks in the plant (Williams 2000:77).

Work schedules can also weaken or preserve segregation. Employers set up most jobs for which they employed women as daytime jobs, and assumed that jobs that involve night shifts and rotating shifts would employ men. Jobs with regular daytime hours are more accessible for people who also have primary child care responsibility (i.e., women) because off-hours child care is harder to find (Garey 1999; Hofferth 1999). Only 3 percent of child care centers provide care in the evenings (although from 13 to 20 percent of family day care providers do so), and finding child care for rotating shift jobs is even harder (Hofferth 1999:25). For this reason, nonstandard work schedules are likely to have an exclusionary effect on women (Padavic 1991). Also partly for child care reasons, more women than men work part time. Designing customarily male jobs as part time would make them accessible to women and men who have substantial child care responsibilities.

Finally, an organization's orientation to time can have a segregative effect. Consider the practice of calling meetings at the last minute or allowing them to run late. Such a lack of predictability and discipline around the use of time causes problems for workers whose nonwork lives do not allow for flexibility. Women's greater responsibility for the home front means that they will miss more meetings than men do in such "time-unbounded" organizations. Missing chances to make contributions and appearing less committed than people who can stay late makes them less viable candidates for advancement into mostly male high-level jobs (Meyerson and Fletcher 1999).

In sum, a variety of employer practices can affect the levels of segregation in an organization. Employment policies can enhance workers' access to sex-atypical jobs. Importantly, they can avoid filling jobs through the informal networks, and they can implement personnel practices that minimize the exclusionary impact of conscious or unconscious tendencies to stereotype. In general, however, decision makers sometimes subvert reforms because they find it easier or more beneficial for their own careers to conduct business as usual rather than to implement changes, which can incur costs (Cohn 2000). Even employers who have no desire to discriminate have higher priorities than ferreting out possible sources of sex inequality in their organizations and eliminating them (Bielby and Baron 1986). Thus, employers subject to pressure from government or the courts are more likely to pursue inclusionary policies.

Workers' Actions

The other group whose actions contribute to sex segregation is workers. Two theories contend that jobs are sex segregated because women and men prefer different occupations. It is easy to see why men might choose male-dominated lines of work and reject predominantly female occupations: Predominantly male occupations pay more, provide more autonomy, and offer better chances for advancement.

But why would women choose "female" jobs? The standard answer appears in the opinion of the judge who decided that Sears, Roebuck had not discriminated against women and explained their absence from high-paid commission-sales jobs as follows:

> Women tend to be more interested than men in the social and cooperative aspects of the workplace. Women tend to see themselves as less competitive. They often view noncommission sales as more attractive than commission sales, because they can enter and leave the job more easily, and because there is more social contact and friendship, and less stress in noncommission selling. (*EEOC v. Sears, Roebuck & Co.* 1988)

We contend that the judge greatly overstated the importance of socialization, while ignoring Sears's segregative personnel practices. Here, we assess the evidence for the two theories of sex segregation that underlie the judge's opinion: human-capital theory and gender-role socialization theory.

Human-Capital Theory of Sex Segregation. Human-capital theory's account of sex segregation makes three assumptions. The first is that workers are rational actors who make fully informed choices about education and employment in order to maximize their lifetime earnings. The second is that investments in education and experience increase workers' productivity, for which their employers compensate them. The third assumption is that the sexual division of labor that was common in the first two-thirds of the twentieth century still prevails. In other words, women plan on specializing in unpaid family work and on being supported by a man. If these assumptions are valid, it follows that men will invest more than women in acquiring skills and experience that employers value, and women will invest more than men in acquiring skills and experience that will attract a partner and foster domestic success. If women's top priorities are attracting an economically successful mate and raising a family, they will invest in less education, training, and experience than men do and limit their time in paid jobs (see, for example, Polachek 1981). These different strategies would foster sex segregation for three reasons. First, women would be less qualified for customarily male jobs. Second, women would prefer occupations that are easy to reenter because they involve general skills that would not get rusty while they are at home raising children. Third, women would opt for jobs that demand the least effort in order to save their energy for their families. In short, the human-capital explanation of segregation holds that tens of millions of women have chosen to be secretaries, cashiers, teachers, nurses, and waitresses as a rational response to their expected family roles.[9]

Given women's primary responsibility for domestic work and child rearing, the idea that women give their family roles priority is plausible. Nowadays, though, the majority of mothers participate in the labor force through their prime working years, as Chapter 2 shows. Mothers are more likely than nonmothers to work part time, however, so employers' greater likelihood of structuring customarily female jobs rather than customarily male jobs as part time contributes to women's and men's segregation into different jobs.

Apart from the link between women's child-rearing responsibilities and part-time work, however, a variety of studies cast doubt on the human-capital explanation for women's concentration in female-dominated occupations. First, married women are no more likely than single women to work in predominantly female occupations. Second, predominantly male and female occupations require similar amounts of preparation (England, Chassie, and McCormack 1982), and most workers acquire necessary job skills on the job. Thus, it seems unlikely that women's concentration in different occupations from those that employ men represents women's rational decision. If differences in men's and women's levels of human capital (as measured by their education) contribute to the overall level of sex segregation, then the level of segregation should be lower when one controls for education. At the end of the twentieth century, the overall level of sex segregation in the United States was about 52. When Jacobs (1999) controlled education by calculating the segregation index within educational categories (less than high school, high school graduate, some college, college graduate, and some postgraduate education), the average level of segregation remained in the low 50s, with specific indices varying from 42 to almost 61. Thus, a rough control for human capital did not explain the amount of sex segregation in the late 1990s.

Of course, some women—and some men—lack the skills necessary to do predominantly male jobs, such as construction work. But employers' actions can and do redress these training deficiencies. As we have seen, employers are more likely to provide on-the-job training for male employees than female employees, presumably because employers more often train workers in predominantly male jobs (Kilbourne, England, Farkas, Beron, and Weir 1994). When employers provide training, how they organize it can either include or exclude women. Expecting seasoned workers to train new ones can limit women's ability to learn customarily male jobs. For example, a female plumbing apprentice showed up at a job site and asked the men responsible for training her, "'Aren't you guys supposed to train me?' They looked at me, I think there were three of them, and two of them said at the same time, 'We ain't got to show you shit,' and they turned around and walked away" (Eisenberg 1998:48). A meatpacking company made training the responsibility of veteran workers who were all men. They were reluctant to provide it because they regarded women as slow learners, and taking time to train them would reduce the men's own productivity and hence their pay (Fink 1998:99).

Misguided training also can hinder women's success in predominantly male jobs and thus affect their retention. An overly protective attitude toward women sets them apart and prevents them from learning their jobs and establishing their ability to succeed. The paternalism of a police academy instructor who demonstrated "takedown" tactics by throwing male but not female students to the floor meant that women students were denied both a learning opportunity and the chance to show their skill at rebuffing an attack (Prokos and Padavic 2002). Organizing training programs so that training is a management function or organizing it to give coworkers an incentive to conduct high-quality training should improve women's skill levels in customarily male jobs, thereby reducing sex segregation.

Human-capital theory is vulnerable on several additional counts. Importantly, the job characteristics of female jobs are not especially compatible with women's family roles: On average, they are not easier or more flexible than predominantly male occupations (Glass 1990:791; Jacobs and Steinberg 1990). In addition, as Chapter 3 shows, women exert as much effort on the job as men and, on average, are as committed as men to their jobs.

Finally, although the human-capital perspective is commonly invoked to explain women's occupational outcomes, it is rarely invoked to explain men's. How does it hold up as an explanation of men's workplace outcomes? According to the theory, men invest in career-oriented training and skills acquisition, subordinating other goals to this end. Thus, if the human-capital explanation holds, we would expect to find most young college men pursuing coursework that is likely to have the most career payoff. Yet many college men choose majors whose career payoff is likely to be slim. And many spend fewer hours studying (in other words, investing in their human capital) than they do in social activities. Among older men, those who are more oriented to their families or hobbies than their jobs also fail to conform to the theory's assumptions. Thus, the assumptions of human-capital theory are often at odds with how people actually behave. The sexes do make somewhat different choices in college major and in how many hours they work for pay that contribute to sex segregation. But the human-capital explanation of sex segregation does not help us much in explaining variation in sex segregation.

Gender Role Socialization. Differences in the socialization of females and males could contribute to job segregation by encouraging them to pursue different occupations, as Chapter 3 indicates. Socialization could create preferences in each sex for different kinds of work or for working with members of their sex, or it could teach each sex only the skills needed for sex-typical occupations. Or it could engender preferences for different working conditions, as the judge in the Sears case assumed. In a larger sense, by creating a desire to fit into socially acceptable roles—to play the games, wear the clothes, and aspire to the jobs that have been deemed appropriate for one's sex—socialization could perpetuate workplace segregation.

Examples of social practices that might contribute to gender-role socialization are ubiquitous. Consider the theme-based "Barbie" and

"Hot Wheels" personal computers that Mattel released in the fall of 2000. The Barbie PC supplied only half as much educational software as that accompanying the Hot Wheels PC. The Hot Wheels software taught human anatomy, three-dimensional visualization, and logic; the Barbie software did not (Headlam 2000). More generally, the media regale all of us with different images of men and women, so it is easy to imagine how girls and boys might come to prefer different occupations.

The long-term effects of childhood socialization on career outcomes are unknown, however. Not all children necessarily absorb sex-traditional messages from toys and media images. Preschool girl soccer players who named their team "Barbie Girls," for example, used the Barbie symbol to "celebrat[e] girl power," rather than the female passivity that some observers expect Barbie doll play to promote (Messner 2000:777). Moreover, society provides counterimages, from "riot grrrls" to a "kids and careers" website that presents games with the sexes in a variety of jobs, although the availability of these counterimages varies by economic status, region, race, and ethnicity.

While gender-role socialization may lead children and youth to aspire to jobs that are culturally viewed as appropriate for their sex, such aspirations are highly unstable; in fact, young people's occupational aspirations are weakly related to the occupations they hold as adults (Jacobs 1999:137). Moreover, adults—especially women—move back and forth between mostly female and mostly male occupations (Jacobs 1999:137-38). The weak association between youthful aspirations and actual jobs casts doubt on the importance of the gender-role socialization of children for sex segregation among adults.

A more important challenge to the socialization explanation of sex segregation is that it assumes that all females are socialized differently from all males and that all men thus will pursue customarily male jobs and all women will pursue customarily female ones. Although there is great variation in gender-role socialization among both boys and girls, researchers have not examined whether exposure to one or another kind of socialization has any ramifications for the sex type of the jobs people pursue. Past research largely fails to support this theory's assumptions, and its logic seems less plausible as women spend more of their adult lives in the labor force and as women's earnings become increasingly essential for their families.

Opportunities and Constraints. Far more influential than the messages we pick up as children are the opportunities we encounter as adults. The young women who began moving into traditionally male jobs in the 1970s and 1980s demonstrate this point. Most were raised by parents who subscribed to traditional gender roles (dad at work, mom at home), and the messages these women received from television (*Ozzie and Harriet, Leave It to Beaver,* and *The Flintstones*) reinforced this traditional socialization. Yet this did not deter them from taking higher-paying male-dominated jobs when they became open to women. Occupations' sex labels can also override the influence of childhood socialization in the opposite direction, as was the case for a woman who had several years' experience working construction jobs with her uncle. Nonetheless, when she applied for a job at Home Depot, she indicated a cashier's job because she thought "that's where women went" at Home Depot (Sturm 2001:155). In other words, she applied for the job that she believed was available to her.

Our knowledge of what people want in their jobs and how workers get into jobs is inconsistent with explanations of sex segregation that claim women freely choose traditionally female occupations. Although there are small sex differences in the job characteristics workers value, with males attaching greater importance to earnings and leisure and females attaching greater importance to working with people and helping others, by and large, women value the same job characteristics as men: good pay, autonomy, and prestige (Konrad et al. 2000; Marini et al. 1996).[10] Indeed, almost all workers seek these characteristics, but they settle for the best jobs available to them. Employers and society tend to limit women to a narrower set of options than men have.

When employers make customarily male jobs available to women, women usually flock to them (Cohn 1996:88). Despite conservative beliefs about gender in the late nineteenth century, the British Post Office found 12 women for every job vacancy in gender-atypical but well-paid and secure jobs (Cohn 1996:88). During World War I, African American female domestic workers seized the chance to work in industry, manufacturing everything from gas masks and airplane wings to tires and shoes (Jones 1985:166-67). The military also illustrates how segregation levels can drop when jobs are opened to women. As the number of male recruits fell in the 1970s, the military turned to women, eliminating some exclusionary policies (Segal 1995). As a result, the number of women in military service more than quadrupled between 1972 and the end of the century—from less than 45,000 to over 200,000 (U.S. Department of Defense 1999), and women entered many occupational specialties that were formerly off-limits to them. Similarly, changes in law school admission policies drew female applicants in the 1970s (Epstein 1993). In 1972, no women applied to work in the mines of Kentucky's Peabody Coal Company, the nation's largest producer of coal. But in 1978, the word was out that Peabody was hiring women, and 1,131 women applied for mining jobs (*Working Women* 1981). Coal mining was just one of the customarily male occupations that hundreds of thousands of women entered in the 1980s. Given the opportunity, women took jobs as bartenders rather than cocktail waitresses, as pharmacists rather than drugstore clerks, as bank managers rather than bank tellers, and as insurance sales agents rather than receptionists (Reskin and Roos 1990).

Laws and regulations (or even simple statements in classified ads indicating that the employer is an equal opportunity employer) are important partly because they tell women that jobs are open to them. Antidiscrimination laws and affirmative action regulations encourage women to apply for jobs that they might otherwise have thought were off-limits. Some beneficiaries of new government policies mentioned that such policies played a role in their getting nontraditional jobs. A case in point is a woman who wanted one of the better-paying all-male jobs in a meatpacking plant. After arguing with her boss for months, she got the job after she told him: "Hey, I want that job down there and if I don't get it, I'm going to sue the hell out of you" (Fink 1998:108).

The reactions of coworkers to the entry of sex-atypical workers are a further source of influence on women's share of customarily male jobs. When men enter traditionally female occupations such as nurse or teacher, their female coworkers generally welcome them (Williams 1995). In contrast, the response of men to women intruders varies widely, from helpful to hostile. Hostile coworkers may drive women out, thus preserving segregation, whereas supportive ones help retain women, thus undermining segregation.

Some male workers have resisted women's entry into traditionally male jobs through hazing, heckling, sabotage, and worse. In the past, many male unions and professional associations refused to admit women, but nowadays resistance is more likely to come from informal work groups or just a few individuals.

Such resistance may be subtle and even unintentional (Martin 2001). Talk about sex in a predominantly male work setting can make women feel unwelcome, for example, even though this is not necessarily men's goal. When a female rapid-transit conductor went to the crew room for her meal break during an 11-hour shift, she encountered several male coworkers she didn't know watching a rape scene in a *Death Wish* movie:

> I was so beside myself that I just walked over and changed the channel. One changed it back and someone said, "That's the best part. . . ." I went towards the television again, and someone . . . physically pushed me away from [it]. I left my food, I couldn't keep eating. I started crying and walked out of the crew room. (Swerdlow 1989:379)

Such behavior is not limited to blue-collar worksites. When a sociologist asked a female stock trader whether coworkers called her Deborah or Debbie, she answered, "They mostly just call me 'bitch'" (Levin 2001:122). A woman attorney heard a judge comment when he learned that a woman was joining his division: "I hear we're getting another bleeder" (Padavic and Orcutt 1997:694).

We do not know either how common such negative reactions are or whether they deter women from remaining in sex-atypical jobs. Despite the negative treatment of her coworkers, a woman meatpacker was determined to stay: "Those sons of bitches aren't going to do this. They're not going to get by with this. They're not going to get me to quit" (Fink 1998:97). Research showing that women move into and out of predominantly male occupations in a "revolving door" is consistent with the notion that some women leave male occupations because they run into male opposition (Jacobs 1999). Yet many women who confront such hostility remain in male jobs, either because they like the work or because they need the higher pay associated with traditionally male jobs (Padavic and Reskin 1990).

Many women in customarily male jobs meet with neutrality or support from male workers. A different female meatpacker in the same plant as the woman in the last paragraph described finding a "protector":

> Pete, the forklift driver who moved boxes of bellies, called me over. . . .
> With a friendly hand on my shoulder, he told me to ask him if I wanted
> anything . . . and he would help me. . . . [Then] the other forklift drivers
> warmed up. (Fink 1998:105-106)

Similarly the rapid-transit worker whose crew mates watched *Death Wish* had coworkers who taught her the ropes (Swerdlow 1989:384). A woman plumbing apprentice made a mistake that caused flooding and described her supervisor's reaction: "He said, 'You think I haven't made mistakes? . . . Everybody makes them. Everybody makes big ones. And you know, you can't kill yourself over it, just forget it'" (Eisenberg 1998:105). As with the effect of hostile reactions from coworkers, we do not know whether such positive reactions encourage women to remain in sex-atypical jobs.

In sum, some male workers try to exclude women from traditionally male jobs. Others create an uncomfortable environment simply by behaving in ways that are normal in all-male settings. Still others welcome women into their ranks. Thus, there is considerable variation in how coworkers respond. Unfortunately, research has yet to determine whether or how these different responses influence the degree of sex segregation. Nor does research give us a sense of the importance of coworkers' reactions in maintaining segregation relative to other factors, such as earnings.

The larger point is that explanations for sex segregation that emphasize women's socialization and women's free choices do not have much support. The most privileged members of our society are able to choose their life's work, and men's aversion to customarily female jobs—either because they are predominantly female or because the pay is low—contributes a great deal to levels of sex segregation. But no one would argue that choice is equally important in explaining the job outcomes of poor men, immigrants, and members of other disadvantaged groups.[11] Like men, women accept the best jobs that are open to them. When employers open traditionally male occupations to women, neither custom nor occupational sex labels deter many women from accepting them.

Summary

To varying degrees, workers are segregated on the basis of sex as well as other characteristics into different and unequal jobs. From a theoretical standpoint, we know the kinds of processes that contribute to varying levels of segregation. Workers' credentials, experience, and economic need matter, as does their sense of what possibilities are open to them. Yet even when workers have a hand in perpetuating sex segregation, they are not the most powerful actors involved. A single worker's decision is inconsequential for the level of segregation. In contrast, employers and the government have the resources to alter segregation levels. For this reason, employers' personnel practices are particularly important. We have seen that these personnel practices themselves depend on the presence of economic and regulatory pressures.

As we have noted, some long-standing explanations for segregation have not been adequately tested. When segregation was universally high, such explanatory research was not possible (you can't explain a constant). Now that segregation levels vary widely across different work settings, we should see more research testing the theories reviewed in this chapter.

Notes

1. A photograph of an office filled with typists was captioned "Clerical work—quite a new job for Negro Girls," and the caption for a photograph of women at sewing machines explained, "Laundry and domestic work didn't pay so they entered the garment trade" (Callahan 1992:37).

2. Although these were paid jobs, the conditions were such that it has been described as "legalized slavery" (Amott and Matthaei 1996:79).

3. This list omits the most female-dominated occupation in the United States—homemaker—because our society does not consider it to be a real job.

4. "Occupational race segregation" refers to the segregation of people of different races into different occupations.

5. Unfortunately, the ILO report does not provide a direct comparison for men. Because there are seven times as many male-dominated as female-dominated occupations, most male workers do not have to face competition from women (Anker 1998: 219).

6. Most women hear about only a tiny fraction of the jobs for which they are qualified. And even when women learn of and apply for a job, the employer chooses whether to hire them and for which job.

7. In response, some flight attendants made buttons saying, "Fly yourself!" (Ireland 2001).

8. Because laws construed discrimination as originating in out-group *hostility*, the courts have permitted differential treatment based on a preference for one's own sex (McGinley 1997).

9. Karen Nussbaum, head of the AFL-CIO's Working Women department, called this idea the "lemming theory" of sex segregation, in reference to the mouse-like animals in Scandinavia that periodically march to the sea, where they inexplicably drown themselves.

10. Among workers in customarily male occupations, women attach at least as much importance to earnings as men do, either because women who care about high earnings are attracted to predominantly male occupations, or because having the same employment opportunities as men leads workers to express the same occupational values, regardless of their sex (Konrad et al. 2000:607, 610).

11. A poignant example of having to choose from limited options comes from a 1956 ad in the "situations wanted" section of the classifieds: "Colored girl, college grad with B.S. degree in math, desires office job, clerical, filing, or day's work."

5

Moving Up and Taking Charge

Until 30 years ago, few employers considered women for promotions that would take them outside the female clerical or assembly-line ghettos. Now women receive promotions as often as men, although they occupy only a tiny fraction of the nation's very top jobs. When they are in higher-level jobs, many women do not have the authority that is typical of these positions. This chapter first examines promotion differences between women and men and then focuses on two aspects of women's and men's differential access to authority: women's greater chances of encountering a "glass ceiling" barring them from jobs that grant power and authority and women's lesser chances of being able to exercise authority even when they hold jobs that normally confer it. We conclude by discussing explanations and remedies for the sex differences we find.

Women, Men, and Promotions

Promotions matter to workers and employers. Given the centrality of work in peoples' lives, career advancement is key for how they think about themselves. Many regard getting ahead at work as a way of showing that they are worthwhile and productive. For their part, employers use promotions to retain valued workers, to fill higher-level positions with workers familiar with the company, and to give workers an incentive to work hard.

National surveys that ask about promotions—the General Social Survey (GSS) and the National Longitudinal Survey of Youth (NLSY)—indicate a small to moderate gender gap in promotions. The GSS asked a random sample of workers across all ages whether they had ever been promoted by their current employer. In 1991 (the most recent year available), 48 percent of men had been promoted, compared to only 34 percent of women (Kalleberg and Reskin 1995). In contrast, in 1998 the NLSY asked workers in their mid-30s and early 40s if their current employer had promoted them within the previous two years. These data indicate that men had a very slight edge over women (21.6 percent of men compared to 20.6 percent of women) (U.S. Bureau of Labor Statistics 1999b). Because the NLSY data concern only recent promotions of workers in midcareer, they do not pick up sex differences during the early years of a career, when most promotions occur. Men are promoted at a faster rate during those years, after which the sex gap disappears (Cobb-Clark and Dunlop 1999). Thus, compared to the large differences in promotion rates in the early 1980s (men averaged .83 promotions compared to women's .47; Spaeth 1989), the promotion gap has narrowed considerably.

Among federal government workers, women have been promoted at a higher rate than men: Whereas women made up 45 percent of the federal workforce in 1998, they accounted for 52 percent of all promotions. However, most of women's promotions were in the low- and midlevel ranks, not the senior ones, 62 percent of which went to men, who were 55 percent of the federal workforce (U.S. Office of Personnel Management 1999).

The size of sex differences in promotion rates also depends on characteristics of workers. Consider education. Women high school graduates and women with less than a high school education are far more likely to be promoted than similarly educated men. The reverse is true for college graduates and above. About 35 percent of men college graduates were promoted in 1996, compared to only about 29 percent of similar women. The difference is even more pronounced among those with postgraduate schooling: 34 percent of such men had been promoted, compared to 21 percent of such women (Cobb-Clark and Dunlop 1999).

Being married increases the chances of a man being promoted, but has the opposite effect for women. Having a preschooler also has contrary effects for men and women: Fathers of preschoolers have higher rates of promotion than the average man, and mothers of preschoolers have lower rates than the average woman. Thus, the sex gap in promotions is greater among married than single workers and among parents of preschoolers compared to others (Cobb-Clark and Dunlop 1999).

Women's and men's promotion rates depend partly on their race and ethnicity, with black women particularly disadvantaged relative to white men. Among workers in their mid-30s to early 40s in 1998, for example, only 17 percent of black women had been promoted, compared to 22 percent of white men (U.S. Bureau of Labor Statistics 1999b).

Promotion opportunities also vary by occupation. When the media depict people who are promoted, they tend to present high-status workers moving up, such as law firm associates becoming partners or midlevel managers rising to executive positions. But most workers are not in management or professional jobs. Recall from Chapter 4 that the most common job for men is truck driver and for women it is secretary. Most promotions are from low- to slightly higher-level positions. Moreover, many workers hold jobs with no promotion possibilities (Davis, Smith, and Marsden 2000). Thus, for many workers, the problem is not the glass ceiling blocking them from top jobs (which we discuss later), but the sticky floor that traps them in low-mobility jobs (Berheide 1992). Generally, female and male workers in the less-skilled occupations—operatives, laborers, and service workers—are less likely to be promoted than workers in higher-skill jobs (Cobb-Clark and Dunlop 1999).

Of people aged 32 to 39 in 1996, men had an advantage among professionals, service workers, and operators (Cobb-Clark and Dunlop 1999). In one professional group—lawyers—men were two to three times more likely to have been promoted to partnership than women (Gorman 2001; Rhode 2001). Not surprisingly, women lawyers tend to be less satisfied with their advancement opportunities and more likely to think that promotion decisions in their firms were made unfairly (Catalyst 2001).

Even in traditionally female jobs (nurse, librarian, elementary school teacher, social worker, and the like), men do not confront blocked opportunities because of their sex. According to male workers, their employers singled them out for an express ride to the top on a "glass escalator" (Williams 1995). Findings from a nationally representative sample from the 1980s confirm this finding: the more women in an occupation, the greater men's—particularly white men's—chances of moving into supervisory positions (Maume 1999:501). In fact, the odds are that after having spent 12 years in a predominantly female occupation, 44 percent of white men will have been promoted into managerial ranks, compared to only 17 percent of black men, 15 percent of white women, and 7 percent of black women.

Although men as a population seldom encounter barriers to promotion, they nevertheless can face promotion-related problems. Employers may regard men who are unwilling to pursue advancement opportunities because of family reasons as lacking career commitment, just as they perceive women who make similar choices. A senior computer programmer unwilling to be promoted out of his 35-hour-a-week job explained:

> I have a six-year-old and a two-year-old. School ends for the older one at 2:30 every day, plus they have "early release" at noon every other

Wednesday. My wife can only take so much time off work, and after-school programs only go so far. This isn't a point in my life when I can add the work hours that would come with a promotion, but my boss doesn't understand that. (Jim Madsen, personal communication, 2001)

Men who do not seek advancement, regardless of the reason, may suffer professionally because they violate gender stereotypes of men as oriented to advancement. Some of the men in traditionally female jobs that Williams studied faced pressure to accept promotions, such as the children's librarian who received negative evaluations for not "shooting high enough." He recalled that, "I wasn't doing the management-oriented work that they thought I should be doing. And as a result . . . [I] had a lot of bad marks . . . against me" (Williams 1995:88). Thus, both sexes face promotion problems, but the nature of these problems can vary for men and women.

In sum, sex inequality in access to promotions has declined: If we compare all women and men, the differences between them are small. One group of men appears to face greater obstacles to promotion: men with high school diplomas or less. Segregation probably accounts for this difference: These men are concentrated in lines of work that offer fewer advancement opportunities than those in which women are concentrated.

In other groups, men have an advantage over women: Among those educated to the college degree level and beyond, married people, and parents of preschoolers, men enjoy a promotion advantage. Nowadays, women are not systematically disadvantaged: Some are doing about the same as men, some do better, and some do worse, particularly black women, whose chances of promotion are worse than white men's chances.

Women, Men, and Authority

When it comes to exercising authority on the job, women still fare worse than men. Exercising **authority** means having legitimate power to mobilize people, to get their cooperation, and to secure the resources to do the job (Kanter 1983). Typically in a bureaucracy, authority resides in the job, not in its occupant's personal qualities. A person with job authority sets policy or makes decisions about organizational goals, budgets, production, and subordinates (for example, about hiring, pay, and work schedules).

Women's lesser authority in the workplace appears in two guises. First, women are less likely than men to occupy the high-level positions that offer opportunities to exert power. This blocked mobility to influential jobs has been called a **glass ceiling.** Second, even when women hold positions that typically confer authority, they have less power than men, regardless of whether they are managers, professionals, or blue-collar workers.

The Glass Ceiling in Management

Men are greatly overrepresented among the elite group of top job-holders in organizations, a phenomenon that has been described as a glass ceiling. Although managerial occupations, by definition, confer authority, if women are blocked from the top managerial ranks, they are unable to make the major business or policy decisions. The occupational category of manager includes jobs with wide variation in status and authority, ranging from the extremely low level (such as coffee shop manager) to the extremely top level (such as chief executive officer). And despite improvements, women managers are still greatly underrepresented in the top slots.

In general, the higher the level of authority in an organization, the less likely women are to be represented. In 2000, women held fewer than 13 percent of the corporate officer slots across all Fortune 500 companies, up from about 9 percent in 1995 (Catalyst 2000a). Of the 10 highest-earning companies in 1999, women's share of officer positions ranged from none at Exxon to 31 percent at Phillip Morris. Between those extremes were Citigroup (14 percent); AT&T, Ford, General Motors, Wal-Mart, and Boeing (around 10 percent); and General Electric and IBM (about 6 percent). Although in 50 of the Fortune 500 companies women held one-quarter or more of corporate officer positions, in 90 others no women were represented in these positions.

Women's representation is even lower—just 6 percent—in the "clout" positions that offer the greatest power—chief executive officer [CEO], chair, vice chair, president, chief operating officer, senior executive vice president, and executive vice president. At the very top of the job hierarchy, CEOs in the top 500 corporations, there were just five women in 2001.

Positions on corporate boards of directors provide another route to exercising genuine power, and here, too, women remain sharply underrepresented, holding only 12 percent of such seats in the Fortune 500 firms in 2000. Eighty-one of these companies had no women board members (Catalyst 1999).

Industries vary in employing women in positions that confer authority. In industries that employ mostly women, women are more likely to be found in top-level occupations (Catalyst 1999). For example, in 1999 only

EXHIBIT 5.1

Managerial Employment by Sex and Race, 1970-2000

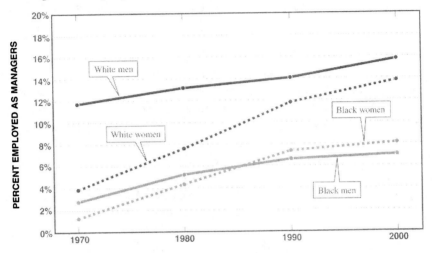

Source: U.S. Census Bureau 1972, table 2; U.S. Census Bureau 1982a; authors' calculations from the March 1998, 1999, and 2000 Current Population Surveys.
Note: Figures for 2000 are averages of 1998, 1999, and 2000 Current Population Survey data.

3.3 percent of officers in the male-dominated computer peripherals industry were women, but a quarter of officers in the publishing and printing industry were. A study of the United States, Canada, Norway, and Sweden found that women had far greater access to positions of authority in service industries than in industrial ones (Clement and Myles 1994).[1]

Sex Differences by Race and Ethnicity. Sex differences in the likelihood of being in managerial occupations vary by race and ethnicity. Exhibit 5.1 shows improvements over the past 30 years for black women and men and particularly strong gains for white women. At the turn of the twenty-first century, white women were almost as likely as white men to be managers. Among African Americans, women had a slight edge over men in their likelihood of holding managerial positions. White men were still twice as likely to be managers (15.8 percent of white men found employment as managers) as were black women (8.1 percent) or black men (7 percent).

A different source that uses a category called "officials and managers" provides more detailed race and ethnic information, but because this category differs from "managerial occupations," the data deviate somewhat from those depicted in Exhibit 5.1. These data from the Equal Employment Opportunity Commission show that men in 1999 were better represented than coethnic women among all race/ethnic groups for which data were available (U.S. Equal Employment Opportunity Commission 2001b). The sex gap was largest among whites (16.1 percent of white men held such jobs compared to 8.8 percent of white women). It was smallest among Hispanics (5.2 percent of men and 3.7 percent of women) and blacks (5.5 percent of black men and 3.9 percent of black women). The gap between Asian/Pacific Islander women and men (9.5 percent of men and 5.4 percent of women) and that between American Indian/Alaskan Native men and women (8.5 percent of men and 5.3 percent of women were officials and managers) fell between these extremes.

The Managerial Glass Ceiling in Government Employment. Among government workers, too, men have a substantial edge in access to top jobs, although the disparity is smaller than in the private sector. Women accounted for about 52 percent of the workforce in state governments in 1999, but only 30 percent of those serving as top-ranking policy leaders (Center for Women in Government 1999). In the federal government—the nation's largest employer—women made up 45 percent of the workforce at the turn of the twenty-first century and have greatly increased their representation in the top jobs. In 1978, women held only 6 percent of higher-level positions; they held 22 percent of senior executive positions in 1998 (U.S. Merit Systems Protection Board 1996:16; U.S. Office of Personnel Management 1999). Thus, the authority gap has been shrinking in the federal government, but despite women's gains, men still hold three-quarters of the best jobs.

These sex differences in federal government employment depend on the race of the worker. Minority women remain concentrated in lower grades than white men or men of their same race/ethnicity (U.S. Merit Systems Protection Board 1996, Figure 4; U.S. Office of Personnel Management 2001). Although minority women made up 37 percent of federal government workers, they filled only 19 percent of senior management positions; minority men made up 23 percent of the workers and only 12 percent of such positions (U.S. Office of Personnel Management 2001). And when it comes to the top executive positions, minority women held about 2 percent and minority men held about 8 percent of these jobs (U.S. Merit Systems Protection Board 1996, Table 4). These differences are not the result of different qualifications: Women with levels of education and experience equivalent to those of men of their same race and ethnicity were in lower-ranked jobs.

The Managerial Glass Ceiling Around the World. Compared to women in most other countries, American women are doing relatively well: Women's representation in top jobs worldwide is under 5 percent (International Labour Organization 1998). In no country are women represented in top-level jobs on a par with their numbers in all administrative and managerial positions. Out of Germany's 70,000 largest companies, fewer than 3 percent of top executives and board members were women. In Brazil, about 3 percent of top executives were women. In the United Kingdom, women were 4 percent of directors and 2 percent of executive directors in the top 100 companies. In Japan, only 2 percent of top managers of large corporations were women, although including small and medium-sized companies brings the figure up to 13 percent. The United Nations estimates that if current trends continue, women will not achieve parity with men in attaining top jobs for almost another 500 years (Seager 1997:70).

The Glass Ceiling in Other Occupations

We noted earlier that one reason women have less authority than men is that they are less likely to be in managerial positions. Of course, there are other positions in which people exercise authority, and we now turn to the glass ceiling in other occupations. Women are underrepresented in top jobs in the professions, the military, and unions. In the field of law, at the beginning of the twenty-first century, women were far more likely to be law firm associates than law firm partners, and it is partners who run the show. Nationally, women were 39 percent of law firm associates, but only 15 percent of partners (Rhode 2001). A study of almost 700 Ontario lawyers found that even women lawyers who served the "important" clients and who generated high billings had lower chances of partnership compared to men (Kay and Hagan 1999). At the pinnacle of the legal profession and certainly at the height of decision-making power are federal court judges, fewer than 1 in 6 of whom are women (Rhode 2001).

Other professions show similar patterns. Female medical school graduates who obtained degrees between 1979 and 1993 made up only 10 percent of medical school faculty (DeAngelis 2000). A "stained glass ceiling" in which women clergy were overrepresented in subordinate, low-status positions exists, according to a national study of over 15,000 Episcopal priests and a smaller sample of Presbyterian clergy (Sullins 2000). In the military, women's representation in the officer ranks was about equal to their representation in the enlisted ranks (Manning and Wight 2000:9), but female and minority officers were concentrated in less-prestigious administrative and supply areas and underrepresented in tactical operations, from which two-thirds of the general and flag officers are drawn (*New York Times* 1999). The Federal Bureau of Investigation (FBI) refused even to hire women as agents until after its director, J. Edgar Hoover, died in 1972 (Johnston 1993). The lingering effect of this practice is that women FBI agents near the end of the twentieth century were far less likely than men agents to be in the highest ranks: 92 percent of criminal investigators in the Bureau's highest grades were men (U.S. Government Accounting Office 1995, Figure I.2).

Unions have increased the proportion of women in top jobs, but room for improvement remains. At the turn of the twenty-first century, women comprised over 40 percent of union members but only 13 percent of the AFL-CIO Executive Council (Gerstel and Clawson 2001:290). The executive vice-president of the AFL-CIO was a Hispanic woman in 2001, but at that time only three women had been elected president at the nation's biggest unions: the American Federation of Teachers, the Association of Flight Attendants, and the American Federation of Television and Radio Artists (Fix 2001).

Sex Differences in Opportunities to Exercise Authority

Women who achieve jobs that typically involve decision-making power cannot always exercise the same level of authority as men. Among workers in Atlanta, Boston, and Los Angeles, women were substantially less likely to hold positions of authority than men, regardless of race or ethnicity (Smith and Elliott 2002). White men had a decided advantage in almost every case: They were four times more likely to hold positions that provided authority than were black and Hispanic women, and three times more likely than Asian women, twice as likely as black or Hispanic men, and slightly more likely than Asian men to hold positions that conferred authority.

What does it mean that women have less decision-making authority than men? A study of decision making among a cross section of workers found that women managers participated in decision making by gathering information and making recommendations, but that men usually made the final decisions (Reskin and Ross 1992). Men more often had the authority to make decisions about bread-and-butter issues such as hiring, firing, promoting, and giving raises, and they were more likely to have had a say in decisions that affected other units. The three-city study we discussed earlier similarly found that among women and men in authority positions, men were more likely than coethnic women to be in jobs offering high levels of authority (Smith and Elliott 2002). Asian men, for example, were two-and-a-half times as likely as Asian women to hold positions of authority, black and Hispanic men almost twice as likely as black and Hispanic women to hold such positions, and white men were half again as likely as white women.

The existence of relatively powerless female managers has led some researchers to question whether women's increasing representation in managerial occupations represents genuine progress or whether they are "glorified secretaries," women with managerial titles but not the responsibilities and authority that usually accompany the titles (Jacobs 1992). A conversation secretly taped by the FBI between the vice-chair and two division presidents in a Fortune 500 corporation illustrates this concept. One executive raised the idea of promoting two women to vice president levels and making another head of a department. Another senior executive responded: "Yeah, [it's] just a title, just a title. Don't mean anything. At least to the outside it does mean something" (Eichenwald 2000).

Coworkers also may actively deny women and minorities the chance to exercise authority. Women in traditionally male blue-collar jobs, for example, encounter problems in exercising authority even when their job explicitly confers it. One woman promoted to construction foreperson while the supervisors were out for a week said:

> It was like *Mutiny on the Bounty*. I mean, I had been working with these guys for months, everybody getting along fine, doing a wonderful job. . . . [But when I was put in charge], by God, . . . if I told them to do something, they'd do their best to find some way not to do it. (Eisenberg 1998:167)

When a female electrician was appointed to a supervisory role at Atlantic City's convention center, the site's business manager objected: "[N]ow is not the time, the place or the year [n]or will it ever be the year for a woman foreman" (Schultz 1998:1723). The men she supervised refused to work under her and stood by laughing while she lifted heavy boxes.

Some workers circumvent a lack of authority by becoming their own boss (Powell 1999:338). Women commonly cite blocks to advancement as a reason for starting their own businesses (Moore and Buttner 1997). In 1997, women-owned businesses made up about one-quarter of all nonfarm businesses in the country, representing an increase of 16 percent in just 5 years, and showed receipts that grew at a faster rate than those of other businesses (U.S. Census Bureau 2001). Businesses owned by minority women, especially Hispanics, have grown at an even faster rate (Moore 1999:371, 375).[2] Yet women-owned firms tend to be smaller and return lower profits than men-owned firms. Over two-thirds had receipts of under $25,000 per year (compared to 53 percent of all firms), and only 2 percent had receipts of over $1 million (U.S. Census Bureau 2001).

Women-run businesses generate less revenue than men-run businesses because they are smaller and are in the service sector. Many female business owners act as **independent contractors**—workers hired on a freelance basis to do work that regular employees otherwise would do in-house. Most employ just themselves—only 16 percent had paid employees.[3] The average annual earnings of a full-time self-employed female worker were only about $14,000, compared to about $29,000 for an employed female worker (U.S. Census Bureau 1998, 1999, 2000a). Another factor that depresses the profits of women-run businesses is that few are able to attract venture capital. Only 5 percent of the $12 billion pool of available venture capital went to women-owned firms in 1999 (an improvement over the 2 percent in previous years; Thomas 2000).

Explanations and Remedies for the Promotion and Authority Gaps

Although there is no longer a systematic promotion gap across the board, there are sectors where it remains. Particularly problematic are the slots high up in organizations: Men are more likely to occupy top positions, and the higher one looks, the bigger the sex disparity. This section examines four explanations for sex inequalities in promotions and authority and the remedies derived from them.

Source: © Jim Borgman; reprinted with special permission of King Features Syndicate.

Segregation

Women's and men's segregation into different jobs contributes to women's blocked mobility to the top jobs. Thus, the more segregated the sexes over time or across work settings, the greater should be men's promotion advantage. The mechanism that converts segregation into a promotion gap is the **internal labor market**. Internal labor markets comprise related jobs (or job families) connected by **job ladders** that are promotion or transfer paths between lower- and higher-level jobs.

Insofar as segregation disproportionately concentrates women in dead-end jobs or jobs with short promotion ladders, it commensurately reduces their promotion chances. Men are more likely than women to be on career ladders (Cassirer and Reskin 2000, table 1). In a mid-1990s court case, the Wall Street firm Salomon Smith Barney paid thousands of dollars to settle a claim that (among other charges) it had systematically channeled men into broker-training programs while directing women into sales assistant jobs that offered little hope of promotion to broker (McGeehan 1998). Academia offers other examples. Women faculty members are overrepresented in non-tenure track positions (i.e., instructor, lecturer) that offer no prospects for rising through the ranks (Grant and Ward 1996). Women faculty in law schools, for example, disproportionately work as instructors who teach legal writing and research and professional skills, and instructors are seldom on the tenure ladder (Reskin, Hargens, and Merritt 2001). Men's greater likelihood of being on career ladders is mirrored in their greater optimism about their chances of a promotion: 61 percent of a national sample of 34- to 41-year-old men in 1998 thought being promoted at their present job within 2 years was possible, compared to 56 percent of women (U.S. Bureau of Labor Statistics 1999b; see also Cassirer and Reskin 2000).

Sex-segregated internal labor markets can also help explain women's lesser access to jobs that confer authority. Employers designed many traditionally female jobs, such as teacher, without job ladders in order to encourage turnover, thereby keeping wages low. (By giving workers an incentive to stay, job ladders discourage turnover.)

For workers whose jobs are on promotion ladders, men tend to be found on longer ladders that reach higher in the organization where authority is concentrated. In contrast, women are concentrated on shorter ladders, with just one or two rungs above the entry level. Clerical work, for example, is often part of a two-rung system. A typical word-processing office in a small firm consists of many word-processing workers and one supervisor; a travel agency employs many reservation agents and one supervisor (Gutek 1988:231).

An illustration of how internal labor markets can affect access to top jobs comes from a grocery chain, whose female employees sued for discrimination because it had promoted almost no women or minorities to store manager. A diagram of this chain's internal labor market (Exhibit 5.2) shows how women's underrepresentation in the top jobs stemmed largely from the sex segregation of lower-level jobs. Job ladders in the predominantly male produce department led to top management. In contrast, the most heavily female departments—bakery/deli and general merchandise— were on short job ladders that were not directly connected to the ladder to top management.

Establishment segregation explains much of women's underrepresentation in the top jobs. Large organizations are more likely to have the resources that allow them to create internal labor markets (Powell 1999). Moreover, their sheer size lets them create more opportunities for deserving workers (Spaeth 1989). Most workers of both sexes work for small employers, not corporations, but women's greater concentration in small, entrepreneurial firms and nonprofit organizations reduces their odds of promotion relative to men (Cobb-Clark and Dunlop 1999; Kalleberg and Reskin 1995).

EXHIBIT 5.2

Internal Labor Market for Grocery Store Chain

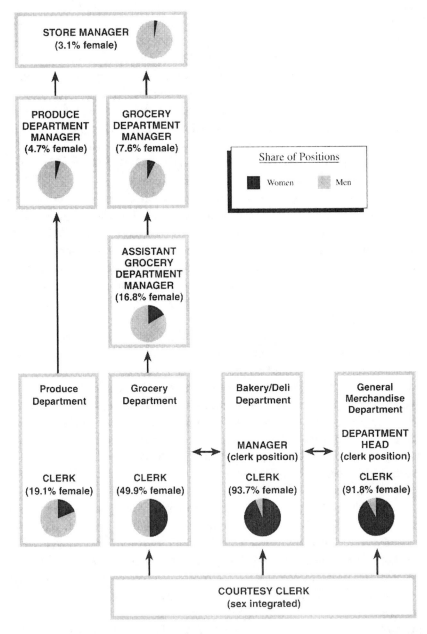

Note: Arrows indicate transfer or promotion paths.

Women's share of top leadership jobs also affects other women's opportunities to move up and take charge. Jobs that have low female representation at the top tend to have poor female representation at all levels of management (Cohen, Broschak, and Haveman 1998). For instance, junior women in law firms that had higher proportions of women partners had better employment experiences: Compared to those in firms with few senior women, they perceived fewer differences between women and men workers and regarded women as more capable of achieving success (Ely 1995).

Women's share of nonmanagerial jobs also matters. In companies that fill managerial jobs by promoting from within rather than by recruiting from outside the company, a strong representation of women in nonmanagerial positions increased female employees' share of managerial jobs (Reskin and McBrier 2000:224). This was particularly true in largely male industries, where the recruitment pool outside the company was also mostly male. (Of course, if the insider pool has few women and the outside pool has many, women's chances of becoming managers are greater if the firm engages in recruiting from outside.)

Segregation further contributes to women's underrepresentation in the upper echelons of management and the professions by obscuring women's accomplishments. Women tend to hold "staff" positions, such as human relations and public relations, that offer fewer opportunities to demonstrate competence. Among corporate officers, for example, men occupy 93 percent of the more important "line" positions, which entail profit and loss responsibility, compared to only 7 percent of women (Catalyst 2000a). Staff positions involve little risk and therefore provide few opportunities for workers to display their talents to senior managers. When top executives are looking for people to promote to senior management, they seldom pick vice presidents of personnel management or public relations. They pick vice presidents in product management or sales, who are usually men. By denying women jobs in which workers make important decisions, segregation produces an authority gap.

Women in heavily female industries tend to have greater access to jobs that confer authority than do women in male-dominated industries, as we noted previously. Perhaps the companies' greater experience with female workers makes them less likely to stereotype women and better able to spot talented individuals. Furthermore, jobs in female-intensive industries pay less and are thus less desirable to men. Because of the small pool of male competitors, women get more opportunities to exercise authority than they would in male-dominated industries. In any event, sex segregation contributes to this outcome by concentrating women in some industries.

In general, lowering segregation within establishments would go a long way toward equalizing the sexes' access to advancement and authority. Chapter 4 discussed ways organizations can decrease segregation. Until it is eliminated, however, steps can be taken to ensure that the contributions of workers relegated to staff jobs are noticed and rewarded with promotions. For example, workers who bring profitable clients or resources into their firms are commonly called "rainmakers." Evaluations that contain "rainmaking equivalency quotients" calibrate the accomplishments of workers in departments that do not produce profits to those in departments that do, thus allowing staff workers the possibility to advance into the upper ranks (Meyerson and Fletcher 1999; see also Nelson and Bridges 1999:340).

The problem posed by women's concentration on job ladders with low mobility potential can be addressed through companies' creation of "bridge" programs to help workers switch job ladders—for example, move from a clerical ladder to an administrative one—without penalty. In response to a consent decree, for example, Home Depot partially automated its promotion system. Current employees enter into a computer their job qualifications, which are automatically incorporated into the applicant pool for all jobs that fit their preference and qualifications profile, regardless of the employee's originating department (Sturm 2001:459).

Sex Differences in Human Capital

As Chapter 3 explained, the logic behind human-capital theory assumes that sex differences in commitment, education, and experience make women less productive than men (Becker 1985). Lower productivity should lead to poorer promotion rates and fewer opportunities to exercise authority. As we showed in Chapter 3, women's career commitment does not differ from men's, and women are fast catching up in educational attainment with men. The human-capital claim that women's lesser experience contributes to their underrepresentation at the top of career hierarchies deserves a more careful look, however.

According to this explanation, women as a group lack the experience needed to advance into positions that confer authority. Sociologists conceptualize different levels of experience between two groups in a workplace in terms of the seniority composition of the organization. Many demographic factors affect the sex composition of an organization, and how rapidly these factors change depends on the turnover rate of female and male workers in the higher ranks, the sex composition of the younger pool of workers, the growth (or decline) of jobs in the field, and the sheer number of jobs in the top ranks (Hargens and Long 2002).

Organizations vary on these demographic dimensions. In settings where turnover is high and career spans are short, it should not take as long for the sex composition to become more equal if employers ignore sex in employment decisions; in settings where turnover is low and career spans are long, it takes longer. Thus, the sex composition of the U.S. Supreme Court will change more slowly (because justices have lifetime appointments) than will the sex composition of top jobs in an organization that replaces corporate officers every two or three years. Commenting on the small number of job slots in the top ranks of her firm, an African American woman engineer at General Electric said, ". . . there are only so many management slots. It gets to the point where your moves are lateral, not vertical" (Walsh 2000). Establishments with more top slots or greater turnover in managerial jobs offer more opportunities. Thus, even in the complete absence of discrimination today, it can take decades for women to achieve parity with men in the top ranks when turnover is low.

There is merit to this logic and to the human capital claim that women as a group receive less training and have less experience both within an establishment and within the labor force. These differences need to be equalized for the sex gap in promotions and authority to disappear. On the other hand, it is important to recognize that employers as well as workers contribute to how much and what kinds of experience workers acquire. In many settings, employers prevent women from acquiring experiences needed for advancement. For example, military promotion to the rank of commissioned officer is usually reserved for people with ground combat experience, but Congress and the military ban women from combat (Manning and Wight 2000:18). In banking, managers who hope for a top spot need extensive experience in commercial lending. Only recently have substantial numbers of women bank managers been given the chance to work in commercial lending, so few women could acquire the expertise needed to rise beyond middle management. In the same way, the sex segregation of blue-collar production jobs denies women the experience they need to rise to management positions in manufacturing firms. Moreover, the biases of people responsible for training can block opportunities. A black female electrician recalled her "training": "I did all the grunt work—digging ditches, moving trash, unloading tractor trailers for days in and days out. You didn't use your tools that much. I had to . . . clean out their toilets and mop their floors. . . . The electricians would tell me, 'This is the way you move up'" (Eisenberg 1998:149).

In an increasingly global economy, international experience is crucial for advancement in many firms. Eighty percent of the human resources executives in a study of 75 Fortune 500 companies said that developing global talent will be a top priority over the next five years (Catalyst 2000b). Women, however, are far less likely than men to receive international assignments. Women are 49 percent of all managers and professionals but are only 13 percent of American managers who are sent abroad (Catalyst 2000b). Many companies think twice before sending a woman to a foreign assignment, partly because they fear that sexist attitudes abroad will hinder their employee's ability to get the job done. For example, a woman with excellent performance evaluations and rapport with clients said that her career was stalling because of management's refusal to have an African American woman represent it overseas (Hesse-Biber and Carter 2000:164).

What remedies based on human capital explanations are likely to work? Women still lag behind men in the years of experience that would put them in line for the top positions. Clearly, if a qualification such as training or experience truly is essential to do a high-level job, women who don't have it won't advance. Thus, adding women at lower levels where they can gain experience and enter the pipeline leading to future high-level jobs is necessary for progress. But it is not sufficient. Also necessary is the removal of barriers that block women's access to training and experience. For example, because having *job-specific* experience is important for promotions, employers who concentrate women in different jobs than men will reduce these women's job-relevant experience, thereby lowering their promotion chances. As for experience abroad, the courts have ruled that customer preference does not justify treating women and men employees differently. To the extent that employers take seriously a commitment to abide by antidiscrimination laws and to create an equal-opportunity environment, concerns about customers' or foreign firms' comfort levels will be more or less a barrier. Enforcement matters, too: If regulatory agencies more closely monitored women's opportunities for assignments overseas, for example, women would face fewer such barriers. In sum, the equalization of women's and men's opportunities for moving up and taking charge varies depending on organizations' personnel policies and practices and on enforcement agencies' activities.

Sex Differences in Social Networks

As Chapters 3 and 4 showed, filling jobs through social networks ("word-of-mouth" recruiting) tends to reproduce the characteristics of the existing workforce because people's networks tend to include others like themselves (Lin 2000). As this chapter has shown, at the highest levels, most organizations are male dominated. Thus, if the pool of people being considered is made up of members of decision makers' social networks, women usually will be disadvantaged. A woman manager alluded to the advantages men have in networks by describing what she called the "armpit track" into the upper reaches of management: "They put [a man] under their armpit and say come fly with me up to the executive suite" (Bell and Nkomo 2001:153).

Most employers fill managerial jobs through informal networks, according to a nationally representative survey of establishments described in Chapter 3. Half had frequently recruited managers via referrals or direct invitations to apply; only 7 percent had not used these methods, and the establishments using informal recruitment methods were less likely to have women in managerial positions than organizations that used "open" recruitment methods (Reskin and McBrier 2000:221-22).

Some organizations have sought to remedy social-network exclusion by actively seeking to expose workers to a broader array of networks. Encouraging the formation of networks of women and minority employees from across the organization is one way to do this (Sessa 1992; Walsh 2000). Caucus groups at the Xerox Corporation, for example, helped promote women's upward mobility (Sessa 1992).

Mentoring programs can help get around social network exclusion by providing connections to influential people in the organization who can advocate for people they mentor, teach them the ropes, and provide them with "reflected power" (the status that comes with being associated with powerful people; Kanter 1977; McGuire 2000:501). Having a powerful person publicly support a woman helps protect her from blatant and subtle discrimination. Moreover, mentoring allows some outsiders into the networks of powerful people, which provides them with information on job openings and corporate politics. Workers with mentors experience clear advantages over other workers: They are promoted at a higher rate, earn more, have greater work satisfaction and commitment, and have more power at work (Lin 2000:787; Ragins 1999:347).

Organizations' Personnel Practices

Organizations improve women's access to promotions and to top jobs when they engage in practices that minimize decision makers' abilities to act on their stereotypes and preferences. In Chapters 3 and 4, we noted how all decision makers automatically come up with mental schemas in evaluating others. If decision makers, who typically are male, have the discretion to act on these stereotypes or any preferences for certain types of people—usually people like themselves—then women's prospects for advancement will be diminished. Women's prospects improve in organizations that check this discretion.

Supervisors' stereotypes of women as lacking the qualities needed in higher-level jobs—which abound—can damage women's promotion chances. A large body of research documents how stereotypes of women as less able than men to make hard-nosed decisions and as lacking the qualities needed for leadership roles hinder women's career progress (Heilman 1995:8-9). Consistent with this evidence are women's reports of stereotypes interfering with promotions. Women coal miners, for example, said that supervisors' negative stereotypes about their work capabilities affected their success in obtaining higher-skilled mining jobs (Tallichet 2000). One told how foremen "have it in their minds that we are the weaker sex." The mine superintendent told her that "men have a more mechanical approach" to their work and that the women were stuck in the menial rather than the more skilled mining jobs because it was "natural." At a major accounting firm, decision makers' stereotypes meant that women were routinely passed over for assignments that would provide the experience they needed to move up. According to a member of the task force studying the problem:

> The pervasive issue was people in leadership positions in our firm
> [who] were exclusively male making assumptions about women, like
> "I wouldn't want to put her on that kind of client because it's a dirty
> manufacturing environment, and that's just not the right place for her"
> or "That client's in a real nasty part of town." Or making assumptions
> on behalf of the client, like "Well, the client's not really going to be
> comfortable with her." If you asked the people who were doing that if
> they were doing that, I think they'd say no. It was very subliminal and
> unconscious, but it was happening a lot. (Sturm 2001:494)

Motherhood can also disqualify women from authority positions in settings where employers hold stereotypes that pregnancy and motherhood "soften" women (Williams 2000:69). An attorney complained that since she returned from maternity leave, her superiors refused to give her the high-level work she had been doing: "I want to say, look, I had a baby, not a lobotomy" (Williams 2000:69). A self-study by Deloitte & Touche revealed that some managers admitted they kept top assignments from women out of fear that they might quit for family reasons (Williams 2000:89). One woman summed up the problem: "Let's face it, how is an employer going to think a woman is manager material if he thinks her maternal instincts have primacy over business priorities?" (Kleiman 1993). If allowed to influence job assignments, stereotypes like these seriously undermine women's authority on the job as well as their chances for advancement.

A tendency to act on such stereotypes is more common in some situations than others (Powell 1999:91; Reskin 2002). When women are already fairly well represented in the higher ranks, for example, decision makers tend to act in a more gender-neutral way in conferring promotions, resulting in less bias in favor of men (Perry, Davis-Blake, and Kulik 1994). Thus, as we noted earlier, female managers' promotion chances are better for jobs that already have some women (Cohen et al. 1998), in part because the women who came before have shown that women can perform the job.

Staffing jobs in which the nature of the work is uncertain or ambiguous presents a situation likely to bring out favoritism toward men because decision makers attempt to eliminate uncertainty by promoting people who have social characteristics like their own (Kanter 1977). Kanter called this practice **homosocial reproduction.** Presumably, employers believe that similar people are likely to make the same decisions they would. This belief—along with in-group favoritism, discussed in Chapter 3—leads employers to seek to advance others who are the same sex, race, ethnicity, social class, and religion and who belong to the same clubs, share the same sexual orientation, attended the same colleges, and enjoy the same leisure activities. Homosocial reproduction is especially likely in risky ventures, such as launching a new TV series. Denise Bielby and William Bielby (1992) argued that, because most studio and network executives are male, they view male writers and producers as "safer" than women with equally strong qualifications and are more likely to give men rather than women long-term deals and commitments for multiple series. Executives' acting on stereotypes about someone who seems different—a woman, perhaps, or a Hispanic—results in a cadre of top managers who look alike and think alike.

Organizations can shrink the promotion and authority gaps by replacing informal personnel practices with formal ones that restrict opportunities to act on bias. Firms with written rules and procedures, written hiring and firing procedures, written job descriptions, written performance records, and written evaluations have a better record in placing women in management jobs than firms that do not, because these bureaucratic practices discourage favoritism (Reskin and McBrier 2000:223-24).[4]

Using formal criteria can also help ensure that decisions are based only on relevant information for each candidate and not on casual impressions or hearsay, which stereotypes tend to distort (Reskin 2002). The case of Ann Hopkins, who had been denied partnership in the former Big Six accounting firm of Price Waterhouse, offers an example. Despite having brought more money into the firm than any other contender for promotion had done, Hopkins was denied promotion to partner. According to the Supreme Court, which ruled in her favor in 1990, the senior partners based their evaluation on her personality and appearance and ignored her accomplishments. Hopkins had been advised that her chances for promotion would improve if she would "walk more femininely, talk more femininely, wear makeup, have [her] hair styled and wear jewelry" (White 1992:192). Formal evaluation procedures based on established criteria would have allowed her accomplishments to take center stage.

Similarly, a lack of formal personnel practices meant that Lucky Grocery Stores did not formally post announcements of promotion opportunities because male store managers thought they knew which employees were interested in promotion. The result was that few women were promoted, prompting a successful lawsuit by women who had been passed over (*Stender et al. v. Lucky* 1992). A contrasting case shows how formalized procedures can enhance equality: After a lawsuit, Home Depot instituted a program whereby managers must interview at least three applicants for every position, thus minimizing the possibility that jobs are "wired" for certain candidates.

Employers have many incentives for revamping organizational cultures that impede the career progress of women and minorities (Powell 1999:332). A stake in complying with laws and government regulations is one reason. Meeting the needs of an increasingly diverse customer base is another. A desire to recruit and retain the best workers is a third powerful motivation to disrupt systems that discourage these workers. For example, when Proctor & Gamble followed up on highly valued employees who had quit, it discovered that two-thirds were women and that many had quit out of frustration with their advancement opportunities. Because it wanted to keep its best employees, the company revamped its promotion system and saw women's quit rates fall to the level of men's and their satisfaction levels rise substantially (Parker-Pope 1998). Similarly, when Deloitte and Touche learned that women who quit cited a lack of mentors, having been barred from plum assignments, work-family balance problems, and having been excluded from informal networks and from social events with clients, it instituted policies to eradicate the glass ceiling and to make jobs more flexible. As a result, women's turnover rates dropped from 26 to 15 percent (Williams 2000:90).

The social forces within an organizational culture that maintain sex differences in opportunities to move up and take charge are resistant to change, however, and formal policies are not a panacea. In some firms, especially smaller ones, these policies are merely symbolic, and decision makers still choose managers through social networks (Reskin and McBrier 2000).

Raising the price that employers pay to discriminate has prompted some firms to eliminate several of the obstacles described in this chapter. Despite the wastefulness of excluding potentially productive people from influential jobs on the basis of their sex and color, many employers have done just that. Organizations have multiple goals, and they act on the ones that have the highest priority. Because the bottom line is usually the top priority, fines and other financial sanctions raise equal opportunity on employers' agendas.

Litigation increases this price. Although individual lawsuits rarely result in court wins (because the plaintiff loses or because the case results in a settlement, not a verdict), large awards in class action cases spur employers to reconsider their employment practices. For example, a 1991 lawsuit led Marriott Corporation to pay $3 million to women managers who had been denied promotions. At fault was the company's informal promotion policy and a work culture that "froze women out" (Goozner 1991). Lawsuits against grocery store chains in the 1990s also have resulted in large settlements: Publix supermarkets agreed in 1997 to pay over $81 million to settle a lawsuit claiming that it had kept women in dead-end jobs, Albertson's paid $29 million in 1996, and Safeway paid $7.5 million in 1994.

Legislation can reduce the authority gap when it is implemented and enforced. Congress established the Glass Ceiling Division within the U.S. Department of Labor in 1991 with the charge to eliminate barriers to women's and minorities' promotions to top posts. Its "glass ceiling reviews" of some companies with federal contracts and its awards to exemplary companies are expected to increase voluntary compliance with the law (U.S. Employment Standards Administration 1997).

Summary

We have seen considerable variation in women's progress in closing the promotion and authority gaps over the past 30 years. The promotion gap has narrowed considerably. For some populations and in some settings, it seems to have disappeared; for other groups and in other settings, it is still appreciable. Thus, women who haven't completed high school now have an advantage over similar men, but men who are college educated and married still have an advantage over similar women. Another group that stands out is black women, who face a disadvantage in promotions compared to white men. As for the authority gap, women have made some gains, but their representation in top jobs in management and the professions is uneven. Will the outlook be better for the college students of today? We don't know. History shows that women's and minorities' access to jobs that confer authority does not improve automatically. It improved during the 1970s through the efforts of federal agencies, advocacy groups, and companies voluntarily establishing Equal Employment Opportunity programs (Reskin 1998). It then stalled in the 1990s. Further progress depends on similar efforts and on organizations' recognition of the gains to be made from instituting programs to ensure equality in access to top jobs for all their workers.

Notes

1. Compared to women in the United States and Canada, Norwegian and Swedish women were less likely to hold jobs involving authority (Clement and Myles 1994). The high level of part-time employment among the women in these countries accounts for this difference (Kalleberg and Reskin 1995).
2. Note that growth rates are high because the numbers these percentages are based on are so small.
3. These few firms accounted for 88 percent of the gross receipts for women-owned businesses.
4. A different strategy for getting around the negative effects of favoritism draws on people's tendency to create "us" and "them" categories (Reskin 2002). Organizations can encourage workers to identify with sex- and race-integrated *task* groups, so that the "us" category becomes "we who are working on this project" (Brewer 1997).

6

Sex Differences in Earnings

From the earliest records of paid work, which date from the fourteenth century, employers have paid men more than women. Accompanying this earnings disparity today are sex differences in fringe benefits, pensions, and Social Security payments.[1] Sex differences in earnings occur in every occupation and in every country, although the magnitude of the disparities differs. This chapter examines the trends in earnings disparities, their causes, and ways to reduce these sex differences.

The Cost of Being Female

The disparity in earnings between men and women is usually measured by the ratio of women's to men's earnings. This **earnings ratio,** which is calculated by dividing women's average or median earnings by men's, indicates how much women earn for each dollar a man earns. The shortfall between how much men earn and how much women earn is termed the **pay gap.** Early evidence of such a gap is seen in Paris tax records for the year 1313. Among 4,495 Parisian taxpayers, women's wealth was two-thirds of men's (Herlihy 1990:149), a ratio that is remarkably similar to the pay gap during much of twentieth century in the United States.[2] As is true today, the size of the gap varied, depending on the kind of work people did. It was largest among workers who pursued the most lucrative occupations—goldsmiths and tavern keepers—in which men were three times as wealthy as women. At the other extreme, laundering and dressmaking, women had 90 percent as much wealth as men. The gap was small in these occupations because men had almost no wealth.

The pay gap did not disappear with the spread of industrialization. Statistics on textile workers in 1883 revealed that among workers under the age of 16, girls slightly outearned boys. Girls below age 11 earned a halfpence a week more than boys, and girls from ages 11 to 16 received two pence a week more than boys. But after reaching age 16, males had a decided advantage: Employers paid 16- to 20-year-old women 70 percent of what they paid young men. Within six months of turning 16, boys would have made up for all those extra halfpennies and pennies that younger girls had received. Among adult workers, employers paid women less than half—sometimes only one-third to one-fourth—of what adult men earned (Pinchbeck 1930:193-94).

Trends in the Pay Gap in the United States

In the early years of industrialization in the United States, employers exacted a large wage penalty from female workers. In the first part of the nineteenth century, for example, women working full time in agricultural and manufacturing industries earned between 29 and 37 cents for every dollar a man earned (Goldin 1990). Men's wages were low, and women could barely support themselves on a fraction of men's pay. In the 1860s, one woman was forced to take extreme measures:

> I had no money and a woman's wages were not enough to keep me alive. I looked around and saw men getting more money, and more work, and more money for the same kind of work. I decided to become a man. It was simple. I just put on men's clothing and applied for a man's job. I got good money for those times, so I stuck to it. (Matthaei 1982:192)

The pay gap narrowed by the mid-nineteenth century, partly because the increased use of machinery reduced the importance of strength. By 1885, manufacturers paid women about half what they paid men (Goldin 1990, table 3.1). The pay gap narrowed further through the first three decades of the twentieth century.[3] Contributing to the decline in pay inequality were women's increasing education relative to men, which enabled them to perform better-paying jobs, and the growth of white-collar jobs for which employers sought female workers (Goldin 1990).

The relative earnings of women and men from 1955 to 2000 are summarized in Exhibit 6.1. The bars, which represent the female-to-male earnings ratio, show that the gap fluctuated between about 59 and 64 percent between 1955 and 1980. Not until 1985 did the earnings ratio surpass its 1955 level of 63.9 percent. The trend lines for each sex help explain the narrowing of the pay gap. The line for men's earnings shows that men's earnings rose between 1955 and 1970, followed by stagnation and slight decline. Women's line shows that their earnings slowly climbed until

EXHIBIT 6.1

Trends in Median Earnings by Sex, 1955-2000

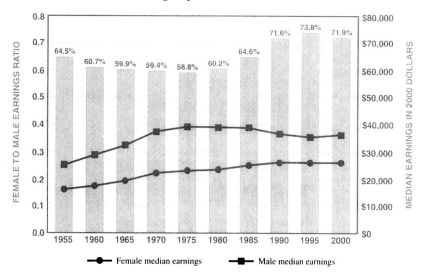

Female median earnings   Male median earnings

Sources: Nelson and Bridges 1999, figure 3.1; authors' calculations from the March 1998, 1999, and 2000 Current Population Surveys.
Note: Data are for full-time, year-round workers. Values for 1955 are incomes; all others are earnings. Figures for 2000 are averages of 1998, 1999, and 2000 Current Population Survey data.

1970, stagnated in the 1970s, and then gradually rose again. Among the reasons the gap narrowed substantially in the 1980s (discussed later in this chapter) was that men's real earnings fell at the same time that women's wages grew.

We cannot assume that the pay gap will continue to close. In fact, among managers employed full time, the wage gap grew between 1995 and 2000 in 7 out of the 10 industries studied by the U.S. Government Accounting Office (U.S. Government Accounting Office 2002). In the communications industry, for example, in 1995 women earned 86 percent of men's wages, but they earned only 73 percent in 2000.

By 2000, the earnings ratio for full-time, year-round workers had narrowed to 72.2 percent. Thus, for every $10,000 that employers paid the average man in 2000, they paid the average woman only $7,222.[4]

Race, Ethnicity, and the Pay Gap. People's earnings vary by their color, as well as their sex. When employers began paying African Americans for

EXHIBIT 6.2

Earnings Ratios for Median Annual Earnings of Full-Time, Year-Round Workers, by Sex, Race, and Hispanic Origin, 2000

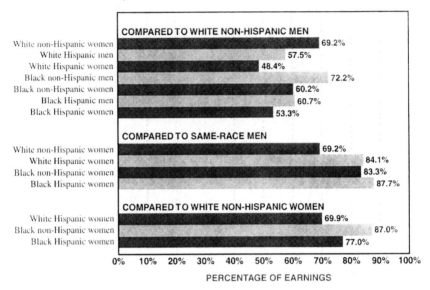

Source: Authors' calculations from the March 1998, 1999, and 2000 Current Population Surveys.
Note: Figures are averages of 1998, 1999, and 2000 Current Population Survey data.

their work in the nineteenth century, they paid them substantially less than they paid whites. This practice continued through much of the twentieth century (Jones 1998:308). Segregation into different jobs based on workers' race and sex was pervasive, and many of the lowest-paying jobs were reserved for African Americans of both sexes (Bose 2001:114; Jones 1998:301-336). The nineteenth century brought new groups of workers into the racial/ethnic labor-market hierarchy (Amott and Matthaei 2001:238), and employers—who regarded women and men of Mexican, Philippine, Puerto Rican, and Asian descent as cheap sources of labor—confined them as well to low-paying jobs (Moore and Pinderhughes 2001).

Male and female non-Hispanic whites continue to outearn same-sex members of other groups, as Exhibit 6.2 shows. All women earn less than men of their own race and ethnicity, and all earn less than non-Hispanic white men. Black and white Hispanic women are the biggest losers relative to non-Hispanic white men, with their earnings depressed because of

EXHIBIT 6.3

Median Earnings of Full-Time, Year-Round Workers as a Percentage of Non-Hispanic White Men's Earnings, by Sex, Race, and Hispanicity, 1955-2000

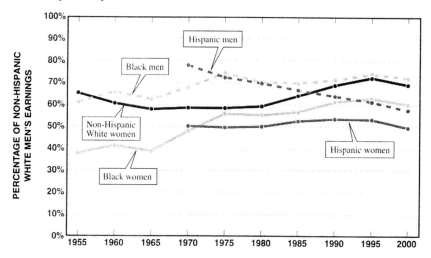

Sources: Farley 1984, figure 3.2; U.S. Census Bureau 1981b, table 6; U.S. Census Bureau 1983, tables 37 and 39; U.S. Census Bureau 1988, tables 27 and 29; U.S. Census Bureau 1991, table 24; U.S. Census Bureau 1996, table 7; Harrison and Bennett 1995, table 4A.1; authors' calculations from the March 1998, 1999, and 2000 Current Population Surveys.
Note: 2000 figures are averages of 1998, 1999, and 2000 Current Population Survey data.

both their race or ethnicity and their sex. We cannot compare Asian Americans and other race-ethnic groups because their small numbers in the data make earnings estimates unreliable. In general, wages for Asian American men tend to be closest to non-Hispanic white men's, and wages for Asian American women tend to be slightly above those of non-Hispanic white women (Reskin and Padavic 1999).

Trends in the earnings ratio by sex, race, and Hispanic origin since 1955 are shown in Exhibit 6.3. In general, among full-time, year-round workers, the gap between non-Hispanic white men and most other groups has been slowly closing. However, by the end of the twentieth century, no group earned more than three-quarters of non-Hispanic white men's earnings. Black women showed the greatest gains—they earned less than 40 percent of non-Hispanic white men's earnings in 1955 and 60 percent at the end of twentieth century—although their progress stalled after 1980 (Corcoran 1999:5). They currently average almost $16,000 less annually than non-Hispanic white men. The gap between Hispanic women and non-Hispanic white men also narrowed between 1975 and 1990, but it has since stabilized, leaving a shortfall of nearly $20,000 per year. Non-Hispanic white women also narrowed the gap until 1995, at which point they lost ground, so that they currently earn about $12,000 less per year than their male counterparts.

The Pay Gap Over the Life Span. The pattern we described earlier for British textile workers in 1833 still holds true: The younger workers are, the closer women's earnings are to men's. At the end of the twentieth century, the median weekly earnings of 16- to 24-year-old women who worked full time, year-round were 89 percent of the earnings of same-age men (U.S. Census Bureau 1998, 1999, 2000a). Employers paid the average 25- to 34-year-old woman who worked full time about 82 percent of what they paid her male counterpart. Compared to the overall pay gap of 72 percent, 82 percent may not sound so bad. But in dollars, the average young woman aged 18 to 34 employed full time, year-round lost $5,558 per year because of her sex. For older workers, the pay gap is wider, with women between 35 and 44 averaging 70 percent of the pay of men their age, and those between 55 and 64 averaging 64 percent of the pay of men their age.

The Pay Gap Within Occupations. Men outearn women in all occupations, but in some the sexes' pay is much closer to parity than in others. As Exhibit 6.4 shows, women who worked full time selling securities and financial services, for example, earned just 64 percent of what men made each week ($597, compared to men's $937), and female financial managers averaged only 65 percent of men's weekly earnings ($700 vs. $1,070). In predominantly female occupations, men's earnings advantage was smaller. Among cashiers, for example, an occupation that is over three-quarters female, women averaged 90 percent of men's earnings. In many of the occupations in which women's weekly earnings are closest to men's, both sexes' pay tends to be low.

Among the highest earners in America, women lose hundreds of thousands of dollars annually because of their sex. Of the five most highly compensated officers in each of the Fortune 500 companies, top-level women's salaries were just 73 percent of those of their male counterparts, and their bonuses were less than 70 percent of men's (Catalyst 1998, table 8). In four major "Grand Slam" tennis events, men's prize money in 1999 exceeded women's in most countries: Australian women winners

EXHIBIT 6.4

Women's Median Weekly Earnings as a Percentage of Men's Earnings for Full-Time, Year-Round Workers in Selected Occupations

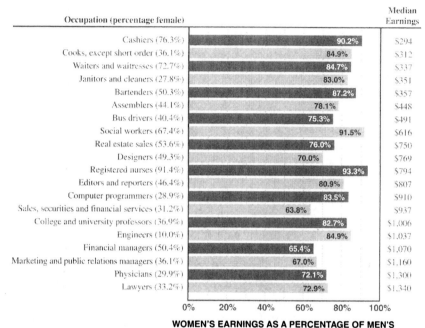

Occupation (percentage female)		Median Earnings
Cashiers (76.3%)	90.2%	$294
Cooks, except short order (36.1%)	84.9%	$312
Waiters and waitresses (72.7%)	84.7%	$337
Janitors and cleaners (27.8%)	83.0%	$351
Bartenders (50.3%)	87.2%	$357
Assemblers (44.1%)	78.1%	$448
Bus drivers (40.4%)	75.3%	$491
Social workers (67.4%)	91.5%	$616
Real estate sales (53.6%)	76.0%	$750
Designers (49.3%)	70.0%	$769
Registered nurses (91.4%)	93.3%	$794
Editors and reporters (46.4%)	80.9%	$807
Computer programmers (28.9%)	83.5%	$910
Sales, securities and financial services (31.2%)	63.8%	$937
College and university professors (36.9%)	82.7%	$1,006
Engineers (10.0%)	84.9%	$1,037
Financial managers (50.4%)	65.4%	$1,070
Marketing and public relations managers (36.1%)	67.0%	$1,160
Physicians (29.9%)	72.1%	$1,300
Lawyers (33.2%)	72.9%	$1,340

0%   20%   40%   60%   80%   100%

WOMEN'S EARNINGS AS A PERCENTAGE OF MEN'S

Source: Authors' calculations from the March 1998, 1999, and 2000 Current Population Surveys.
Note: Figures are averages of 1998, 1999, and 2000 Current Population Survey data.

received 94 percent as much as men winners, French women 90 percent, and at Wimbledon (England), 83 percent; only the U.S. Tennis Open paid equally for women and men winners (Hiestand 1999).

The Earnings Ratio Across the Nation and Around the World

In every state in the United States and every country in the world, men outearn women, although the size of the gap varies widely. In 2000, women averaged 84 cents for every dollar a man earned in Hawaii and 80 cents on the dollar in Maryland. In contrast, in Utah and Louisiana, women earned just 65 cents on the dollar (Institute for Women's Policy Research 2000).

Because men tend to work more days per week and more weeks per year, the size of the wage gap depends on the unit of time being considered. Thus, women worldwide earned 60 to 70 percent of men's monthly earnings, between 70 and 75 percent of men's daily and weekly earnings, and between 75 and 80 percent of men's hourly earnings (Anker 1998:30). According to United Nations statistics for 1997, women's wages in the industry and service sectors were between 53 and 97 percent of men's, with a median of 78 (Elson 2000, chart 4.2; these figures are based on hourly, weekly, or daily earnings). These median earnings ratios resemble those for the United States, where women's median weekly earnings in 1998 were about three-quarters of men's (U.S. Women's Bureau 2000, table 1).

The earnings ratio is lowest in the North African and the Middle-Eastern countries of Libya, Iraq, Saudi Arabia, Bahrain, United Arab Emirates, Oman, and Qatar, where employed women earn less than 20 percent of men's earnings (D. Smith 1999:44-45). These countries also tend to have low female labor force participation rates, signaling societal ambivalence about the propriety of women's labor market participation more generally (D. Smith 1999:123). At the other extreme, the earnings ratio was highest in Sweden, Cambodia, and Tanzania, where women earned between 80 and 90 percent of men's earnings. The small earnings gap in Sweden and in other Scandinavian countries reflects centralized wage setting, where government tribunals set wages for an industry or occupation (Anker 1998:34; Rosenfeld and Kalleberg 1991), and investment in public child care, which frees women to work more hours (but see Sorensen 2001:114). In contrast, the reason for the small gap between the sexes in Cambodia and Tanzania is the same as that for the small wealth gap among Parisian launderers and dressmakers in 1313—men's low earnings.

As is true for the United States, the pay gap has been shrinking worldwide. Although recent data are hard to come by for most nations, in 22 out of 29 countries with available data, women's wages rose relative to men's in industry and services between 1980 and 1997 (Elson 2000, chart 4.5).

In sum, the pay gap in the United States and around the world has varied across time and place. The size of the gap in this country varies by workers' race/ethnicity, their age, their occupation, and the place they live and work. Non-Hispanic white men's earnings exceed other workers', with black and Hispanic women particularly disadvantaged. Older women pay a greater pay penalty for being female than younger women, although the amount of the gap is sizable even for young women.

Although men outearn women in all of the 503 occupations for which the U.S. Census Bureau gathers data, the gap is smaller in occupations that are predominantly female. Earnings trends over the second half of the twentieth century show gradual improvement, although the size of the gap has been stable in recent years.

Explaining the Pay Gap

As we have seen, men outearn women, on average, regardless of their race or ethnicity, marital status, age, education, and occupation, and this pattern holds around the world. This section asks why. Coming up with explanations for the earnings disparity between the sexes is easy.[5] For example, the documentary video, "You've Come a Long Way, Maybe" draws a laugh from our students when a man on the street explains to an interviewer that men outearn women because "men are smarter and more intelligent," to which he adds after a pause, "more intelligent and smarter." Social scientists, who are in the business of explaining social phenomena, have also advanced multiple explanations for men's generally higher earnings. Finding evidence that supports these explanations is a different matter. To support an explanation, research must show both that the hypothesized explanatory factor affects how much both sexes earn and that the factor is associated with workers' sex. If the evidence shows either to be false, then that factor does not play a role in the pay gap.

Before summarizing the explanations, we should point out that although we tend to try to explain variation in the size of the earnings ratio, the size of the ratio depends on *both* how much women earn (the numerator of the ratio) and how much men earn (the denominator). This means that earnings ratios may differ across places or over time because of factors that influence either men's earnings or women's earnings. The narrowing of the earnings gap in the United States is a case in point. Most of the decline in the pay gap in the 1980s stemmed from men's falling earnings as well-paying manufacturing jobs disappeared. More recent declines reflect both the erosion in men's average earnings and the growth in women's earnings.

We illustrate theoretical explanations for the pay gap between the sexes with examples from a hypothetical workplace—Acme Chip, Inc.— in which male workers average $646 weekly and women workers average $491 (which happen to equal men's and women's weekly median earnings in 2000), and the range of earnings for each sex is from $219 to $720.

Chris Britt
The Seattle Times
Copley News Service

Source: © Copley News Service and Chris Britt; used by permission.

Thus, although men outearn women, on average, there are men and women at both ends of the earnings distribution.

Workers' Productivity

Let's begin with explanations that focus on the abilities and preferences of workers. Consider how employers set pay, according to traditional neoclassical economic theory: Their desire to maximize profits leads them to set wages as low as possible. According to this theory, Acme Chip Company does not care whether its workers are male or female (or whether they are high school dropouts or hold doctoral degrees in chipology). If this theory is correct, men will outearn women who are doing the same job *only* if men, as a group, work harder or are more skilled at producing chips. This means that in this hypothetical firm, although some women outproduce some men, if men earn more it means that more male workers are high producers and more females are low producers.

Time Spent Working. Why should men be more productive chipmakers than women? Social scientists have come up with several possible reasons.

One is that men, as a group, may simply put in more hours at producing chips than women do. In fact, across all racial/ethnic groups, men put in more hours paid work per week and more weeks per year than women do (U.S. Census Bureau 1998, 1999, 2000a). Moreover, how much time people work significantly affects their earnings. Thus, men's longer hours contribute to the earnings gap. This becomes clear if we compare the size of the pay gap across different groups. In 1999, women employed full time, year-round earned 72.2 percent of men's annual earnings, but the ratios for weekly earnings—76.5 percent—and hourly earnings—83.8 percent—were substantially closer to parity (U.S. Women's Bureau 2000, table 1).

There are two primary reasons women work for pay for fewer hours a day and fewer days a year than men. First, as Chapter 7 shows, women bear the primary responsibility for child rearing and other unpaid domestic work. In other words, women spend more time than men doing the unpaid work of taking care of the family's children, cooking the family's meals, and washing the family's chip-making uniforms. (Note also that workers who spend more hours in the chip shop than at the washing machine may become more proficient at chip production, so average sex differences in time at work could widen the productivity gap between the sexes.)

As other people take more of the responsibility for unpaid domestic work, women can devote more time to paid employment. Commercial substitutes for the domestic work that women customarily do for their own families are increasingly available to women who can afford to purchase them. And women are doing more paid work and less unpaid domestic work. For example, 45 percent of women worked full-time in 1990, but 55 percent did so in 1997 (U.S. Women's Bureau 2000:9), a change that helped to narrow the pay gap between the sexes. Policies that encourage men to work fewer hours could also narrow the earnings gap. Most Americans would prefer to work fewer hours (Jacobs and Gerson 1998). Thus, policy initiatives that encouraged shorter workweeks for men and women could win public favor and reduce the earnings gap.

The second reason women spend less time than men at paid work is sex segregation, whose effect on the pay gap we discuss later in the chapter. All of the groups of workers who are especially likely to put in long hours—professionals, high-level managers, and unionized craft workers—are disproportionately male (Jacobs and Gerson 1998). Increasing women's employment in these occupations provides inducements for women to invest more time into their jobs.

Skill. Another reason men might outproduce women is that they are better chip producers. Why should men be better chipmakers than women? Conceivably chipmaking requires upper body strength on which the average man is superior to the average woman. Alternatively, chipmaking may use skills that are related to activities that males were more likely than females to have done for fun as children, such as playing video games. Perhaps men—anticipating a lifelong career in the chip industry and hoping for high pay—spend more years in school studying chipology than women do, on average. Or perhaps male chipmakers are more willing to pass on tricks of the trade to other men than to women. Or perhaps employers provide men with better tools than women have.

To test hypotheses about workers' skill, researchers often use a set of variables in the *Dictionary of Occupational Titles* that attempts to capture the complexity of occupations. Across studies of different populations, neither sex regularly outscores the other on these variables (Farkas et al. 1997:919).[6] Moreover, higher skill levels are not necessarily associated with higher earnings (England, Reid, and Kilbourne 1996:519; Kilbourne, England, and Beron 1994; but see Farkas et al. 1997, table 3). In view of the fact that in most lines of work, skill is acquired on the job and hence is partly a *consequence* of job segregation by sex, it seems safe to conclude that skill differences between the sexes are not an important source of the earnings gap.

Effort. Why would women invest less effort than men do in chipmaking? One possibility is that women, on average, are less concerned with making money and hence feel freer to stop to rest or talk to coworkers, whereas men are hungry ball players who work steadily. This leads to still another question. Why should men, as a group, be more committed to high earnings than women? Some social scientists would answer that society (friends, relatives, neighbors) is more likely to judge men than women by how much they earn, so men experience social pressure to maximize their earnings. There is no evidence that male workers work harder than women do, however (Bielby and Bielby 2002), and some research suggests just the opposite. In laboratory experiments, female subjects did *more* work than male subjects for a prespecified amount of money, and they did it more accurately and more efficiently (Major, McFarlin, and Gagnon 1984). In a nationally representative survey of workers, women reported devoting more effort to their jobs than men reported (Bielby and Bielby 1988; Marsden et al. 1993). Thus, the few studies that have addressed the possibility that men might outearn women because they work harder do not support this explanation. In addition, there is no solid evidence that effort increases earnings.

Because of the difficulty in measuring productivity, most research on the neoclassical explanation assumes that better-educated, more-experienced workers are more productive. If this assumption is valid,[7] we can indirectly gauge the impact on the pay gap of sex differences in productivity by examining whether education and experience are positively related to earnings and if male workers, on average, are more educated and experienced than female workers.

Education. More-educated workers outearn less-educated workers, but social scientists disagree over whether this occurs because education increases workers' skills or because employers favor more-educated workers for other reasons (Blau and Ferber 1992:148). In addition, there is little difference in women's and men's average education. Overall, men average 12.9 years of schooling, compared to women's 12.7.

Women's increased education between 1976 and 1989 accounted for between one-sixth and one-twelfth of the improving earnings ratio, according to economists O'Neill and Polachek (1993:222). Thus, the importance of the sexes' differing amounts of schooling has diminished as their years of schooling and college majors have converged (Blau and Kahn 1997). Women have caught up with men in legal and medical education, for example (Jacobs 2003). Special programs to attract women to engineering and science have been paying off (National Council for Research on Women 2001). More effort is needed to open some fields to women, especially in information technology. Increasing women's access to training for skilled jobs is important for reducing inequality in their earnings. Because most workers are trained on the job, equalizing access to training depends to a considerable degree on the actions of employers and unions who control much of the training for customarily male jobs.

Experience. Economists also treat labor force experience as a proxy for productivity. Up to a point, experience is positively associated with earnings, and men average more job experience than women do, although this disparity has been closing (Roos and Gatta 1999:106). In the late 1980s, men chalked up 4.5 more years of full-time work experience than women, a difference that could explain 30 percent of the pay gap (Blau and Kahn 1997, 2000:9).

The human-capital approach to the pay gap also assumes that men participate in the labor force continuously, whereas women interrupt their participation to raise children. This explanation assumes that women's skills get rusty during any time out of the labor force, which reduces their productivity and earnings when they return to paid jobs. Employment interruptions do reduce women's earnings (Jacobsen and Levin 1995), but their importance in the total pay gap has declined as fewer women interrupt their labor force participation to raise children (Roos and Gatta 1999:109).[8]

As younger cohorts of workers in which the sexes are similar in experience replace older cohorts of workers in which men have accumulated more experience than women, the experience gap will continue to shrink. It would close more rapidly if employers arranged work schedules to make it easier for workers to combine work and family (see Chapter 7).

In sum, sex differences in education and labor force experience favor men and contribute to their higher earnings. As the sexes have become much more similar in their education and labor force experience, this convergence has contributed to the shrinking of the wage gap.

Wage Bargaining. Let's return to Acme Chip's pay practices. Acme may not set a fixed rate per chip; instead it may negotiate pay rates with each worker it hires. If men insist on higher rates than women do or are more successful at bargaining for high pay, they would outearn equally productive women.

Men might command higher per-chip rates or women might settle for lower pay for several reasons. First, women might accept lower pay in exchange for other job qualities that women particularly value. If, for example, Acme provided assistance with child care, and if women valued such assistance more than men, women might be more likely to settle for lower pay. This explanation is part of Adam Smith's theory of **compensating differentials,** which holds that employers set wages in part based on how unpleasant or pleasant the job is, paying more to attract workers to jobs with unpleasant or dangerous working conditions and less if working conditions are good. Although the idea of compensating differentials makes sense, researchers have shown that this theory does not explain the pay gap (Kilbourne, England, Farkas, Beron, and Weir 1994). In fact, one study showed that doing unpleasant jobs *lowered* women's pay (Jacobs and Steinberg 1995).

Second, if other employers in town refuse to hire women, male applicants at Acme would have greater bargaining power than women have. This situation contributed to the higher pay of male janitors compared to female clerical workers at the University of Northern Iowa (Nelson and Bridges 1999).

Third, workers decide what is an acceptable wage based partly on the earnings of members of their reference group (people to whom they compare themselves). Members of people's reference groups tend to be their same sex, so in industries or communities in which other employers tend to pay men more than they pay women, men's standards of a fair rate would exceed women's. Recall the experiments described earlier that showed both female and male college students thought that typically male tasks deserved higher pay than typically female tasks (Major and Forcey 1985). Why should women undervalue women's work? People apparently use same-sex others in deciding whether their pay is fair partly because most of their coworkers are their sex (Major 1989:101). The concentration of customarily female and male jobs in different firms and different departments within firms means that workers can rarely compare the complexity and effort of their jobs and their pay to workers of the other sex. When they can make these comparisons, women do not consider their lower pay fair (Bylsma and Major 1992:198).

The preceding explanations for male workers' higher average pay focus primarily on individual workers' skills, preferences, and decisions about how to invest their time and energy. Economists classify workers as the "labor supply," so these explanations are often labeled **supply-side explanations.**

Not all workers bargain individually with employers over wages, however; some bargain collectively as members of a union. Union membership raises workers' wages across the board, but its impact depends on workers' sex, race, and ethnicity (U.S. Census Bureau 2000c). Non-Hispanic white women represented by unions earn 26 percent more than other women, and similar men earn 15 percent more than men who are not. Black women represented by unions earn 29 percent more than other black women, and black men represented by unions earn 22 percent more than same-race non-unionized men. Among Hispanics, men gain more than women from union membership. Indeed, the biggest gains of union representation go to Hispanic men, who earn 55 percent more than their non-union counterparts, compared to one-third more for Hispanic women.

In the past, men have been more likely than women to be union members and thus more likely to benefit from union pay. In recent decades, declines in blue-collar, male-dominated manufacturing industries have led unions to increasingly court members from female-dominated clerical, education, and nursing occupations. Some unions have gained women members by using participatory and democratic styles of organizing and representing workers (Eaton 1996) and by campaigning for issues important to women, such as pay equity and parental leave (Cobble 1996:335). These efforts have paid off. Undermining stereotypes from the middle of the twentieth century that women workers are "unorganizable," unions have won about 60 percent of elections in mostly female units, compared to only one-third in units where women made up less than half the workers (Bronfenbrenner and Juravich 1998; Cobble 1996:354). Over the past 20 years, the majority of new union members have been women (Karen Nussbaum, personal communication, 2001), and women currently make up over 40 percent of the unionized workforce (AFL-CIO 2001).

We do not know how important any sex difference in individual or collective wage bargaining might be for the earnings gap. Individuals can reduce their disadvantage by finding out what others who do the same job earn before bargaining for pay. A more widespread solution would base earnings on credentials or other objectively measurable attributes and by making earnings public within firms. Collective bargaining necessarily has broader effects, both by expanding the number of workers who benefit and by making public the pay-setting process.

Employers' Discriminatory Actions

All supply-side explanations assume that in setting pay Acme Chip, Inc., is indifferent to workers' sex; it cares only about how productive they are or how much they cost to employ. Most social scientists question the assumption that employers set pay solely on the basis of productivity, and the evidence is on their side.[9] So let's alter our original hypothetical example to recognize that some employers treat men and women differently because of their sex. Explanations for the pay gap that focus on employers' decisions are termed **demand-side explanations.** If employers treated equally productive men and women differently, they would be engaging in **pay discrimination.**

Statistical Discrimination. Assume that Acme Chip cannot recruit enough high-quality workers who are willing to work on a **piece-rate** basis (that is, pay based on the number of chips produced). To attract workers, it must offer workers monthly salaries. Acme wants to set pay based on workers' productivity, but it knows of no easy way to predict how productive new hires will be. So Mr. Acme looks at how much workers earned when the company paid them on a per-chip basis. If he notices that men outearned women, he might set the pay of all new female employees at the average for his female employees and that of new male hires at the average pay of his male employees. This strategy would **statistically discriminate** against women by paying every woman less than every man on the basis of generalizations about women and men as groups. Although this strategy would both underpay and overpay some members of each sex, on average, it would underpay women compared to men. Employers statistically discriminate in order to avoid the cost of obtaining information about individuals. Generalizations that prompt statistical discrimination are often based on stereotypes.

Both quantitative studies and interviews with employers confirm that many employers statistically discriminate against women (Bielby and Baron 1986; Browne and Kennelly 1999). Statistical discrimination is illegal under Title 7 of the 1964 Civil Rights Act (see Chapter 3). The main avenue for reducing its effect is through better enforcement of that law.

Gender Ideology and Stereotypes. Gender ideology in many parts of the world holds that men need higher pay because they support families. This ideology supported the movement in the United States for a family wage (May 1982). Although support for this ideology has weakened in the United States (Brewster and Padavic 2000), the consequences of past pay practices continue to plague women workers. As we noted in Chapters 3 and 5, organizations are slow to change past practices, and changes often do not challenge fundamental assumptions. Thus, if 50 years ago Acme Chip set women's pay lower than men's on the stereotyped assumption that women worked for pin money, and if they never reviewed their pay practices for bias, men would still outearn women. Occasionally, we see the present-day results of past social values. Pay rates in California in the 1980s, for example, reflected the belief in the 1930s that women had lower economic needs than men had (Kim 1989:43; Nelson and Bridges 1999). A recent investigation of US Airways by the Office for Federal Contract Compliance of the U.S. Department of Labor also shows the ramifications of past practices. After agreeing to provide $390,000 in back pay and salary adjustments to 30 female managers, US Airways attributed the underpayment to "anomalies in the company's early history [that were] exacerbated by the [company's] financial difficulties of the early 1980s" (Swoboda 1998).

Stereotypes about the sexes that portray women as having attributes and abilities that differ from men's can affect the earnings gap if employers act on them in hiring, placement, or promotion decisions. Stereotypes that women are better at some tasks and men at others, for example, can lead employers to hire women into customarily female jobs and men into customarily male ones. Because customarily male jobs pay more, this lowers women's pay relative to men's. Work organizations that institute formalized personnel practices (such as written job descriptions) and hold decision makers accountable for their decisions improve women's chances of being hired into customarily male and better-paying jobs by reducing decision makers' freedom to act on stereotyped beliefs (Heilman 1995).

Employers' Pay Practices. Some employers produce a wage gap by rewarding the same credentials, the same level of performance, or the same amount of work with higher pay for men than women. Case studies of a bank, a public university, a state government, and a retail chain that had been sued in court for pay discrimination revealed that men's higher pay was not the result of market pressures (Nelson and Bridges 1999). For example, although the university testified that it paid its all-male physical-plant workers more than its all-female secretaries because the local labor market had pushed up the wages of blue-collar workers, in fact, the university had persuaded the other major employer in town not to hire its clerical workers, thereby preventing the market from raising women's pay. These case studies convinced the researchers that pay disparities between the sexes resulted from organizational politics and policies.

Aversion to Female Workers and Wage Discrimination. Now consider the possibility that Mr. Acme dislikes women and that this distaste makes him prefer to employ men. According to economist Gary Becker (1971), Mr. Acme would pay any female workers the "market wage" set by supply and demand. In order to avoid having to employ women, he would pay an above-market wage to men to attract them. The result would be higher average pay for men than for women doing the same job. If Mr. Acme's hypothetical aversion to female workers (or, to use Becker's term, "taste" for male workers) leads him to hire only men for a particular job, he would be discriminating in hiring or job assignment. If his aversion to women or preference for men leads him to pay men more than women, he would be discriminating in pay.

Public Policy and Wage Discrimination. The explanations that we have discussed so far assume that pay is set in a free market according to the laws of supply and demand or that employers' attitudes produce the wage disparity. Neither of these explanations recognizes the ultimate importance of public policy for the pay gap. Even in our "free market" economy, government policies affect how much workers earn. Governments set minimum pay, sometimes prescribe the pay for specific jobs, and occasionally regulate the relationship between women's and men's pay. When the U.S. federal government began employing women in 1864, Congress legislated substantially lower pay for women than men (Reskin 2001), setting the country on a path of officially mandated pay discrimination. The United States was not alone in officially discriminating against women. Britain's first minimum-wage law, passed in 1909, set a lower minimum wage for women than for men (Westover 1986:60).

Although Michigan and Montana passed equal pay laws as early as 1919, pay discrimination based on sex was a standard employment practice. Not until 1963, almost 100 years after Congress enacted the 1864 statute requiring unequal pay, did Congress officially ban unequal pay based on sex. The 1963 Equal Pay Act (EPA) made it illegal for employers to pay workers differently because of their sex for jobs that require equal skill, effort, and responsibility and are performed under similar working conditions.[10]

The EPA was symbolically important because it made an official statement against pay discrimination. In practice, however, the impact of the EPA has been limited because pervasive job and establishment segregation limits the number of workers the law protects. Also, the burden of enforcement falls largely on the victims of pay discrimination, and complainants risk retaliation by their employers (Reskin 2001). Over the years, women have lost more cases than they have won (Nelson and Bridges 1999:37). Of over 10,000 wage discrimination complaints filed with the EEOC or states' Commissions on Fair Employment Practices in 2000, just 22 percent were resolved in favor of the complainant. Nonetheless, the EPA presumably discourages some employers from underpaying women, and it offers redress for some victims of pay discrimination. Some examples are a 1990 back-pay award by Bethlehem Steel to female clerical workers, whom it had paid $200 a month less than men doing the same work (National Committee on Pay Equity 1991:3). Since 1997, the Office of Federal Contract Compliance has collected $10 million in Equal Pay Act settlements from companies such as Texaco, US Airways, Pepsi-Cola, and Gateway (Barko 2000). Other cases involved Swift Transportation, which agreed to back pay of almost a half million dollars to six female driver managers, who complained that they were paid less than men in the same jobs (U.S. Equal Employment Opportunity Commission 2000a), and a juvenile rehabilitation facility in Pittsburgh, which consented to a $280,000 back pay award to several female counselors, whom it paid less than males by not permitting women to work overtime (U.S. Equal

Employment Opportunity Commission 2000b; U.S. Employment Standards Administration 2000). When government regulatory agencies have proactively enforced the law it has been a more effective remedy for pay discrimination.

In sum, discrimination by employers plays a major role in the pay gap. Sometimes this happens because of an employer's explicit sex bias. More often it probably reflects a combination of unconscious bias, the devaluation of women's work, and the legacy of past practices when unequal treatment was customary and legal. Probably employers' most important impact on the size of their pay gap is the extent to which they segregate women and men in different jobs. We turn now to the effects of segregation on the earnings gap.

Sex Segregation

So far, we have assumed that Acme Chip assigns men and women to the same job—producing chips. As you saw in Chapter 4, however, job-level sex integration is rare. So let's bring Acme into line with American employers and assume that it assigns women and men to different jobs.

Segregation lowers women's pay relative to men's: The more segregated a country, an occupation, an industry, or a firm, the more women and men will be concentrated in different jobs. And the more women in a job, the less both its male and female incumbents earn (Jacobs 1999; Reid 1998).

In assessing the impact of segregation on earnings, researchers have examined the effect of women's share of an occupation, job, industry, or establishment (in other words, the percentage of workers who are female) on women's and men's earnings. Depending on the study, the data, the statistical method, and the other variables that researchers take into account, some or even most of the pay gap between women and men results from occupational segregation (Cotter et al. 1997:714; Kilbourne, England, and Beron 1994). Industrial segregation accounts for between 12 and 17 percent of the gap (Sorensen 1989:74), and job segregation—which captures segregation both across occupations and establishments—accounts for 89 percent of the earnings gap (Petersen and Morgan 1995, table 4). In short, predominantly female lines of work pay less than predominantly male lines of work.

Additional evidence of the effect of job segregation comes from other studies. Consider men's higher payoff to education (see Exhibit 6.5). Even among workers with the same amount of schooling, men substantially

EXHIBIT 6.5

Median Annual Earnings of Full-Time, Year-Round Workers by Education, Sex, Race, and Hispanic Origin, 1999

	WOMEN			
Education	**All Races**	**White**	**Black**	**Hispanic**
Overall	$27,137	$27,600	$25,082	$20,242
Less than high school	$15,704	$15,661	$13,544	$13,879
High school graduate	$21,970	$22,247	$20,609	$19,923
Some college	$26,456	$26,850	$25,209	$24,236
Associate's degree	$30,129	$30,302	$27,198	$24,744
Bachelor's degree	$36,340	$36,672	$34,692	$31,996
Master's degree	$45,345	$45,772	$41,780	$43,718
Professional degree	$56,726	$59,223	*	*
Doctoral degree	$56,345	$58,577	*	*

	MEN			
Education	**All Races**	**White**	**Black**	**Hispanic**
Overall	$38,427	$40,138	$30,926	$25,242
Less than high school	$22,576	$22,981	$21,619	$18,960
High school graduate	$32,098	$33,147	$27,408	$25,291
Some college	$37,245	$38,463	$31,961	$31,446
Associate's degree	$40,474	$40,928	$31,206	$36,212
Bachelor's degree	$51,005	$51,606	$40,805	$41,467
Master's degree	$61,776	$61,691	$52,308	$50,410
Professional degree	$96,275	$96,863	*	*
Doctoral degree	$76,858	$80,359	*	*

Source: U.S. Census Bureau 2000b; table 10.
Note: The categories of white and black include both Hispanics and non-Hispanics; the category Hispanic includes Hispanics of any race.
*No data were available for these categories due to small sample sizes. The all-races column includes Asians and other non black, non-Hispanic groups.

outearn women. Among college graduates and Ph.D.s, some of these sex differences reflect men's and women's concentration in different college majors (Hecker 1998). But what about workers with lower levels of education? Non-Hispanic white men who dropped out of high school earned about as much as women who had between one and three years of college; white non-Hispanic women who had graduated from high school earned almost $4,000 less than non-Hispanic white men who had not. The sex difference was smaller among Hispanics and African Americans, but among both those groups, male high school graduates outearned women with one to three years of college. These differences do not come about because the same employer is paying a male high school graduate as much as it pays a woman with three years of college for the same job. Instead, they reflect the fact that male high school graduates hold different—and typically better-paying—jobs than women with some college, and they often work for different employers.

The fact that men employed full time, year-round averaged $535 in annual earnings for each year's experience compared to $318 for women (U.S. Census Bureau 1998, 1999, 2000a) also shows that men's credentials are compensated at a higher rate than women's (Roos and Gatta 1999:101). (Importantly, the differential payoff the sexes receive for their education and experience has declined, contributing to the decline in the pay gap; O'Neill and Polachek 1993, table 8.) Here again, most of these different payoffs to experience stem from women's segregation into jobs that reward experience at a lower rate than men's jobs do.

In sum, segregation causes a large part of the earnings gap. Why it does so is a matter of debate. We now turn to possible reasons, summarizing available evidence.

Crowding. Traditional economic theory suggests that sex segregation could reduce the pay in customarily female or male occupations by crowding workers of either sex into a relatively small number of occupations. If workers' earnings are set by supply and demand, as neoclassical economists assume, an oversupply of workers in an occupation hypothetically allows employers to pay them lower wages (Bergmann 1986:129-30). Women's exclusion from male occupations hypothetically crowds women into a smaller number of occupations than the number open to men, thus lowering women's pay relative to men's in the occupations into which women are crowded. An intriguing test of whether crowding helps to explain why occupational segregation lowers women's pay examined occupational sex segregation and the earnings across 261 U.S. cities (Cotter et al. 1997). City differences in the earnings ratio led the researchers to conclude that occupational sex segregation accounted for most of the earnings gap. In cities with highly segregated labor markets that crowded women into smaller numbers of occupations, women earned less in all occupations. The authors concluded that all women benefit from living in cities with less occupationally segregated labor markets.

The Assignment of Higher- and Lower-Paying Jobs Based on Workers' Sex. If Acme earmarks for men most of the better-paying jobs (e.g., chip designer, chip supervisor, vice president of chips) and relegates women to lower-paying jobs (chip polisher, chip tester, chip sweeper), then men will earn more than women. We do not know how many employers reserve better-paying jobs for men or why. We do know that higher-paying employers tend to hire men for a particular line of work, whereas lower-paying employers hire women for the same job. We see this every day with respect to food servers. Waiters outearn waitresses primarily because upscale restaurants often hire male servers for higher pay, whereas low-end restaurants hire female servers and pay them less. In fact, a study of elite New York restaurants found that the price of dinner for two was negatively correlated with women's employment as servers. And the difference was more than small change: Servers in more expensive restaurants averaged $45,000 salaries, compared to under $20,000 for those employed in less-expensive restaurants (Rab 2001).

Because U.S. employers often set pay for job titles, segregating the sexes into jobs with different titles can lead to unequal pay. Although researchers can rarely tell why employers do this, the outcome is predictable. Consider the experience of a woman who worked for 25 years cleaning the Russell Senate Office building. She earned $22,000 a year in 2000, whereas men doing essentially the same job earned $30,000. She explained that men's jobs are classified as "laborer," which allow them to advance through five grades, whereas women are classified as "custodial workers" and can advance only two. Nonetheless, she said, "They scrub with a mop and bucket. We scrub with a mop and bucket. They vacuum. We vacuum. They push a trash truck. We push a trash truck. The only thing they do that we don't is run a scrub machine. But that's on wheels, so we could do it too" (Barko 2000:1; see also Beechey and Perkins 1987:64-66).

Early in the twentieth century, a supervisor in a magazine publishing plant explained that men did the machine work, and women folded pages by hand. He commented:

> I could put a girl to work operating the cutting machine if I paid her $18 a week [the male wage]. . . . I could have a woman tend the large folding machine if I paid her the same as the union scale for men. I don't know why I don't, except that I see no good reason why I should. (Tentler 1979:35)

In theory, federal laws and regulations provide a good reason for employers to give all workers access to all jobs that they can perform. The first of such laws is Title 7 of the 1964 Civil Rights Act, which made it illegal for firms with at least 15 full-time employees to discriminate on the basis of race, color, religion, national origin, and sex in hiring, discharge, compensation, and [other] terms, conditions, or privileges of employment.[11] As we explained in Chapter 4, this law bans segregating employees on the basis of these characteristics.

The other regulatory tool that has the potential to reduce segregation and thus shrink the earnings gap is the presidential executive order that requires federal contractors to take affirmative action to ensure that they do not discriminate. As we noted in Chapter 4, the effectiveness of Title 7 and the executive orders banning discrimination and requiring affirmative action has varied, given off-again-on-again enforcement. Vigorous enforcement could go a long way toward reducing the pay gap by reducing segregation.

The Devaluation of Women's Work. Some scholars have suggested that predominantly male jobs pay more than predominantly female jobs because pay-setters believe that female-dominated jobs are less valuable than those in which men predominate. As we indicated in Chapter 1, societies devalue female activities, including customarily female tasks—regardless of what those tasks entail—*because* women do them. For example, our culture tends to devalue caring or nurturant work at least partly because it is done by women (Kilbourne, England, and Beron 1994:1151). This tendency accounts for child care workers' low rank in the pay hierarchy. Once Acme segregates its female and male employees into different jobs, unless it actively guards against the cultural tendency to devalue women's work, it is likely to view jobs primarily held by women as less valuable than those men hold, even when they require the same levels of skill, effort, and responsibility (Treiman and Hartmann 1981:9).

To explore the impact of the devaluation of women's work on the pay gap, researchers have examined the effect of women's share of an occupation on its pay. After taking into account occupational complexity (a measure of the skill an occupation requires), the percentage of workers who were female in the occupation accounted for almost 20 percent of the pay gap between black women and men and 7 percent of the gap between white women and men (Kilbourne, England, and Beron 1994:1170). The pay disparity due to women's share of jobs, net of skill level, is termed **comparable worth discrimination** because among people doing tasks requiring equal skill (that is, those presumably of comparable worth to the employer), workers in more female jobs or occupations earn less because the occupation employs mostly women.

We have seen that employers often undervalue predominantly female occupations. Although the 1963 the Equal Pay Act (EPA) makes it illegal for U.S. employers to pay women less than men in the same job, the courts have held that the EPA does not apply when an employer assigns the sexes to do different jobs, even if they involve the same amount of skill, effort, and responsibility. Thus, it is currently legal for employers to underpay workers in predominantly female lines of work relative to what they pay workers in predominantly male jobs that entail the same skill, effort, and responsibility.

In the 1980s, proponents of fair pay began to advocate **pay equity,** a compensation system that pays workers on the basis of the worth of their work, not the sex or race of the workers who perform it.[12] In the 1980s and 1990s, several states enacted laws requiring pay equity by public employers. But no law prevents private employers from devaluing predominantly female jobs, and the courts have refused to apply the EPA to these situations, arguing that pay differences by private employers are the result of the "market" and of women's choice of occupations that pay less (Nelson and Bridges 1999:25, 360). As long as the sexes are segregated into different jobs, no legal remedy exists for the underpayment of private-sector workers in predominantly female jobs.

Other countries have been more successful in eliminating comparable-worth discrimination. Consider Australia, where government tribunals set minimum wage rates for occupations. Prior to 1969, wage tribunals openly discriminated against women, setting their pay at 75 percent of men's rates. A policy of equal pay for equal work that Australia implemented that year, similar to the United States' Equal Pay Act, made little difference because most women worked in heavily female occupations for which the tribunals still set low wages. Three years later, however, after the tribunals replaced the policy of equal pay for equal work with a policy of equal pay for work of equal value, the earnings ratio increased from 65 percent to 84 percent (Blau, Ferber, and Winkler 1998:357). This dramatic reduction in Australia's pay gap demonstrates the ability of governments to help equalize pay.

On-the-Job Training. Occupational segregation contributes to the pay gap by reducing female workers' chances to acquire skills or engage in tasks that employers reward with higher pay. Men's greater access to on-the-job training (white men had twice as much training on their current job as did black or white women or black men) thus may contribute to men's higher pay. According to one study, the training gap explained 11 percent of the gap between white men and women and 8 percent of the gap between white men and black women (Roos and Gatta 1999:108).

Government-sponsored training programs have a particular responsibility to provide training without regard to trainees' sex.

Summary

For most of the twentieth century, American women's pay was about 60 percent of men's. In 1964, the year the Equal Pay Act went into effect, women employed full time, year-round earned 59.1 percent of what men earned. Over the next quarter century, the pay gap closed to 72.2 percent. This chapter has shown that the disparity between female and male workers' earnings stems both from "supply-side" and "demand-side" factors. On the supply side, men's greater amount of time at paid work contributes to the pay gap. According to supply-side approaches to the pay gap, if women want to earn as much as men, they must act more like men.[13] In practice this means that women will need to cut back further on sleep or leisure time activities and hire out more domestic work and child care or that men will need to take on more domestic work.

On the demand side, the sexes' segregation into different places of work and different jobs and the devaluation of women's work are important reasons for the pay gap. Demand-side explanations imply that employers must behave differently, integrating jobs by sex, eliminating the wage penalty for predominantly female lines of work, and ending pay discrimination. In considering the remedies these explanations imply, we must bear in mind that what women do affects employers' behavior and vice versa. For example, if employers assigned women to more rewarding jobs, women would be willing to work longer hours, and if women worked as many hours a week as men do, statistical discrimination by employers might decline.

Since 1964 when Congress outlawed pay discrimination based on sex, women have been catching up with men's earnings at a little less than a half cent per year. If this rate of progress continues, the sexes will not earn equal pay until 2055. Maintaining this rate of progress depends on occupational sex segregation's continuing decline (but we saw in Chapter 4 that that decline has slowed), women's continuing movement into customarily male fields of study, a continuing increase in women's work experience, and a continuing erosion in men's earnings. Achieving equal pay sooner will require political and economic changes of the sort witnessed in the last third of the twentieth century.

Notes

1. At the turn of the twenty-first century, older women's Social Security payments averaged $697 a month, compared to $904 for men (Hinden 2001).
2. Most of the wealth on which fourteenth-century Parisians were taxed was acquired through the work they did.
3. However, the pay gap in manufacturing has scarcely budged since then. At the end of the twentieth century, women in manufacturing earned 62.7 percent of what men earned (U.S. Census Bureau 1998, 1999, 2000a).
4. To put it another way, for every $10,000 the average woman earned, her male counterpart received $13,850.
5. Fewer than 5 percent of people surveyed in the 1996 General Social Survey declined to answer a series of questions about why women earn less than men (Davis, Smith, and Marsden 2000:508). The sexes favored similar explanations, but women were more likely to agree that the fact that employers tend to give men better-paying jobs than they give women was important, and more men than women assigned some importance to the beliefs that men work harder on the job than women do and that women's family responsibilities keep them from putting as much time and effort into their jobs as men do (GSS data from http://www.icpsn.umich.edu/GSSI).
6. Bear in mind, however, that the notion of skill is socially constructed, and that the invisibility and devaluation of women's work tends to downwardly bias evaluations of their skill levels (Steinberg 1990).
7. Even if education and experience are good measures of productivity, other factors also affect it, such as the work technology available to workers. Because the sexes are segregated into different places of work and different jobs, they almost certainly have access to differentially productive work tools.
8. Recent reductions in labor force interruptions are partly attributable to the 1994 Family and Medical Leave Act (see Chapter 7), which guarantees covered workers the right to return to their jobs after taking time off for family or medical reasons (Waldfogel 1999a, 1999b).
9. In most jobs, employers cannot readily measure their workers' productivity.
10. The law exempted situations in which such payment is based on a seniority system, a merit system, a piece-rate system, or on the basis of any other factors than sex (public law 88-38; 77 Stat. 57).
11. Millions of women who work in establishments with fewer than 15 full-time employees have no legal protection against sex discrimination (Reskin 2001).
12. Initially, this pay policy was termed *comparable worth.*
13. The gap also narrows when men act more like women. This is what happened when the disappearance of customarily male manufacturing jobs pushed men into service sector jobs.

7

Paid Work and Family Work

At one time in history, work and home life were intimately linked: The physical space of work was also the place where family life occurred. Indeed, in many developing societies, this is still the case: Homes and farms are the site of economic enterprise. In modern industrialized countries, in contrast, the link between the two spheres is that they often are in conflict with one another.

After describing changes in the last half of the twentieth century in men's and women's patterns of labor force participation, this chapter turns to the issue of work-family conflict. This notion has two distinct meanings. The first meaning addresses the conflict that workers confront when work demands and home demands compete. We describe three elements of work-family conflict: time shortages, scheduling demands, and work-family spillover. The second is the conflict that employed women and men face in trying to distribute household tasks fairly. In the last section, we address employers' and governments' efforts to help workers resolve these conflicts.

The Decline of the Stay-at-Home Wife and Mother

At the turn of the twentieth century, fewer than 4 percent of married women between the ages of 16 and 65 were in the labor force; by the end of the century, that figure was 59.5 percent (U.S. Census Bureau 1998, 1999, 2000a). Even more dramatic is mothers' rising labor force participation. Today, women are far less likely to interrupt their labor force participation for children than they were 30 years ago. As Exhibit 7.1 shows, the labor force participation of women and men has been converging since 1950. In that year, women's labor force participation over the life cycle dipped sharply during prime childbearing years. Now, in contrast, few women leave the labor force to have children. In 1976, 31 percent of

EXHIBIT 7.1

Labor Force Participants by Age and Sex, 1950 and 2000

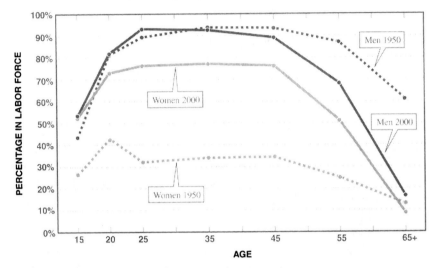

Source: Bloom and Brender 1993, figure 2; authors' calculations from the March 1998, 1999, and 2000 Current Population Surveys.
Note: Figures for 2000 are averages of 1998, 1999, and 2000 Current Population Survey data.

mothers with a child under 1 year old were in the labor force; that percentage was 59 percent in 1998 (66.5 percent for women with college degrees and 73.6 percent for women with graduate or professional degrees; Bachu and O'Connell 2000).

Family-work patterns also have changed considerably in the past 60 years, as Exhibit 7.2 shows. By the end of the twentieth century, both parents were employed in 44 percent of families with children, compared to 35 percent in 1975 (U.S. Census Bureau 1998, 1999, 2000a; Hayghe 1990). Even more dramatically, families with employed husbands and stay-at-home wives accounted for only 19 percent of all families, down from 67 percent in 1940. In addition, high divorce rates and a rise in the number of unmarried mothers since 1970 have increased the ranks of families maintained solely by employed women to 14 percent. Meanwhile, the proportion of father-only families has remained stable at around 3 percent. The diverse group of "all others" includes families in which only wives are in the labor force (about 5 percent) and families with no member in the labor force (about 15 percent). The growth in this no-worker category since 1940 has stemmed primarily from the growth of the retired population.

EXHIBIT 7.2

Employment Patterns of Families, 1940-2000 (in percentages)

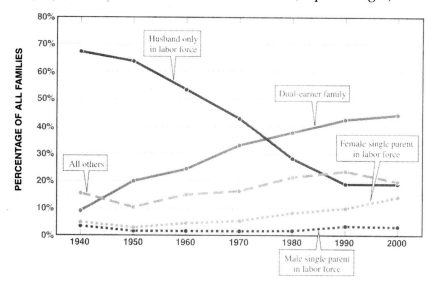

Sources: Hayghe 1990, 1993; authors' calculations are from the March 1998, 1999, and 2000 Current Population Surveys.

Note: Figures for 2000 are averages of 1998, 1999, and 2000 Current Population Survey data.

Work-Family Conflict

Jobs and home both demand enormous commitments of time and energy, and the periods of greatest energy expenditure—the peak years of family formation and of career growth—tend to coincide. Jobs consume about a quarter of the week for the average full-time worker, not including time spent commuting or preparing for work (U.S. Census Bureau 1998, 1999, 2000a). In addition, many working people are responsible for caring for others, such as their children, elderly parents or in-laws, or spouses. Child care requires considerable regular attention, frequently during parents' paid work hours, and children's illnesses cannot be scheduled around work hours.

How successful are people in meeting dual obligations at work and at home? A survey of a large company known for its family-friendly policies found that only one-third of workers of both sexes agreed that it was possible to get ahead at work and still devote enough time to their families (Morris 1997). In a national survey, about 15 percent of employed women and men reported a lack of success at balancing work and family, and over a third felt that they have done a very good job. Most people—about half—fell in the middle, saying that they are somewhat successful at achieving balance (Davis, Smith, and Marsden 2000). Life-stage and family status play important roles in feelings of success in balancing, however. Among dual-earner couples, those with preschoolers were least likely to say that they successfully managed work and family. Only 1 in 10 felt they performed both roles successfully (although slightly older couples with preschoolers felt somewhat more successful; Moen and Yu 1999). Regular hours rather than long hours, a supportive supervisor, and job security also contribute to success in balancing work and family (Moen and Yu 2000). In sum, reconciling the tension between the time demands of work and home is a challenge for many. Even people who report that they successfully manage the balance may nevertheless experience work-family conflict and miss out on leisure time.

Work-family conflict occurs in three important respects, and the next section describes the conflict stemming from time demands, scheduling dilemmas, and the problems that arise when work spills into home life or home demands spill into work life.

Time Shortages

Many American workers feel pressed for time as they try to accommodate the demands of both work and family (Jacobs and Gerson 2001). But the time pressure they feel depends on how much they work for pay and how many demands they face on the home front. A sense of a "time famine" (Hochschild 1989) is particularly characteristic of dual-earner families where both partners work full time: 43 percent said that they always feel rushed (Davis, Smith, and Marsden 2000). The problem is less acute for couples in which one or both partners limit the demands of the work sphere. This is a common strategy: Among married women in the prime working ages of 25 to 54, only 35 percent with children under six work full-time, year-round (Bianchi 2000:407).

The desire of many employers to have totally committed employees causes workers to be pressed for time. For these employers, an ideal worker should put work above all other commitments and activities (Acker 1990; Ely and Meyerson 2000). A variety of organizational practices sustains the notion that the time demands of work should trump all other commitments (Ely and Meyerson 2000). Crisis-oriented work patterns and chaotic work routines that demand workers' constant presence make breaking away from work difficult. So does measuring productivity and commitment by "face time" instead of by the amount of work accomplished. Public actions and declarations that identify as "committed" those workers willing to subordinate family obligations to work are other such practices. An extreme example is the employer who praised a woman for having scheduled a Caesarean-section delivery so she could attend an important meeting (Martin 1990). Workers who face no demands from spouses, aging parents, or children—or who have someone at home who can meet those demands—are more likely to meet this ideal of a committed worker.[1] According to *Fortune* magazine: "in a world built on just-in-time, the ideal employee is the one who is always available, not the one who's constantly torn. . . . The corporate hero is the one free to fly to Singapore on a moment's notice, not the poor schlep who has to get home to relieve the nanny" (Morris 1997:3-4). Many employers have not rethought the organization of work that existed in the 1950s, when most workers had wives who attended to the home front full time. Managers often resist workers' attempts to make more time for family life, as evidenced by this manager's response on hearing that employees wanted better work-family balance:

> Don't *ever* bring up "balance" again! I don't want to hear about it!
> Period! Everybody in this company has to work hard. . . . Just because
> a few women are concerned about balance doesn't mean we change the
> rules. If they chose this career, they're going to have to pay for it in
> hours, just like the rest of us. (Hochschild 1997:71)

Thus, expectations of total devotion to one's job place subtle and not-so-subtle pressure on workers to resist the pull of home obligations.

It doesn't have to be this way. Hours of work are much shorter in many western European countries than in the United States. In the United States, full-time workers average 43.5 hours a week. In contrast, workers covered by collective bargaining agreements in Germany work 37.4 hours a week (some unions have negotiated a 35-hour week [European Industrial Relations Observatory 1999]). In 1997, France passed a law to lower the workweek to 35 hours, and Italy is moving toward a 35-hour week (Hayden 1999). In contrast, U.S. law governing work hours simply requires employers to pay overtime to nonprofessional workers working over 40 hours a week. Length of vacation accounts for some of the difference between the United States and Europe in average work hours. No

U.S. law requires employers to pay for vacation time, a practice common throughout Europe. As a result of shorter workweeks and longer vacations, Dutch and Norwegian workers average 30 percent fewer hours than their U.S. counterparts (Polatnick 2000:3).

We now turn to the time demands people face when they are not on the job. Maintaining one's life and personal relationships also demands time and energy. Everyone must deal with needs of basic upkeep, including obtaining meals, cleaning, shopping, laundry, and possibly yard care and car maintenance. Workers with children or ill family members must manage additional time demands.

Some home demands have diminished in recent years. American women have reduced their hours of housework by almost half since 1965 (Bianchi et al. 2000). They cook less, clean less, wash fewer dishes, and put up with more "dust bunnies" than in the past (Robinson and Milkie 1997). In addition, some services that families—particularly women—used to provide for free for their own households can now be purchased. The use of child care centers, nursing homes, cleaning services, grocery-delivery services, and takeout restaurants has expanded considerably (Glass 2000:134).

Yet these market substitutes do not make up for the shortage of time and can create problems of their own. For one thing, market substitutes are not cheap, and some workers may work longer hours to pay for them (Glass 2000:134). For another, not all services can be hired out, nor do workers necessarily want to hire others to do them. Spending time with their children is one such activity that many working parents want to maintain (Glass 2000). Some researchers believe that the demands of child rearing have escalated, as contemporary parents are expected to monitor children's television watching, volunteer in their schools, supervise their play, get to know their friends, and watch for signs of emotional trouble (Glass 2000:131). These tasks place strong demands on the time of workers who are also parents. In addition, other time-consuming tasks also remain: waiting in line at the post office, staying home to let repair people in, washing and folding laundry, among many others.[2]

In sum, both the work and home spheres demand time, with the result that many workers feel overwhelmed. Although there may be some workers whose home lives are so stressful that they escape to their jobs (Hochschild 1997), for most this is not the case (Bielby 1998:33). Almost two-thirds of both women and men would like to reduce their working hours by about 11 hours per week. When both jobs and home demand many hours, "balancing" or "juggling" is not sufficient (Polatnick 2000).

Scheduling Demands

The sheer number of hours that home and work demand is not the only problem. Another arises when workers are expected to be in two places at the same time. Parent-teacher conferences, doctor appointments, and being home for the plumber occur during standard working hours. When the demands of work occur at the same time as the demands of home, as happens, for example, when the boss demands overtime but the child care center is closed, paid work conflicts with family obligations.

Lack of control over work schedules is a primary source of stress for working parents, especially mothers (Barnett and Rivers 1996). For this reason, workers seek flexibility in their work schedules (Barnett and Rivers 1996; Coltrane 1996). Workers whose employers provide little or no flexibility for dealing with home-work conflicts are less satisfied on their jobs and less committed to their employers (Bond, Galinsky, and Swanberg 1998).

The difficulty of scheduling work and family life is clear among workers subject to mandatory overtime (Gerstel and Clawson 2001). U.S. employers can legally require workers not covered by union contracts to work overtime hours or risk losing their jobs. Although many workers value overtime pay, some have begun to challenge mandatory overtime. Unionized employees at Verizon staged a strike in 2000 that won them the right to overtime notification of at least 2.5 hours beforehand and a mandatory maximum of 7.5 to 15 overtime hours a week, depending on the job category and the particular union local (Moody 2000; Schafer 2000). Similarly, United Airlines has faced strong pressure from its pilots and mechanics to limit the extent of mandatory overtime. Some unionized workers are taking a strong stand because the unpredictability of overtime can wreak havoc on home life. For workers who can find backup child care, overtime pay can go to baby-sitters. Workers must simply miss other events. A national survey in 1996 found that half the respondents (59 percent of men and 42 percent of women) had missed a family event because of work (Reid-Keene 2001).

Scheduling Child and Elder Care. Scheduling difficulties result partly from inflexible child care arrangements. Obtaining adequate child care is a primary source of stress among employed parents. The ranks of relatives who once might have filled in have thinned as women have entered the labor force (Brewster and Padavic 2002). As a result, parents increasingly rely on child care centers (about a quarter of preschoolers are in organized care while their mothers are at work).

However, organized child care is often inadequate to meet working parents' needs. First, most centers operate only during standard business hours and do not provide care for sick children. Only 3 percent of centers offer evening care (Hofferth 1999:25). Second, nonrelative child care is seldom cheap; it constitutes one of the largest shares of work-related expenses, particularly for single parents and poor families. In 1995, poor mothers of preschoolers spent 29 percent of their family income on care, compared to 6 percent for high-income mothers (U.S. Census Bureau 2000d). Third, not enough affordable facilities exist to meet the demand. According to one estimate, if child care were fully funded, the employment rate among mothers would increase by 10 percent (Blau and Hagy 1998).

Insufficient child care affects people's ability to adequately attend to their work or family responsibilities (Harris Poll 1998). The high cost and inaccessibility of child care force some parents to leave their children home alone. One out of 10 children between 6 and 9 years old whose mothers are employed are regularly left without any child care at all (Capizzano, Tout, and Adams 2000). Another 1 in 10 is cared for by their mother at work. Some parents schedule different shifts—for example, one spouse working nights and the other days—in order to manage child care. This arrangement takes a toll on marriage, however: Divorce rates are above average because spouses see so little of each other (Presser 2000).

Working Americans increasingly face another family demand that can conflict with the timing of paid work: care of elderly relatives. Although most of the elderly population care for themselves, family members are responsible for almost all of the long-term care of the noninstitutionalized disabled elderly.[3] People who care for children and elderly parents at the same time have been dubbed the "sandwich generation" because they are caught between two generations, both of whom need care. Caregivers of the elderly help with day-to-day activities such as shopping and preparing meals, arranging for outside services, and responding to emergencies. Advances in medical technology that keep people alive longer plus the aging of the baby boom generation point to the increasing need for long-term care in the future (Bogenschneider 2000).

Demands on workers to care for elderly relatives can make work life difficult. Yet in 1997, only one-quarter of wage and salary employees received any kind of help from employers in caring for elderly relatives (Bond et al. 1998). Salaried workers fared better. Indeed, almost half of Fortune 1000 firms now assist some of their salaried employees (Hewitt Associates LLC 2000). What elder-caregivers most want is "free time, time for myself" (U.S. Women's Bureau 1998), yet the most common help employers offer is resource and referral services (Hewitt Associates LLC 2000). Some workers encounter opposition by supervisors when they try to use a benefit (Intracorp 1998). The consequences of inadequate support in caring for elderly relatives for some workers are lost sleep, lost leisure, and in some cases, loss of a full-time job. Caring for a disabled parent for just 10 hours a week is associated with a substantial drop in women's paid work hours, and residing with a disabled parent cuts the chance of working at all by 55 percent (Ettner 1995).

In sum, domestic life and employment are incompatible when they require that a person be in two places at once. Domestic life—especially child rearing—can involve schedules that do not mesh well with work schedules. The scheduling problem is most severe for workers who have others who depend on them at home, but many workers without dependents would like greater flexibility in their hours of work. In a later section, we consider employers' responses to workers' desire for more flexible schedules.

Work-Family Spillover

Both the work and family spheres can bring problems, worry, and demands—as well as satisfactions and rewards. In the days when the sexual division of labor made many women responsible only for the home and men only for earning a living, the concerns of each domain tended to stay there. But with the erosion of the breadwinner/homemaker sexual division of labor, each sex often has responsibilities on both fronts. In addition the boundaries between work and home have become more permeable: paid work tends to spill over beyond the boundaries of the workday, and home life tends to spill over into the workplace.

Among the ways that home life interrupts parents' paid jobs are fielding telephone calls from children and teachers, arriving late to work because of an emergency trip to the veterinarian or the pediatrician, missing work because school closes for a snow day or because their child is performing in a school event, or lacking concentration because of a problem that needs attention on the home front. The intrusion of home life into work time can decrease workers' effectiveness and increase their tardiness, absenteeism, and stress levels (Galinsky, Friedman, and Hernandez 1991).

Work life also intrudes into home time. Recent advances in information technology have increased some workers' ability to work from home, a development that is double-edged (Epstein et al. 1999:126). On the one hand, working from home provides parents the flexibility to accommodate school and child care schedules. Many professional workers find this option an advantage. An attorney illustrates how technology facilitates her relationship with her child:

> I have a little three-year-old daughter, so I try to spend more time [with her] and go to her plays and other things. We've got a portable telephone, a telephone in the car, and a fax; you can actually get everything done. . . . You can go anywhere as long as you have a fax machine and a telephone. (Epstein et al. 1999:126)

However, it also shows how hard it is to escape one's work. Technology combined with an economy in which companies compete by providing round-the-clock services has increased the pressure on professional workers to be available outside the office (Glass 2000). Fax machines, modems, e-mail, and cell phones mean technologies exist that cross traditional boundaries between work and family. An attorney whose clients insist that they be able to contact him by e-mail said: "You have to check every five minutes! . . . It doesn't just affect me at the office, it affects my life" (Hymowitz and Silverman 2001). Another attorney said that her cell phone hadn't freed her at all; rather, it had just given her a longer tether (Epstein et al. 1999:126).

Nonprofessional workers, too, work from home doing a variety of clerical and blue-collar jobs, such as entering insurance claims on a computer, knitting sweaters on a machine, or making costume jewelry. Some of the same advantages apply—in particular, increased flexibility—but the disadvantages are even greater than for professionals, because for these workers, the volume and scheduling of work are irregular, the pay is low, and workers receive few or no benefits (Prugl and Boris 1996).

There are other downsides to doing paid work from home for professional and nonprofessional workers. Parents working from home are less visible in their organization, which may reduce their promotion chances. They may also experience difficulty in doing paid work while also caring for children, because children generally require attention when they are not asleep. Finally, **home work** apparently reinforces a traditional division of domestic labor: female paid home workers tend to spend more time on housework than comparable women who leave home to work; male home workers do not (Jurik 1998).

The Sexual Division of Labor and Work-Family Conflict

Although it is clear that family structure and women's labor force participation have changed dramatically in the twentieth century, the sexual division of domestic labor has not kept pace. Today, about 60 percent of married women share responsibility for the breadwinner role, but men, by and large, have been slower to share domestic responsibilities. Women's responsibility for domestic tasks appears early in a relationship: When she enters into marriage or cohabitation, a woman adds 4.2 hours a week, on average, to her household labor while a man decreases his household labor by 3.6 hours per week (Gupta 1999). In 1995, employed women spent a total of 63 hours in paid work, domestic work, child care, and commuting, compared to 61 hours for employed men, a two-hour difference in total productive activity (Godbey and Robinson 1999: 335). Although both sexes benefit from the satisfaction and sometimes status and power that a paid job provides, women tend to experience more stress than men in coping with the double day (Moen and Yu 2000). Employed women are more likely than men to accommodate others' needs by adjusting their work and home schedules (Sanchez and Thomson 1997). Men also face the stresses of the double day, but not to the same extent as women. For some men, participation in housework is still optional (Coltrane 1996). Even in couples that share much of the domestic work, women still tend to hold the ultimate responsibility for making sure that necessary tasks are accomplished.

Men in the United States do more routine housework than they used to, but women still perform twice as much (Bianchi et al. 2000). Indeed, school-aged children perform almost as much routine household labor as fathers (Blair 1992). There is variation in this general pattern, however. Couples in which wives' earnings approximate their husbands' tend to divide domestic work most equally (Blair and Lichter 1991). This may help explain the fact that African American men tend to share housework more equally with their wives than do white men (Orbuch and Eyster 1997). Men whose wives hold shift-work jobs or are on flextime schedules tend to do more housework than other men (Presser 1994). The more hours men work for pay, the smaller the share of housework and child care they do (Ishii-Kuntz and Coltrane 1992).

Men whose wives are employed full time do more housework than other men, but even in couples where both partners are employed full time, such women spend almost three hours a week more on domestic tasks than men do (see Exhibit 7.3). In addition, women and men tend to be responsible for different tasks. Preparing meals and housecleaning consume the largest share of each sex's domestic labor, but in keeping with the traditional sexual division of domestic labor, women devote about three hours more per week to these tasks than men do. They also spend about two hours more per week ironing and cleaning up after meals, whereas men put in two hours more per week than women on outdoor chores and household repairs and maintenance.

A more equitable division of labor improves marriages. Besides taking some of the pressure off of women, men's greater participation in housework enhances marital satisfaction (Barnett and Hyde 2001; Orbuch and Eyster 1997), and it increases wives' sense of fairness, lowering their likelihood of depression (Bird 1999).

A growing number of men—especially younger men—are questioning traditional roles and their father's pattern of spending too little time at home (Cohen 1993). Married fathers spend significantly more time with children than their counterparts did in 1965—1.3 hours a day in child care or a combination of child care and another task, up from about three-quarters of an hour (Bianchi 2000). Controlling for other factors, men under 35 were far more likely to cut back on paid work hours in order to be with their young children than were older men, and this

EXHIBIT 7.3

Hours Spent on Household Tasks per Week for Full-Time Workers by Sex, 1998

Household Task	Men	Women	Men's Hours as a Percentage of Women's Hours
Preparing meals	2.2	4.3	49.7%
Meal cleanup	0.4	0.8	52.9%
House cleaning	2.0	2.8	71.5%
Laundry, ironing	0.6	1.9	31.4%
Outdoor chores	1.6	0.4	400.0%
Repairs, maintenance	1.4	0.7	200.0%
Garden and animal care	0.7	0.7	91.6%
Other household tasks	1.0	1.0	100.0%
Total housework	*9.9*	*12.6*	*78.4%*

Source: Bianchi and Robinson 2001.

difference was particularly pronounced for young men with egalitarian attitudes (Kaufman and Uhlenberg 2000:942). Yet even young fathers with egalitarian attitudes worked for pay over 40 hours a week. Married men generally greet the arrival of their first child with a two-week increase per year in their hours of paid work (Nock 1998:80), and new fathers take only five days off work on average (Hyde, Essex, and Horton 1993).

Women do more domestic work than men throughout the world, although the size of the gender gap varies (Elson 2000; Shelton 1999). Women spend 10 times more hours than men on household chores in Japan; from three to five times more in Spain, Poland, and Israel; and about twice as many in Australia, Canada, Finland, the United Kingdom, the Netherlands, Austria, and Denmark (Seager 1997:61). Around the world, women employed full time still perform more unpaid work in the home than employed men (Elson 2000:101). Even in Sweden, which scholars consider one of the world's most "woman-friendly" nations (Nyberg 2000), employed mothers in the early 1990s performed 70 percent of the core domestic housework.

Cross-national research shows a tendency for the division of household labor between the sexes to become slightly more equal as women's opportunities to earn wages expand (Crompton and Harris 1999:116). In the United States, the closer husbands' earnings are to their wives', the more housework men do.

In contrast, in some "macho" cultures (for example, Greece, Honduras, and Kenya), men who earn less than their wives do not perform housework, presumably because they are threatened by their wives' earning power (Safilios-Rothschild 1990). Similarly, in the United States, men who are economically dependent on their wives tend to do less housework than other men (Brines 1994).

One U.S. study that gathered data by having couples report what they were doing and how they felt when they were "beeped" by the researchers found that husbands were much more likely than wives to be engaged in leisure activities when at home. Early evenings, in particular, varied by sex: Husbands tended to unwind and begin leisure activities, while wives focused on housework and child care (Larson and Richards 1994:66). This pattern is likely to continue in the next generation: Teenage boys do half as much housework as teenage girls (Juster and Stafford 1991), and their tasks tend to be gender traditional, with boys performing chores such as yard care and girls doing cooking and cleaning (Antill et al. 1996).

Despite the problems women face in fulfilling both their customary obligations as homemakers and their newer responsibilities as paid workers, for most the cost is worth it. Even in the face of time shortages, scheduling conflicts, and spillover, being employed benefits women and their families. First, women's employment is essential for many families' economic well-being; it can make the difference between household self-sufficiency and just getting by. In married couples where both members work full time year-round, wives contribute over 43 percent of the total household earnings (U.S. Census Bureau 1998, 1999, 2000a). Second, combining work and family has positive emotional effects. Success in one role—for example, a promotion at work—can buffer a woman from difficulties in another role, such as problems in a marriage.

Responses to Work-Family Conflicts

Attempts to resolve work-family conflicts tend to center on the practical problems of juggling work and family life, particularly the child care problem. In the United States, the responsibility for finding ways to accommodate both work and family roles has fallen primarily on individuals. Only when the problems have become so severe that they impair work performance or retention have employers helped to shoulder some of the burden. Some employers have implemented programs such as flexible schedules, help with child care, and home work. When there are political gains to be had, the government has stepped in to help families cope. In this section, we examine individuals' responses and then turn to the programs that employers and governments have implemented.

Individual Solutions

Most workers experience the incompatibility between work and home demands as their own individual problem. Thus, we talk about workers "balancing," "juggling," "integrating," or "navigating" work and family (Polatnick 2000). According to the CEO of Bell South, "People have always had to make choices about balancing work and family. It has always been a personal issue, and individuals have to solve it" (Morris 1997:11). Despite some employers' efforts (which we discuss later), the structure of work and many employers and managers put the task of juggling squarely in workers' hands. Thus, most workers are on their own in resolving the dilemmas created by work-family conflict.

Some workers respond to work-family conflict by limiting family demands. In the early twentieth century, most women professionals coped by remaining single. Today, U.S. women postpone childbearing and have few children, trends that have reduced fertility to below replacement levels (Clarkberg 1999). Among the highest paid officers and directors of Fortune 500 companies in 1989, for example, 40 percent of the women were childless compared to fewer than 5 percent of men (University of California at Los Angeles/Korn-Ferry International 1993). More recent data for executives in Fortune 1000 companies show almost as many women were childless (36 percent); unfortunately, no data were available for men (Catalyst 1996).[4]

Affluent workers can reduce the time they spend on domestic tasks by hiring others to perform them. Little research addresses how the women they hire—often immigrant, racial and ethnic minorities, and working class or poor—accommodate the demands of the double day (Coltrane 2000; Glenn 1996).

Other women, especially those with young children, adapt to work-family conflict by limiting their time in paid work. Of all women aged 25 to 54, only half were employed full time, year-round, in 2000, compared to three-quarters of men (U.S. Census Bureau 2000a). Among married people with children under 15 years old, only 40 percent of women in their prime working years worked full time, year-round, compared to 83 percent of men (U.S. Census Bureau 2000a). Not surprisingly, many mothers who can afford to do so curtail their work hours in order to accommodate domestic tasks and childrearing. Just one-third of new mothers who had been working full time previously return to full-time work six months after the birth of their first child (Klerman and Liebowitz 1999). Thus, individuals' attempts to resolve the work-family dilemma contribute to higher rates of part-time work among employed women than men (U.S. Census Bureau 1998, 1999, 2000a).[5]

Although part-time employment helps relieve the difficulty of managing both spheres, it is not an ideal solution for many women. First, not all women can afford a part-time income. Second, professional careers are rarely structured to allow part-time work. Third, part-time jobs frequently lack benefits and do not offer advancement possibilities (Williams 2000).[6]

Lawyers who have tried to remain on career tracks while cutting back their work hours to "part time" (which means 45 to 50 hours a week in the legal profession [Ballard 1999]) illustrate the problem of a part-time career. Although most law offices (92 percent) reportedly have part-time policies, fewer than 3 percent of all lawyers practice part time (Lufkin 1997). The culture of the legal profession equates long hours with dedication; people—especially women—who deviate from this ideal fall off the partnership track (Epstein et al. 1999). Women attorneys in Boston's largest firms who reduced their hours "got fewer challenging cases, fewer opportunities for partnership, and less pay" (Ballard 1999). In jobs outside the legal profession, as well, a reduction in hours worked is also likely to throw workers off the promotion track (Kalleberg and Reskin 1995; Williams 2000).

In sum, for many women, career goals and family goals conflict, with success in one domain coming at the price of success in the other. Very few women are able to achieve the combined levels of college graduation, marriage, parenthood, and earnings that men take for granted. Among white women who graduated around 1972 (the most recent group to have completed its childbearing years), only between 13 and 17 percent had attained these things. Among the women who had achieved well-paying jobs, half were childless at about age 40 (Goldin 1995:33). Moreover, mothers suffer a pay penalty of about 7 percent per child, regardless of whether they are in high-level jobs (Budig and England 2001). Thus, some women pay a price by sacrificing family for career; others sacrifice career (or at least wages) for family.

The same applies to men: Success in one sphere often comes at the price of the other. The traditional gender role prescription that men place career ahead of families means that many men sacrifice time with their families. One survey of parents and children found that more fathers than mothers felt they spent too little time with their children, and the children concurred: When asked about wanting more time with their employed parents, more children answered yes about their fathers than about their mothers.

Unlike women's wages, men's wages do not suffer from having children, however. In fact, their pay either is unaffected or increases with the birth of a child. A study of Chicago lawyers found that women who faced work-family constraints were less likely to be promoted to partner positions, but that experiencing the same constraints did not hurt men's careers (Hull and Nelson 2000). Because individuals craft their solutions in a society that still assumes women's obligation to home and men's to the workplace, the workplace costs of the solutions workers come up with—cutting back on work hours—tend to disproportionately fall on women, and the "homeplace" costs are greater for men.

Employer-Sponsored Programs

In many firms in the United States and abroad, employers have devised strategies to accommodate family responsibilities. According to a survey of over 300 organizations, the percent of employers providing a formal program of spouse or partner employment assistance for some of its workers has grown from under one-quarter in 1990 to over one-third in 1998 (Employee Relocation Council 2000). This section discusses two employer-sponsored programs designed to improve recruitment, absenteeism, and turnover.[7] Such programs are now helping some workers cope with work-family conflict.

Assistance With Child Care. Most employees receive no child care help from their employer. In the mid-1990s, only 4 percent of all full-time employees in private establishments were eligible for child care assistance (U.S. Bureau of Labor Statistics 1998). As Exhibit 7.4 shows, large companies are more likely than small ones to provide benefits; however, most workers—especially workers of color—are employed in small companies.

By and large, workers who are harder to recruit and retain receive far more child care benefits than more readily replaceable workers. In the mid-1990s, 10 percent of full-time professional and technical workers had access to one of the child care benefits shown in Exhibit 7.4, but only 4 percent of clerical and sales workers and only 2 percent of blue-collar and service workers did (U.S. Bureau of Labor Statistics 1998).

EXHIBIT 7.4

Percentage of Full-Time Employees Eligible for Selected Family
Benefits by Establishment Size, 1996-1997

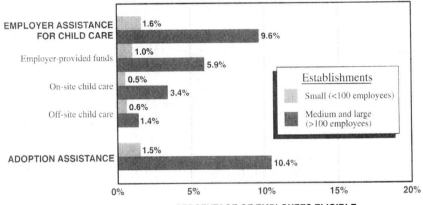

Source: U.S. Bureau of Labor Statistics 1999c, 1999d.

Flexible Scheduling. Flexible scheduling can have two very different meanings. When it is at the employer's discretion, it typically means that workers have no fixed schedules because their work hours depend on the employers' needs. This form can wreak havoc on attempts to balance work and family. Flexibility at McDonald's restaurants, for example, means that workers are supposed to be flexible about working late or leaving early depending on how busy the outlet is (Leidner 1993:51). In 1997, 19 percent of male workers and 14 percent of women worked an irregular schedule (e.g., evenings, nights, rotating schedules, split shifts), but only 4 percent did so for child care reasons. For the vast majority of such workers, their jobs required irregular schedules (Beers 2000).

In contrast, flexibility at the worker's discretion means that workers have some choice in arranging their schedules, which facilitates work-family balance. The traditional organization of work in which most workers are present at the same time is changing. In 1997, over 25 million workers—27.6 percent of all full-time wage and salary workers—made use of flexible work arrangements by varying the times they chose to arrive at and leave work, a rate double what it was in 1985, according to a national study (Beers 2000). Flexible scheduling is most common among executives, administrators, and managers, with 42 percent of such workers using it. Men were slightly more likely than women to opt for flexible scheduling (29 percent of men and 26 percent of women), as were parents of children under age 6 compared to nonparents (30 percent versus 27 percent).

Far less common are options that let employees work at home on a regular basis. One-third of employers with over 100 workers offer this option to some employees, and 24 percent allow workers to adjust their starting and quitting times on a daily basis (Galinsky and Bond 1998).

Workers who have a say in their hours of work find flexible schedules useful in arranging child care and family life. Both women and men are almost unanimous in the belief that employers should allow workers more flexible hours in order to handle family responsibilities (91 percent of women and 88 percent of men [Davis, Smith, and Marsden 2000]). Nine out of 10 parents desire access to compressed workweeks, flextime, job sharing, and part-time jobs that include benefits (Hewlett and West 1998).

Summary. Some employers help at least some employees reconcile family and work. This does not solve work-family conflict for most workers, however. First, the workforce has been polarizing into two groups: privileged workers (managers and professionals) and others who include nonprofessional regular employees and contingent workers (those with no job security, often in temporary or part-time jobs) who are hired and fired according to employers' labor needs. Employers tend to make family benefits available only to privileged workers (Hochschild 1997). Second, most people work for small companies that cannot afford to implement family-friendly changes.

Government-Sponsored Programs

Some countries have addressed work-family conflicts by helping workers accommodate their dual responsibilities. Other advanced industrial countries have left the United States in the dust in this respect. For example, Germany instituted maternity leave in 1883, as did Sweden in 1891, and France in 1928. The United States did not pass legislation until 1993 (Ruhm and Teague 1997). Part of the reason that the United States lags behind other countries is ideological. Americans, with their high value on individualism, see raising the next generation as a private rather than a public concern. In contrast, European countries believe that society bears some responsibility for family well-being and will gain from investing in the next generation. Two policy statements from the Swedish government illustrate this commitment (Kimball 1999:429-30):

Parents and children should have enough time to spend with each other, at the same time enjoying a reasonable economic standard.

Women and men should be able to combine a meaningful working life with active parenting.

Family Leave Policies. Western Europe's industrialized nations are leaders in providing paid extensive parental leaves during children's early years and in supporting high-quality out-of-home care for children (Gornick and Meyers 2001:4). Many developing countries also support generous paid parental leaves. Jamaica, for example, provides 8 weeks at the minimum wage, Nicaragua provides 12 weeks at 60 percent of the worker's wage, Zimbabwe provides 3 months at 70 percent of worker's wage, and Benin provides full pay for 14 weeks (Kamerman 2000). In most countries, parental-leave programs are funded through social insurance or general tax revenues, although a few require contributions from employers (Ruhm and Teague 1997). Mandated maternity or parental leave is now common among the member countries of the Organisation for Economic Co-operation and Development (OECD), as Exhibit 7.5 shows. The average leave (both maternal and parental) is 10 months. More than half of these countries provide at least 70 percent of the new parents' wage, and another seven provide between 50 and 70 percent (Kamerman 2000:8). Paternity leave, ranging from 2 days to 6 months, is paid in eight countries. Twenty-one countries provide supplementary leave (sometimes called child-rearing leave), allowing workers to extend the leave and to facilitate adoptions. Some countries are beginning to offer family leaves for attending to sick family members (Kamerman 2000:8).

Norway's and Sweden's parental-leave plans are the most extensive. Norwegian parents can combine a year of paid leave with an 80 percent wage replacement. Swedish parents can take a year at 80 percent of pay after a child's birth, another 90 days at a lower rate of pay, and 18 months of unpaid leave to be used until the child's eighth birthday (Gornick and Meyers 2001:4; Kamerman 2000).

In contrast to Western European countries, government-mandated parental leave in the United States is paltry. The 1993 **Family and Medical Leave Act** (FMLA) requires employers to hold the jobs of workers for up to 12 weeks after a pregnancy, adoption, or family medical emergency. Importantly, the law does not require paid leave, so it is of no help to parents who cannot afford unpaid leave. In the mid-1990s, 64 percent of employees who were eligible for a needed leave could not afford to take

EXHIBIT 7.5

Duration of Maternity Leave in Weeks and Percentage of Earnings Replaced

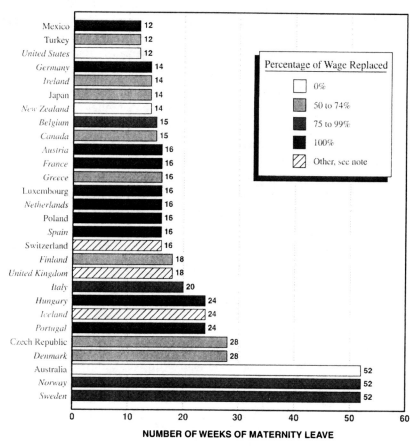

NUMBER OF WEEKS OF MATERNITY LEAVE

Source: Kamerman 2000.
Note: Italicized countries provide parental leave. The amount of earnings replaced in Switzerland varies by political district. Earnings in the United Kingdom are replaced at 90% for six weeks and at a flat rate for twelve weeks. Earnings in Iceland are replaced at a flat rate, plus a dependent benefit.

one (Commission on Family and Medical Leave 1996). The FMLA covers some employees in establishments that employ at least 50 employees who worked at least 1,250 hours in the past year. Because most U.S. workers work in small businesses, as we noted, about half of all U.S. workers are not covered (Commission on Family and Medical Leave 1996). Moreover, the act excludes same-sex domestic partners. Informal barriers, which we discuss later, can also discourage workers from taking the leave. In sum, the United States has taken its first step toward reducing work-family conflict. But it's a small step. The 12 weeks the U.S. law provides is shorter than in most European countries, it excludes more than half of U.S. workers, and its unpaid status sets it off from the European Commission countries, all of which provide income support (Ruhm and Teague 1997).

Maternity- and family-leave policies can help reduce work-family conflict, but they can also reinforce the existing sexual division of labor at home and at work. Traditional gender roles, men's higher pay, and informal workplace norms mean that wives, not husbands, usually take the leave. Although women's leaves under the FMLA tend to range from 29 to 84 days, men's leaves ranged from 1 to 7 days (Commission on Family and Medical Leave 1996, table 5F:271). In the western European welfare states, fathers took only 3 to 10 percent of paid parental leave days (Gornick and Meyers 2001). In an attempt to increase male participation in the double day, some Nordic countries have instituted a "use it or lose it" provision in their parental-leave law. Each parent has to use at least 1 month or else sacrifice 1 month of the total (Kamerman 2000). When the second author of this book taught a course in Sweden in the late 1990s, however, her students said that men often save their month of leave for skiing or hunting seasons.

Barriers to Taking Parental/Family Leave. Workplace culture can create informal barriers to workers taking advantage of unpaid and paid family leave policies. Two such barriers are the cues employers send workers that discourage them from taking leave and the refusal of some supervisors to allow leaves (Flack 1999). Despite some companies' nominal support for work-family balance, informal norms are often at variance with this sentiment. According to one commentator: "It's fine to have the kids' pictures on your desk—just don't let them cut into your billable hours" (Morris 1997). The corporate tendency to equate long work hours with commitment dooms many work-family programs to failure. Men who violate the social expectation that their careers are of foremost importance are likely to be sanctioned. One man described how his experienced male coworkers told him that taking paternity leave would ruin his image in the boss's eyes: "Almost to a man, the other guys said, 'No, no. You don't take paternity leave ...' " (Levine and Pittinsky 1997:30; see also Fried 1998). Workers' reluctance to take advantage of family leave or flexible scheduling is not surprising. Many companies equate "face time" with productivity and long work hours with commitment (Fried 1998; Hochschild 1997). Yet the assumption that physical presence in the workplace signifies productivity is questionable (Perlow 2000). According to the CEO of the Eli Lilly company, "Historically we looked at whose cars were in the parking lot at 7 p.m. and we made the assumption that they belonged to corporate heroes hard at work. In truth, some of those people were probably poorly organized or spending time on the wrong things" (Morris 1997).[8]

Supervisors' support of corporate work-family balance programs is critical for their success (Flack 1999). Lower-level supervisors can perpetuate an informal culture that is at odds with the formal policy because they have a great deal of discretionary power to determine access to leaves beyond the legally mandated limit (Fried 1998:54). One staff person in a company known for its family-friendly policies repeatedly ran into conflict with her supervisor about taking her child to weekly doctor appointments. The supervisor insisted that she find someone else—a grandmother, a sitter, someone—who could take the child because he feared that allowing flexibility would open the floodgates: "If I let Connie take Wednesday afternoons, I'll have Laura asking me for time off next. She's got three-year-old twins. . . . Rena['s] . . . dad just had a stroke. We have a *business* to run" (italics in original; Hochschild 1997:140). Supervisors' and managers' reluctance reflects the fact that their employers hold them accountable for their department's productivity. As a manager in a financial services corporation said of his firm's flextime policy, "The challenge . . . is the extra time it takes [me] to track productivity, schedule work, assign ad hoc assignments, et cetera. We [managers] already work overtime just to maintain our own workload, but add the [work-family] options, and you have more effort and more pressure" (Flack 1999).

Child Care Policies. We have seen that taking care of children makes it difficult for workers to combine paid work and family work, and the extent to which employers and governments alleviate this difficulty varies worldwide. The vast majority of European countries offer more comprehensive options than the United States does. High-quality care for preschoolers in Europe is considered a government responsibility, regardless of parents' employment status. In France, nursery schools for children over age 3 are free and open most of the working day; almost all 3- to 5-year-olds attend. Infant-care facilities and before- and after-school programs further facilitate French parents' ability to fully participate in the labor force (Folbre 2000). Belgium provides care for 95 percent of 3- to 5-year-olds, Italy provides care for 90 percent, and Denmark's figure is 85 percent. Sweden's policy requires local governments to make child care available to any working parent (Ellingsoeter 1999:42). The U.S. child care system—such as it is— involves both federal and state programs. The federal government offers a child- and dependent-care tax credit for all eligible workers, but most other programs are available only to low-income families and are not broad enough to serve all eligible children. At the federal level, 39 percent of the 1998 total child care spending of $11 billion went to the Head Start program and 28 percent went to block grants to states that target the funds to the poor. Neither program addresses the needs of working- and middle-class families (Folbre 2000).

In conclusion, nations' policies to provide family leave, guaranteed benefits for part-time work, and publicly funded child care have the capacity to help women and men meet both their work and family responsibilities. But if policy provisions, employers, or gender-role norms discourage men from taking leaves, these policies can reinforce women's subordinate position in the labor market and their relegation to the home. For example, whereas Germany's policy of providing a 3-year paid parental leave applies to mothers and fathers, men rarely take it, which means that the policy essentially pays women to leave the labor force, thus reinforcing the sexual division of labor.

Summary

In the first half of the twentieth century, when men were generally responsible for paid work and women for domestic work, both women and men who worked for pay were affected by work-family conflict. Both sexes lost out on family time. Women had the additional burden of trying to keep up with domestic tasks. The steady growth of women in the labor force in the second half of the century has meant that contemporary women and men experience this conflict in the form of time shortages, scheduling problems, and work-family spillover. Employers and governments have taken some initiative in providing benefits that help workers "juggle" these responsibilities, and such programs have been beneficial to women and men workers. Nevertheless, in the United States, to the extent that workers resolve work-family conflicts, they are resolved at the individual level.

The burden of this resolution falls more heavily on women than on men, because changes in the domestic division of labor have not kept pace with the sexes' converging labor force participation. In other words, the "revolution" in women's increased labor force participation has not been accompanied by a comparable "revolution" in men's increased participation in domestic labor (Hochschild 1989). Solutions in which women shoulder most or all of the burden of the double day preserve inequality at home and in the workplace.

There are reasons to predict that the domestic division of labor will become more equitable. Forty percent of married women want their husbands to do more housework, and men, in fact, are doing more than in the past. Men's contributions to routine housework have increased since 1965, and couples with men under age 30 share the domestic burden more equally (Robinson and Godbey 1999). Moreover, although the costs to women of the slow pace of change are quite high, so are the costs to men. Slow-to-die societal expectations for men limit their options both at home and at work. Some men acutely feel the disconnection that arises between themselves and their children when their jobs require them to sacrifice family time. One man described the shame he felt when he overheard his daughter's friend say to her, "I didn't think you had a daddy" (Morris 1997:9). Seven out of every 10 men aged 20 to 39 said that they would be willing to give up some pay in exchange for more time for their families (Radcliffe Public Policy Center 2000). Men as well as women are dissatisfied with work-family arrangements that place most of the responsibility for care work on women.

There are also grounds for optimism that employers may take on more responsibility for relieving work-family conflict. Increasing numbers of employers are implementing work-family balance programs or are experimenting with different ways of organizing work time, especially if these bring improvements to their "bottom line." One large employer instituted uninterrupted quiet times, for example, which freed up hours for personal use and also increased efficiency (Bailyn, Fletcher, and Kolb 1997). Some employers have recognized that work-family policies can improve profits. Of over 1,000 large companies nationwide that offered various forms of flexible work arrangements, three-quarters considered the arrangements to be cost-neutral or worth the cost (Galinsky and Bond 1998).

Whether government policy on family leave and child care assistance will become more proactive is unclear. Achieving passage of the FMLA was a long and difficult battle. Many policy analysts feared that its passage would draw hostile reactions from employers that might forestall future efforts. But most employers report satisfaction with it. They indicate minimal abuse by employees, do not have difficulty administering it, and are not unduly troubled by implementation costs (Commission on the Family and Medical Leave 1996). But genuinely reducing inequality at home and in the workplace will require more extensive public initiatives. If the Fair Labor Standards Act were amended to require overtime pay for professional and managerial employees, for example, we would almost certainly see shorter hours for these workers (Jacobs and Gerson 1998). Government-provided child care would ease work-family conflict for millions of workers. The income tax system could be made more progressive so that additional working hours yield less additional income, thus discouraging workers from acceding to lengthy workweeks. In the absence of such policies, or even public discussions of such ideas, however, most workers will continue to cope with work-family conflict on their own.

Notes

1. Men traditionally have been more able than women to fulfill the role of "ideal worker" because women shouldered the responsibility for meeting the demands of home and family (Williams 2000).
2. A work transfer from the marketplace to the domestic sphere has transpired over the past half century. Patients who once recuperated in hospitals, for example, are now discharged more quickly to be cared for by family members. Before World War II, people telephoned their neighborhood grocer, who delivered the groceries. Today, most consumers perform this labor (Glazer 1993).
3. Most elder-caregiving responsibility falls to wives and daughters: Almost three-quarters of unpaid white and black caregivers are female, as are two-thirds of Hispanics and half of Asians. Many of these (41 percent) have children of their own to care for (U.S. Bureau of Labor Statistics 1998).
4. The causal relationship between childlessness and career success is impossible to establish. Employers may confine women with children into certain jobs because they think women's families may interfere with job performance.
5. Not all part-time workers voluntarily opt for part-time work. In the years spanning 1998 to 2000, approximately 12 percent of women and 23 percent of men who worked part time could not find a full-time job (U.S. Census Bureau 1998, 1999, 2000a).
6. Part-time employment rates are lower in the United States than in many OECD countries (Dunn and Skaggs 1999:326), where guaranteed health care benefits rectify one part-time work problem. In the Netherlands, for example, the law requires that part-time workers be treated equally in regard to pay scales, access to benefits, and opportunities for promotion (Hayden 1999).

7. Failures in child care arrangements caused between 6 and 15 percent of mothers to lose time from work in the previous month during 1990 (Hofferth et al. 1991:346).

8. When such realizations lead employers to advise employees to "work smarter, not harder," they may be ignoring the possibility that the problem is the absolute amount of work rather than time management (Morris 1997).

References

Abelson, Reed. 2001. "Companies Turn to Grades, and Employees Go to Court." *New York Times,* March 19, pp. A1, A12.

Acker, Joan. 1990. "Hierarchies, Jobs, Bodies: A Theory of Gendered Organizations." *Gender & Society* 4:139–58.

———. 1999. "Gender and Organizations." Pp. 177-194 in *Handbook of the Sociology of Gender,* edited by J. Chafetz. New York: Kluwer Academic/Plenum.

AFL-CIO. 2001. *The Union Advantage: Unions Are Important for Women.* www.aflcio.org

Alfano, Peter. 1985. "Signs of Problems Amid the Progress." *New York Times,* December 14, pp. 25, 28.

American Council on Education and UCLA Higher Education Research Institute. 2001. "The American Freshman: National Norms for Fall 2000." *Chronicle of Higher Education,* Jan. 26. www.chronicle.com/stats/freshmen/htm

Amirault, Thomas. 1992. "Training to Qualify for Jobs and Improve Skills, 1991." *Monthly Labor Review* 115:31–36.

Amott, Teresa L. and Julie A. Matthaei. 1996. *Race, Gender, and Work: A Multicultural Economic History of Women in the United States, Revised Edition.* Boston: South End.

———. 2001. "Race, Class, Gender, and Women's Works." Pp. 234–242 in *Race, Class and Gender,* 4th ed., edited by M. L. Andersen and P. H. Collins. Belmont, CA: Wadsworth.

Anker, Richard. 1998. *Gender and Jobs: Sex Segregation of Occupations in the World.* Geneva: International Labour Organization.

Antill, John K., Jacqueline J. Goodnow, Graeme Russell, and Sandra Cotton. 1996. "The Influence of Parents and Family Context on Children's Involvement in Household Tasks." *Sex Roles* 34:215–236.

Aven, Forrest F., Barbara Parker, and Glenn McEvoy. 1993. "Gender and Attitudinal Commitment to Organization: A Meta-Analysis." *Journal of Business Research* 26:63–73.

Bachu, Amara and Martin O'Connell. 2000. "Fertility of American Women, June 1998." *Current Population Reports. U.S. Census Bureau.* (Sept.) Washington, DC: U.S. Government Printing Office.

Bailyn, Lotte, Joyce K. Fletcher, and Deborah Kolb. 1997. "Unexpected Connections: Considering Employees' Personal Lives Can Revitalize Your Business." *Sloan Management Review* 38 (Summer):11–19.

Baker, Ross K. 1977. "Women Finally Break Into Government Jobs in the 1800s, but the Pay Is Poor, the Jobs Menial, and Men Hostile." *Smithsonian* 8:82–91.

Ballard, Nancey. 1999. *Facing the Grail: Confronting the Cost of Work-Family Imbalance. Report of the Boston Bar Association on Professional Challenges and Family Needs.* Boston: Boston Bar Association.

Barko, Naomi. 2000. "The Other Gender Gap." *The American Prospect* 11 (15), June 19-July 3. www.prospect.org/print-friendly/print/V11/15/barkon.html.

Barnett, Rosalind C. and Janet S. Hyde. 2001. "Women, Men, Work, and Family." *American Psychologist* 56:781–796.

Barnett, Rosalind C. and Caryl Rivers. 1996. *She Works/He Works: How Two-Income Families Are Happier, Healthier, and Better Off*. New York: HarperCollins.

Barr, Donald A. and Elizabeth H. Boyle. 2001. "Gender and Professional Purity: Explaining Formal and Informal Work Rewards for Physicians in Estonia." *Gender & Society* 15:29–54.

Barrett, Frank J. 1996. "The Organizational Construction of Hegemonic Masculinity: The Case of the US Navy." *Gender, Work, and Organization* 3:129–142.

Baxandall, Rosalyn, Linda Gordon, and Susan Reverby. 1976. *America's Working Women*. New York: Vintage.

Becker, Gary S. 1971. *The Economics of Discrimination*. Chicago: University of Chicago Press.

———. 1985. "Human Capital, Effort, and the Sexual Division of Labor." *Journal of Labor Economics* 3 (Supplement): S33–58.

Beechey, Veronica and Tessa Perkins. 1987. *A Matter of Hours: Women, Part-Time Work and the Labour Market*. Cambridge, UK: Polity.

Beers, Thomas M. 2000. "Flexible Schedules and Shift Work: Replacing the '9-to-5' Workday?" *Monthly Labor Review* 123:33–40 (June).

Bell, Ella and Stella Nkomo. 2001. *Our Separate Ways: Black and White Women and the Struggle for Professional Identity*. Boston, MA: Harvard Business School Press.

Belzer, Michael H. 2000. *Sweatshops on Wheels: Winners and Losers in Trucking Deregulation*. New York: Oxford University Press.

Bennett, Claudette E. 1992. *The Asian and Pacific Islander Population in the United States: March 1991 and 1990*. U.S. Census Bureau, Current Population Survey, Population Characteristics. Washington, DC: U.S. Government Printing Office.

Berg, Maxine. 1985. *The Age of Manufactures: Industry, Innovation, and Work in Britain, 1700–1820*. Oxford, UK: Basil Blackwell.

Bergmann, Barbara R. 1986. *The Economic Emergence of Women*. New York: Basic Books.

Bergmann, Barbara R. and William Darity, Jr. 1981. "Social Relations, Productivity, and Employer Discrimination." *Monthly Labor Review* 104:47–49.

Berheide, Catherine W. 1992. "Women Still 'Stuck' in Low-Level Jobs." *Women in Public Services: A Bulletin for the Center for Women in Government* 3 (Fall).

Bianchi, Suzanne. 1995. "Changing Economic Roles of Women and Men." Pp. 107–155 in *State of the Union: America in the 1990s*, vol. 1, edited by R. Farley. New York: Russell Sage.

———. 2000. "Maternal Employment and Time with Children: Dramatic Change or Surprising Continuity?" *Demography* 37:401–414.

Bianchi, Suzanne, Melissa Milkie, Liana Sayer, and John P. Robinson. 2000. "Is Anyone Doing the Housework?: Trends in the Gender Division of Household Labor." *Social Forces* 79:191–228.

Bianchi, Suzanne and John P. Robinson. 2001. Unpublished data.

Bielby, Denise D. and William T. Bielby. 1988. "She Works Hard for the Money: Household Responsibilities and the Allocation of Work Effort." *American Journal of Sociology* 93:1031–59.

———. 1992. "Cumulative Versus Continuous Disadvantage in an Unstructured Labor Market." *Work and Occupations* 19:366–87.

———. 1996. "Women and Men in Film: Gender Inequality Among Writers in a Culture Industry." *Gender & Society* 10:248–270.

Bielby, William T. 1998. "Firm Commitments." *Contemporary Sociology* 27:32–34.

———. 2000. "Minimizing Workplace Gender and Racial Bias." *Contemporary Sociology* 29:120–29.

Bielby, William T. and James N. Baron. 1986. "Men and Women at Work: Sex Segregation and Statistical Discrimination." *American Journal of Sociology* 91:759–99.

Bielby, William T. and Denise D. Bielby. 2002. "Telling Stories About Gender and Effort: Social Science Narratives About Who Works Hard for the Money." Pp. 193–217 in *New Directions in Economic Sociology*, edited by M. F. Guillen, R. Collins, P. England, and M. Meyer. New York: Russell Sage.

Bielby, William T., Denise D. Bielby, Matt Huffman, and Steven Valasco. 1995. "Who Works Hard for the Money? 'Efficiency Wages,' Work Organization, and Gender Differences in the Allocation of Effort." Paper presented at the Annual Meeting of the American Sociological Association. Washington, DC.

Bird, Chloe. 1999. "Gender, Household Labor, and Psychological Distress: The Impact of the Amount and Division of Housework." *Journal of Health and Social Behavior* 40:32–45.

Blackwelder, Julia K., 1997. *Now Hiring: The Feminization of Work in the United States, 1900–1995*. College Station, TX: Texas A&M University Press.

Blair, Sampson Lee. 1992. "Children's Participation in Household Labor: Child Socialization Versus the Need for Household Labor." *Journal of Youth and Adolescence* 21:241–58.

Blair, Sampson Lee and Daniel T. Lichter. 1991. "Measuring the Division of Household Labor: Gender Segregation of Housework Among American Couples." *Journal of Family Issues* 12:91–113.

Blau, David M. and Alison P. Hagy. 1998. "The Demand for Quality in Child Care." *Journal of Political Economy* 106:104–146.

Blau, Francine D. and Marianne A. Ferber. 1992. *The Economics of Women, Men, and Work*. Upper Saddle River, NJ: Prentice Hall.

Blau, Francine D., Marianne A. Ferber, and Anne E. Winkler. 1998. *The Economics of Women, Men, and Work*. Upper Saddle River, NJ: Prentice Hall.

Blau, Francine D. and Lawrence M. Kahn. 1997. "Swimming Upstream: Trends in the Gender Wage Differential in the 1980s." *Journal of Labor Economics*, 15:1, pt. 1:1–42.

———. 2000. "Gender Differences in Pay." *Working Paper 7732*. Cambridge, MA: National Bureau of Economic Research. www.nber.org/papers/w7732.

Blauner, Robert. 1972. *Racial Oppression in America*. New York: Harper and Row.

Bloom, David E. and Adi Brender. 1993. "Labour and the Emerging World Economy." *Population Bulletin*, October.

Bodenhausen, Galen V. and C. Neil Macrae. 1996. "The Self Regulation of Intergroup Perception; Mechanisms and Consequences of Stereotype Suppression." Pp. 227–53 in *Stereotypes and Stereotyping*, edited by C. N. Macrae, C. Stangor, and M. Hewstone. New York: Guilford.

Bogenschneider, Karen. 2000. "Has Family Policy Come of Age? A Decade Review of the State of U.S. Family Policy in the 1990s." *Journal of Marriage and the Family* 62:1136–59.

Bond, James T., Ellen Galinsky, and Jennifer E. Swanberg. 1998. *The 1997 National Study of the Changing Workforce.* New York: Families and Work Institute.

Bose, Christine E. 2001. *Women in 1900: Gateway to the Political Economy of the 20th Century.* Philadelphia: Temple University Press.

Braddock, Jomills Henry and James M. McPartland. 1987. "How Minorities Continue to Be Excluded from Equal Employment Opportunities: Research on Labor Market and Institutional Barriers." *Journal of Social Issues* 43:5–39.

Bradwell v. Illinois. 1873. 83 U.S. (16 Wall.) 130.

Brewer, Marilynn B. 1997. "The Social Psychology of Intergroup Relations: Can Research Inform Practice?" *Journal of Social Issues* 53:197–211.

Brewer, Marilynn B. and Rupert J. Brown. 1998. "Intergroup Relations." Pp. 554–94 in *Handbook of Social Psychology*, edited by D. T. Gilbert, S. T. Fiske, and G. Lindzey. New York: McGraw-Hill.

Brewster, Karin L. and Irene Padavic. 2000. "Change in Gender Ideology, 1977–1996: The Contributions of Intracohort Change and Population Turnover." *Journal of Marriage and the Family* 62:477–87.

———. 2002. "No More Kin Care? Changes in Black Mothers' Reliance on Relatives for Childcare: 1977–1994." *Gender & Society* 16(4):546–63.

Brines, Julie. 1994. "Economic Dependency, Gender, and the Division of Labor at Home." *American Journal of Sociology* 100:652–88.

Britton, Dana. 1997. "Gendered Organizational Logic: Policy and Practice in Men's and Women's Prisons." *Gender & Society* 11:796–818.

———. 2000. "The Epistemology of the Gendered Organization." *Gender & Society* 14:418–34.

———. 2003. *At Work in the Iron Cage: The Prison as Gendered Organization.* New York: New York University Press.

Bronfenbrenner, Kate and Tom Juravich. 1998. "It Takes More Than House Calls: Organizing to Win With a Comprehensive Union-Building Strategy." Pp. 19–36 in *Organizing to Win: New Research on Union Strategies*, edited by K. Bronfenbrenner, S. Friedman, R. W. Hurd, R. A. Oswald, and R. L. Seeber. Ithaca, NY: ILR.

Browne, Irene and Ivy Kennelly. 1999. "Stereotypes and Realities: Images of Black Women in the Labor Market." Pp. 302–326 in *Latinas and African American Women in the Labor Markets*, edited by I. Browne. New York: Russell Sage.

Budig, Michelle and Paula England. 2001. "The Wage Penalty for Motherhood." *American Sociological Review* 66:204–25.

Burns, John F. and Steve Levine. 1996. "How Afghans' Stern Rulers Took Hold." *New York Times*, December 31.

Burstein, Paul. 1991. "'Reverse Discrimination' Cases in the Federal Courts: Mobilization by a Countermovement." *Sociological Quarterly* 32:511–28.

Bylsma, Wayne H. and Brenda Major. 1992. "Two Routes to Eliminating Gender Differences in Personal Entitlement." *Psychology of Women Quarterly* 16:193–200.

Callahan, Colleen R. 1992. "Dressed for Work: Women's Clothing on the Job, 1900–1990." *Labor's Heritage* 4:28–49.

Camp, Tracy, Keith Miller, and Vanessa Davies. 2000. "The Incredible Shrinking Pipeline Unlikely to Reverse." www.mines.edu/fs_home/tcamp/new-study/new-study.html.

Capizzano, Jeffrey, Kathryn Tout, and Gina Adams. 2000. *Childcare Patterns of School-Age Children With Employed Mothers.* Washington, DC: Urban Institute. http://newfederalism.urban.org/pdf/occa41.pdf

Carney, Judith and Michael Watts. 1991. "Disciplining Women? Rice, Mechanization, and the Evolution of Mandinka Gender Relations in Senegambia." *Signs* 16:651–81.

Carrington, William J. and Kenneth R. Troske. 1994. "Gender Segregation in Small Firms." *Journal of Human Resources* 30:503–33.

———. 1998. "Sex Segregation in U.S. Manufacturing." *Industrial and Labor Relations Review* 51:445–64.

Cassirer, Naomi and Barbara F. Reskin. 2000. "High Hopes: Organizational Location, Employment Experiences, and Women's and Men's Promotion Aspirations." *Work and Occupations* 27:438–63.

Catalyst. 1996. *Women in Corporate Leadership: Progress and Prospects.* New York: Catalyst.

———. 1998. *Catalyst Census of Women Corporate Offices and Top Earners as of March 31, 1998.* New York: Catalyst.

———. 1999. *Catalyst Census of Women Board Directors of the Fortune 1000.* New York: Catalyst.

———. 2000a. *2000 Catalyst Census of Women Corporate Officers and Top Earners.* New York: Catalyst. www.catalystwomen.org/press/releases/release111300.html.

———. 2000b. *Passport to Opportunity: U.S. Women in Global Business.* New York: Catalyst. http://www.catalystwomen.org/press/passportmediakit/factsglobal.html.

———. 2001. *Women in Law: Making the Case.* New York: Catalyst. www.catalystwomen.org/press/factsheets/factslaw.html.

Center for Women in Government. 1999. *Appointed Policy Makers in State Government.* www.cwig.albany.edu.

Chen, Martha. 2000. *The Invisible Workforce: Women in the Informal Economy.* Cambridge, MA: Radcliffe Public Policy Center.

Chenut, Helen Harden. 1996. "The Gendering of Skill as Historical Process: The Case of French Knitters in Industrial Troyes, 1880–1939." Pp. 77–110 in *Gender and Class in Modern Europe,* edited by L. L. Frader and S. O. Rose. Ithaca, NY: Cornell University Press.

Chetkovich, Carol. 1997. *Real Heat: Gender and Race in the Urban Fire Service.* New York: Routledge.

Clark, Anna. 1995. *The Struggle for the Breeches: Gender and the Making of the British Working Class.* Berkeley: University of California Press.

Clarkberg, Marin. 1999. "The Price of Partnering: The Role of Economic Well-Being in Young Adults' First Union Experiences." *Social Forces* 77:945–68.

Clement, Wallace and John Myles. 1994. *Relations of Ruling: Class and Gender in Postindustrial Societies.* Montreal: McGill-Queens University Press.

Cobb-Clark, Deborah and Yvonne Dunlop. 1999. "The Role of Gender in Job Promotions." *Monthly Labor Review* 122:32–38.

Cobble, Dorothy Sue. 1996. "The Prospects for Unionism in a Service Society." Pp. 333–58 in *Working in the Service Society,* edited by C. L. MacDonald and C. Sirianni. Philadelphia: Temple University Press.

Cohen, Isaac. 1985. "Workers' Control in the Cotton Industry: A Comparative Study of British and American Mule Spinning." *Labor History* 26:53–85.

Cohen, Lisa E., Joseph P. Broschak, and Heather A. Haveman. 1998. "And Then There Were More? The Effects of Organizational Sex Composition on Hiring and Promotion." *American Sociological Review* 64:711–27.

Cohen, Theodore F. 1993. "What Do Fathers Provide? Reconsidering the Economic and Nurturant Dimensions of Men as Parents." Pp. 1–23 in *Men, Work, and Family,* edited by Jane Hood. Newbury Park, CA: Sage.

Cohn, Samuel. 1985. *The Process of Occupational Sex-Typing: The Feminization of Clerical Labor in Great Britain.* Philadelphia: Temple University Press.

———. 1996. "Occupational Sex-Typing." Pp. 87–89 in *Women and Work: A Handbook,* edited by P. J. Dubeck and K. Borman. New York: Garland.

———. 2000. *Race, Gender, and Discrimination at Work.* Boulder, CO: Westview.

Collins, Randall. 1974. *Conflict Sociology.* New York: Academic Press.

Coltrane, Scott. 1996. *Family Man: Fatherhood, Housework, and Gender Equity.* New York: Oxford University Press.

———. 2000. "Research on Household Labor: Modeling and Measuring the Social Embeddedness of Routine Family Work." *Journal of Marriage and the Family* 62:1208–33.

Commission on Family and Medical Leave. 1996. *A Workable Balance: Report to Congress on Family and Medical Leave Policies.* www.dol.gov/dol/esa/public/regs/compliance/whd/fmla/family.htm

Cooper, Patricia. 1991. "The Faces of Gender: Sex Segregation and Work Relations at Philco, 1928–1938." Pp. 320–50 in *Work Engendered,* edited by A. Baron. Ithaca: New York State School of Industrial and Labor Relations, Cornell University.

Corcoran, Mary. 1999. "The Economic Progress of African American Women." Pp. 35–60 in *Latinas and African American Women in the Labor Market,* edited by I. Browne. New York: Russell Sage.

Corcoran, Mary, Colleen M. Heflin, and Belinda L. Reyes. 1999. "The Economic Progress of Mexican and Puerto Rican Women." Pp. 105–138 in *Latinas and African American Women in the Labor Market,* edited by I. Browne. New York: Russell Sage.

Cotter, David A., JoAnn DeFiore, Joan M. Hermsen, Brenda M. Kowalewski, and Reeve Vanneman. 1997. "All Women Benefit: The Macro-Level Effect of

Occupational Integration on Gender Earning Equality." *American Sociological Review* 62:714–34.

Crompton, Rosemary and Fiona Harris. 1999. "Attitudes, Women's Employment, and the Changing Domestic Division of Labour: A Cross-National Analysis." Pp. 105–127 in *Restructuring Gender Relations and Employment: The Decline of the Male Breadwinner,* edited by R. Crompton. New York: Oxford University Press.

Davidoff, Leonore and Catherine Hall. 1987. *Family Fortunes.* London: Hutchinson.

———. 1998. "'The Hidden Investment': Women and the Enterprise." Pp. 239–93 in *Women's Work: The English Experience 1650–1914,* edited by P. Sharpe. New York: Arnold.

Davies, Margery W. 1982. *Woman's Place Is at the Typewriter: Office Work and Office Workers, 1870–1930.* Philadelphia: Temple University Press.

Davis, James A., Tom W. Smith, and Peter V. Marsden. 2000. *General Social Surveys, 1972–2000* [machine-readable data file]. NORC ed. Chicago: National Opinion Research Center, producer. Storrs, CT: The Roper Center for Public Opinion Research. http://csa.berkeley.edu:7502/archive.htm.

DeAngelis, Catherine D. 2000. "Women in Academic Medicine: New Insights, Same Sad News." *New England Journal of Medicine* 342 (6): Feb. 10.

Diaz v. Pan American World Airways, Inc. 1971. 442F. 2d 385 (5th Cir.), cert. den. 404 U.S. 950.

Domosh, Mona and Joni Seager. 2001. *Putting Women in Place: Feminist Geographers Make Sense of the World.* New York: Guilford.

Dublin, Thomas. 1993. *Farm to Factory: Women's Letters, 1830–1860,* 2d ed. New York: Columbia University Press.

Dunlop, John E. and Victoria A. Velkoff. 1999. "Women and the Economy in India." Bureau of the Census. Economics and Statistics Administration. (January). Washington, DC: U.S. Government Printing Office.

Dunn, Dana and Sheryl Skaggs. 1999. "Gender and Paid Work in Industrial Nations." Pp. 321–39 in *Handbook of the Sociology of Gender,* edited by J. S. Chafetz. New York: Kluwer Academic/Plenum.

Earle, Alice Morse. 1896. *Colonial Dames and Good Wives.* Boston: Houghton Mifflin.

Eaton, Susan C. 1996. "'The Customer Is Always Interesting': Unionized Harvard Clericals Renegotiate Work Relationships." Pp. 333–58 in *Working in the Service Society,* edited by C. L. MacDonald and C. Sirianni. Philadelphia: Temple University Press.

EEOC v. Sears, Roebuck & Co. 1988. 628F. Supp. 1264 (N.D. Ill. 1986), affirmed 839 F. 2d 302 (7th Cir.).

Eichenwald, Kurt. 2000. *The Informant.* New York: Random House Inc. Excerpt found at www.thislife.org/pages/trax/text/adm2.html.

Eisenberg, Susan. 1998. *We'll Call You if We Need You.* Ithaca, NY: ILR.

Eisenhart, Margaret. 1996. "Contemporary College Women's Career Plans." Pp. 232–35 in *Women and Work: A Handbook,* edited by P. J. Dubeck and K. Borman. New York: Garland.

Ellingsoeter, Anne Lise. 1999. "Dual Breadwinners Between State and Market."
Pp. 40–59 in *Restructuring Gender Relations and Employment: The Decline of the Male Breadwinner,* edited by R. Crompton. New York: Oxford University Press.

Elson, Diane. 2000. *Progress of the World's Women 2000.* New York: United Nations Development Fund for Women. www.undp.org/unifem/progressww/2000/index.html.

Ely, Robin J. 1995. "The Power in Demography: Women's Social Construction of Gender Identity at Work." *Academy of Management Journal* 38:589–634.

Ely, Robin J. and Debra E. Meyerson. 2000. "Theories of Gender in Organizations: A New Approach to Organizational Analysis and Change." *Research in Organizational Behavior* 22:105–153.

Employee Relocation Council. 2000. *The Family Issues Research Report.* Washington, DC: The Employee Relocation Council.

England, Paula. 1996. "Occupational Skill, Gender, and Earnings." Pp. 68–71 in *Women and Work: A Handbook,* edited by P. J. Dubeck and K. Borman, New York: Garland.

England, Paula, Marilyn Chassie, and Linda McCormack. 1982. "Skill Demands and Earnings in Female and Male Occupations." *Sociology and Social Research* 66:147–68.

England, Paula, Lori L. Reid, and Barbara S. Kilbourne. 1996. "The Effect of the Sex Composition of Jobs on the Starting Wages in an Organization: Findings From the NLSY." *Demography* 33:511–21.

Enloe, Cynthia. 2000. "Climates and 'Cultures': What Feminists See When They Look at Women's Lives Inside the State." Talk at Radcliffe Institute for Advanced Study. Nov. 29.

Epstein, Cynthia F. 1993. *Women in Law.* Urbana: University of Illinois Press.

Epstein, Cynthia F., Carroll Seron, Bonnie Oglensky, and Robert Saute. 1999. *The Part-Time Paradox: Time Norms, Professional Lives, Family, and Gender.* New York: Routledge.

Erickson, Bonnie H., Patricia Albanese, and Slobodan Drakulic. 2000. "Gender on a Jagged Edge: The Security Industry, Its Clients, and the Reproduction and Revision of Gender." *Work and Occupations* 27:294–318.

Ettner, Susan L. 1995. "The Impact of 'Parent Care' on Female Labor Supply Decisions." *Demography* 32:63–80.

European Industrial Relations Observatory. 1999. "Working Time Developments—Annual Update 1999." *European Foundation for the Improvement of Living and Working Conditions.* www.eiro.eurofound.ie/2000/02/updates.html.

Farkas, George, Paula England, Keven Vicknair, and Barbara S. Kilbourne. 1997. "Cognitive Skill, Skill Demands of Jobs, and Earnings Among Young European American, African American, and Mexican American Workers." *Social Forces* 75:913–38.

Farley, Reynolds. 1984. *Blacks and Whites: Narrowing the Gap.* Cambridge, MA: Harvard University Press.

Fernandez-Kelly, Maria P. 1983. *For We Are Sold, I and My People: Women and Industry in Mexico's Frontier.* Albany, NY: SUNY Press.

Fink, Deborah. 1998. *Cutting into the Meatpacking Line: Workers and Change in the Rural Midwest*. Chapel Hill: University of North Carolina Press.

Fix, Janet L. 2001. "Labor's Changing Face; Women and the Union Issues They Care About Are on the Move." *The San Diego Union-Tribune*, May 7, p. D1.

Flack, M. Ellen. 1999. *Working the Family In: A Case Study of the Determinants of Employees' Access to and Use of Alternative Work Arrangements, and Their Home to Work Spillover*. Columbus, OH: Unpublished doctoral dissertation, The Ohio State University.

Folbre, Nancy. 1991. "The Unproductive Housewife: Her Evolution in Nineteenth-Century Economic Thought." *Signs* 16:463–84.

———. 2000. "Conditions Are Right for a Bold Initiative." *The Nation* 271 (July 3).

Freeman, Carol. 2000. *High Tech and High Heels in the Global Economy: Women, Work, and Pink-Collar Identities in the Caribbean*. Durham, NC: Duke University Press.

Fried, Mindy. 1998. *Taking Time: Parental Leave Policy and Corporate Culture*. Philadelphia: Temple University Press.

Fullerton, Howard N. 1999. "Labor Force Projections to 2008: Steady Growth and Changing Composition." *Monthly Labor Review* 122(11):19–32.

Galinsky, Ellen and James T. Bond. 1998. *The 1998 Business Work-Life Study: A Sourcebook*. New York: Families and Work Institute.

Galinsky, Ellen, Dana E. Friedman, and Carol A. Hernandez. 1991. *The Corporate Reference Guide to Work-Family Programs*. New York: Families and Work Institute.

Garey, Anita. 1999. *Weaving Work and Motherhood*. Philadelphia: Temple University Press.

Gerstel, Naomi and Dan Clawson. 2001. "Unions' Responses to Family Concerns." *Social Problems* 48:277–97.

Glass, Jennifer. 1990. "The Impact of Occupational Segregation on Working Conditions." *Social Forces* 68:779–96.

———. 2000. "Envisioning the Integration of Family and Work: Toward a Kinder, Gentler Workplace." *Contemporary Sociology* 29:129–43.

Glazer, Nona Y. 1993. *Women's Paid and Unpaid Labor: The Work Transfer in Health Care and Retailing*. Philadelphia: Temple University Press.

Glenn, Evelyn N. 1996. "From Servitude to Service Work: Historical Continuities in the Racial Division of Paid Reproductive Labor." Pp. 115–56 in *Working in the Service Society*, edited by C. MacDonald and C. Sirianni. Philadelphia: Temple University Press.

Goldin, Claudia. 1990. *Understanding the Gender Gap*. New York: Oxford University Press.

———. 1995. "Career and Family: College Women Look to the Past." *Working Paper 5188*. Cambridge, MA: National Bureau of Economic Research.

Goode, William J. 1982. "Why Men Resist." Pp. 131–47 in *Rethinking the Family*, edited by B. Thorne and M. Yalom. New York: Longman.

Goozner, Merrill. 1991. "$3 Million Sex-Bias Accord at Marriott." *Chicago Tribune*, March 6, sec. 3, p. 3.

Gorman, Elizabeth H. 2001. *Gender and Organizational Selection Decisions: Evidence from Law Firms*. Cambridge, MA: Unpublished doctoral dissertation, Harvard University.

Gornick, Janet C. and Marcia K. Meyers. 2001. "Support for Working Families." *American Prospect* 12 (Jan. 1–15): 1–14.

Gould, Robert E. 1974. "Measuring Masculinity by the Size of a Paycheck." In *Men and Masculinity*, edited by J. Pleck and J. Sawyer. Englewood Cliffs, NJ: Prentice Hall.

Graham, Hugh D. 1990. *The Civil Rights Era: Origins and Development of National Policy, 1960–1972*. New York: Oxford University Press.

Grant, Linda and Kathryn B. Ward. 1996. "Women in Academia." Pp. 165–67 in *Women and Work: A Reader*, edited by P. J. Dubeck and K. Borman. New Brunswick, NJ: Rutgers University Press.

Gray, Jane. 1996. "Gender and Uneven Working-Class Formation in the Irish Linen Industry." Pp. 37–56 in *Gender and Class in Modern Europe*, edited by L. L. Frader and S. O. Rose. Ithaca, NY: Cornell University Press.

Gross, Edward. 1968. "Plus Ca Change: The Sexual Segregation of Occupations Over Time." *Social Problems* 16:198–208.

Gupta, Sanjiv. 1999. "The Effects of Transitions in Marital Status on Men's Performance of Housework." *Journal of Marriage and Family* 61:700–711.

Gutek, Barbara. 1988. "Women in Clerical Work." Pp. 225–40 in *Women Working: Theory and Facts in Perspective*, edited by A. H. Stromberg and S. Harkess. Mountain View, CA: Mayfield.

Hanawalt, Barbara A.. 1986. "Peasant Women's Contribution to the Home Economy in Late Medieval England." Pp. 3–19 in *Women and Work in Preindustrial Europe*, edited by B. A. Hanawalt. Bloomington: Indiana University Press.

Haney-Lopez, Ian. 1996. *White by Law: The Legal Construction of Race*. New York: New York University Press.

Hargens, Lowell and J. Scott Long. 2002. "Demographic Inertia and Women's Representation Among Faculty in Higher Education." *Journal of Higher Education* 73 (July/August): 494–517.

Harris Poll. 1998. "Child Care: People's Chief Concerns." (Jan.) www.publicagenda.org.

Harrison, Roderick J. and Claudette E. Bennett. 1995. "Racial and Ethnic Diversity." Pp. 141–210 in *State of the Union: America in the 1990s*, vol. 2, edited by R. Farley. New York: Russell Sage.

Hayden, Anders. 1999. "Taking Up the Challenge: Europe's New Movement for Reduced Work Time." www.web.net/32hours/takingup.htm.

Hayghe, Howard V. 1990. "Family Members in the Work Force." *Monthly Labor Review* 113:14–19.

Headlam, Bruce. 2000. "Barbie PC: Fashion Over Logic." *New York Times*, January 20, p. G4.

Hecker, Daniel E. 1998. "Earnings of College Graduates: Women Compared with Men." *Monthly Labor Review* 121:62–71.

Heilman, Madeline E. 1995. "Sex Stereotypes and Effects in the Workplace: What We Know and What We Don't Know." *Journal of Social and Behavioral Sciences* 10(6):3–26.

Heim v. State of Utah. 8 F 3d. 1541 (10th Cir. 1993).

Herlihy, David. 1990. *Opera Muliebria: Women and Work in Medieval Europe.* Philadelphia: Temple University Press.

Hesse-Biber, Sharlene and Gregg L. Carter. 2000. *Working Women in America: Split Dreams.* New York: Oxford University Press.

Hewitt Associates, LLC. 2000. "More Employers Offer Work/Life Benefits to Gain Edge in Tight Labor Market." Lincolnshire, IL: Hewitt Associates LLC. www.hewitt.com/hewitt/resource/newsroom/pressre1/2000/05-04-00.htm.

Hewlett, Sylvia Ann and Cornel West. 1998. *The War Against Parents: What We Can Do for America's Beleaguered Moms and Dads.* Boston: Houghton Mifflin.

Hiestand, Michael. 1999. "Serving Notice of Dissatisfaction: Female Pros Volley for Equal Money." *USA Today,* June 4.

Hindon, Stan. 2001. "Raw Deal for Women? Effects of Privatizing Social Security Fiercely Disputed." *American Association for Retired Persons Bulletin* 42 (Sept.):18–21.

Hochschild, Arlie with Anne Machung. 1989. *The Second Shift.* New York: Viking.

Hochschild, Arlie. 1997. *The Time Bind: When Work Becomes Home and Home Becomes Work.* New York: Henry Holt.

Hofferth, Sandra. 1999. "Child Care, Maternal Employment, and Public Policy." *The Annals of the American Academy of Political and Social Science* 563:20–38.

Hofferth, Sandra L., April Brayfield, Sharon Deich, and Pamela Holcomb. 1991. *National Child Care Survey, 1990.* Washington, DC: The Urban Institute.

Hogan, David. 1996. "Immigrant Women in the U.S. and Work." Pp. 41–44 in *Women and Work: A Reader,* edited by P. J. Dubeck and K. Borman. New York: Garland.

Hooks, Janet. 1947. *Women's Occupations Through Seven Decades.* Women's Bureau Bulletin No. 218. U.S. Department of Labor. Washington, DC: U.S. Government Printing Office.

Howell, Martha C. 1986. "Women, the Family Economy, and Market Production." Pp. 198–222 in *Women and Work in Pre-Industrial Europe,* edited by B. Hanawalt. Bloomington: Indiana University Press.

Hull, Kathleen and Robert Nelson. 2000. "Assimilation, Choice, or Constraint? Testing Theories of Gender Differences in the Careers of Lawyers." *Social Forces* 79:229–64.

Hyde, Janet S., Marilyn J. Essex, and F. Horton. 1993. "Fathers and Parental Leave: Attitudes and Experiences." *Journal of Family Issues* 14:616–41.

Hymowitz, Carol and Rachel E. Silverman. 2001. "Can Workplace Stress Get Worse?" *Wall Street Journal,* Jan. 16, pp. B1, B4.

Institute for Women's Policy Research. 2000. *The Status of Women in the States 2000.* IWPR: Washington D.C. www.iwpr.org/states/index.html

International Labour Organization. 1998. *Breaking through the Glass Ceiling: Women in Management.* Report for discussion at the Tripartite Meeting. Geneva: ILO.

———. 2001. "Forced Labour, Human Trafficking, Slavery Haunt Us Still." *World of Work.* No 39:4-6. Geneva: ILO.

Intracorp. 1998. *Too Seldom Is Heard an Encouraging Word: A Study of Work/Life Programs and Corporate Culture's Impact on Utilization.* Philadelphia: Intracorp.

Ireland, Patricia. 2001. "Talk of the Nation" interview with Juan Williams, National Public Radio. (July 3).

Ishii-Kuntz, Masako and Scott Coltrane. 1992. "Predicting the Sharing of Household Labor: Are Parenting and Housework Distinct?" *Sociological Perspectives* 35:629–47.

Jackman, Mary R. 1994. *The Velvet Glove: Paternalism and Conflict in Gender, Class, and Race Relations.* Berkeley: University of California Press.

Jacobs, Jerry A. 1989. "Long-Term Trends in Occupational Segregation by Sex." *American Journal of Sociology* 95:160–73.

———. 1992. "Women's Entry Into Management: Trends in Earnings, Authority, Values, and Attitudes Among Salaried Managers." *Administrative Science Quarterly* 37:282–301.

———. 1995. "Gender and Academic Specialties: Trends Among Recipients of College Degrees in the 1980s." *Sociology of Education* 68:81–98.

———. 1996a. "Gender Inequality and Higher Education." *Annual Review of Sociology* 22:153–85.

———. 1996b. "The Sex Segregation of Occupations: Structural Approaches." Pp. 114–16 in *Women and Work: A Reader,* edited by P. J. Dubeck and K. Borman. New Brunswick, NJ: Rutgers University Press.

———. 1999. "The Sex Segregation of Occupations: Prospects for the 21st Century." Pp. 125–41 in *Handbook of Gender and Work,* edited by G. N. Powell. Thousand Oaks, CA: Sage.

———. 2003. "Detours on the Road to Equality: Women, Work, and Higher Education." *Contexts* 2(1):32–41. Washington, DC: American Sociological Association.

Jacobs, Jerry A. and Kathleen Gerson. 1998. "Who Are the Overworked Americans?" *Review of Social Economy* 56:442–59.

———. 2001. "Overworked Individuals or Overworked Families? Explaining Trends in Work, Leisure, and Family Time." *Work and Occupations* 28:40–63.

Jacobs, Jerry A. and Ronnie J. Steinberg. 1990. "Compensating Differentials and the Male-Female Wage Gap: Evidence From the New York State Comparable Worth Study." *Social Forces* 69:439–68.

———. 1995. "Further Evidence on Compensating Differentials and the Gender Gap in Wages." Pp. 93–124 in *Gender Inequality at Work,* edited by J. A. Jacobs. Thousand Oaks, CA: Sage.

Jacobsen, Joyce P. and Laurence M. Levin. 1995. "Effects of Intermittent Labor Force Attachment on Women's Earnings." *Monthly Labor Review* 118:4–19.

Joekes, Susan and Ann Weston. 1994. *Women and the New Trade Agenda.* New York: United Nations, UNIFEM.

Johnston, David. 1993. "FBI Agent to Quit Over Her Treatment in Sexual Harassment Case." *New York Times,* October 11, p. A7.

Jones, Jacquelyn. 1985. *Labor of Love, Labor of Sorrow.* New York: Vintage.

———. 1998. *American Work: Four Centuries of Black and White Labor.* New York: Norton.

Jurik, Nancy C. 1998. "Getting Away and Getting By: The Experiences of Self-Employed Homeworkers." *Work and Occupations* 25:7–35.

Juster, F. Thomas and Frank P. Stafford. 1991. "The Allocation of Time: Empirical Findings, Behavioral Models, and Problems of Measurement." *Journal of Economic Literature* 29:471–522.

Kalleberg, Arne and Barbara F. Reskin. 1995. "Gender Differences in Promotion in the United States and Norway." *Research in Social Stratification and Mobility* 14:237–264.

Kalleberg, Arne L., Barbara F. Reskin, and Ken Hudson. 2000. "Bad Jobs in America: Standard and Nonstandard Employment Relations and Job Quality in the United States." *American Sociological Review* 65:256–78.

Kamerman, Sheila B. 2000. "Parental Leave Policies: An Essential Ingredient in Early Childhood Education and Care Policies." *Social Policy Report* 19:3–15.

Kanter, Rosabeth Moss. 1977. *Men and Women of the Corporation*. New York: Basic Books.

———. 1983. "Women Managers: Moving Up in a High Tech Society." Pp. 21–36 in *The Woman in Management: Career and Family Issues*, edited by J. Farley. Ithaca: New York State School of Industrial and Labor Relations, Cornell University.

Kaufman, Gayle and Peter Uhlenberg. 2000. "The Influence of Parenthood on the Work Effort of Married Men and Women." *Social Forces* 78:931–49.

Kay, Fiona M. and John Hagan. 1999. "Cultivating Clients in the Competition for Partnership: Gender and the Organizational Restructuring of Law Firms in the 1990s." *Law & Society Review* 33:517–55.

Kidwell, Claudia Brush and Valerie Steele, eds. 1989. *Men and Women: Dressing the Part*. Washington, DC: Smithsonian Institution.

Kilbourne, Barbara, Paula England, and Kurt Beron. 1994. "Effects of Individual, Occupational, and Industrial Characteristics on Earnings: Intersections of Race and Gender." *Social Forces* 72:1149–76.

Kilbourne, Barbara, Paula England, George Farkas, Kurt Beron, and Dorothea Weir. 1994. "Returns to Skills, Compensating Differentials, and Gender Bias: Effects of Occupational Characteristics on the Wages of White Women and Men." *American Journal of Sociology* 100:689–719.

Kim, Marlene. 1989. "Gender Bias in Compensation Structures: A Case Study of Its Historical Basis and Persistence." *Journal of Social Issues* 45:39–50.

Kim, T. H. and K. H. Kim. 1995. "Industrial Restructuring in Korea and Its Consequences for Women Workers." Pp. 106–155 in *Silk and Steel: Asian Women Workers Confront Challenges of Industrial Restructuring*, edited by H. O'Sullivan. Hong Kong: Committee of Asian Women.

Kimball, Gayle. 1999. *21st Century Families*. Chico, CA: Equality.

Kimmel, Michael. 2000. *The Gendered Society*. New York: Oxford University Press.

King, Mary C. 1992. "Occupational Segregation by Race and Sex, 1940–88." *Monthly Labor Review* 115:30–36.

———. 1993. "Black Women's Breakthrough Into Clerical Work: An Occupational Tipping Model." Presented at the Society for the Advancement of Socioeconomics meeting, New York.

Kleiman, Carol. 1993. "Women End Up Sacrificing Salary for Children." *Tallahassee Democrat*, March 3, p. D8.

Klerman, Jacob Alex and Arleen Liebowitz. 1999. "Job Continuity Among New Mothers." *Demography* 36:145–55.

Kondo, Dorinne K. 1990. *Crafting Selves*. Chicago: University of Chicago Press.

Konrad, Alison M., J. Edgar Ritchie, Pamela Lieb, and Elizabeth Corrigall. 2000. "Sex Differences and Similarities in Job Attribute Preferences: A Meta Analysis." *Psychological Bulletin* 126:593–641.

Kowaleski, Maryanne and Judith M. Bennett. 1989. "Crafts, Guilds, and Women in the Middle Ages: Fifty Years After Marian K. Dale." *Signs* 14:474–88.

Larson, Reed and Maryse H. Richards. 1994. *Divergent Realities: The Emotional Lives of Mothers, Fathers, and Adolescents*. New York: Basic Books.

Lee, Ching Kwan. 1997. "Factory Regimes of Chinese Capitalism: Different Cultural Logics in Labor Control." Pp. 115–42 in *Ungrounded Empires: The Cultural Politics of Modern Chinese Transnationalism*, edited in A. Ong and D. M. Nonini. New York: Routledge.

Leidner, Robin. 1993. *Fast Food, Fast Talk: Service Work and the Routinization of Everyday Life*. Berkeley: University of California Press.

Lerner, Gerda. 1979. "The Lady and the Mill Girl." Pp. 182–96 in *A Heritage of Her Own*, edited by N. F. Cott and E. H. Pleck. New York: Simon and Schuster.

Levin, Peter. 2001. "Temporality, Work, and Gender on a National Futures Exchange." *Work and Occupations* 28:112–30.

Levine, James A. and Todd L. Pittinsky. 1997. *Working Fathers: New Strategies for Balancing Work and Family*. New York: Addison-Wesley.

Lin, Nan. 2000. "Inequality in Social Capital." *Contemporary Sociology* 29:785–95.

Lorber, Judith. 1992. "Gender." Pp. 748–65 in *Encyclopedia of Sociology*, Vol. 2, edited by E. F. Borgatta and M. L. Borgatta. New York: Macmillan.

———. 1994. *The Paradoxes of Gender*. New Haven, CT: Yale University Press.

Lufkin, Martha. 1997. "Part-Time Work's Around, But Few Do It." *National Law Journal* (Aug. 18): C5.

Major, Brenda. 1989. "Gender Differences in Comparisons and Entitlement: Implications for Comparable Worth." *Journal of Social Issues* 45:99–115.

Major, Brenda and Blythe Forcey. 1985. "Social Comparisons and Pay Evaluations: Preferences for Same-Sex and Same-Job Wage Comparisons." *Journal of Experimental Social Psychology* 21:393–405.

Major, Brenda, Dean B. McFarlin, and Diane Gagnon. 1984. "Overworked and Underpaid: On the Nature of Gender Differences in Personal Entitlement." *Journal of Personality and Social Psychology* 47:1399–412.

Manning, Lori and Vanessa R. Wight. 2000. *Women in the Military: Where They Stand*, 3d ed. Washington, DC: Women's Research and Education Institute.

Margold, Jane A. 1995. "Narratives of Masculinity and Transnational Migration: Filipino Workers in the Middle East." Pp. 274–98 in *Bewitching Women, Pious Men: Gender and Body Politics in Southeast Asia*, edited by A. Ong and M. G. Peletz. Berkeley: University of California Press.

Marini, Margaret M., P. Fan, E. Finley, and Ann Beutel. 1996. "Gender and Job Values." *Sociology of Education* 69:49–65.

Marsden, Peter V. and Elizabeth Gorman. 2001. "Social Networks, Job Changes, and Recruitment." Pp. 467–502 in *Sourcebook of Labor Markets: Evolving*

Structures and Processes, edited by I. Berg and A. L. Kalleberg. New York: Plenum.

Marsden, Peter V., Arne L. Kalleberg, and Cynthia R. Cook. 1993. "Gender Differences in Organizational Commitment: Influences of Work Positions and Family Roles." *Work and Occupations* 20:368–90.

Martin, Joanne. 1990. "Deconstructing Organizational Taboos: The Suppression of Gender Conflict in Organizations." *Organization Science* 1:1–21.

Martin, Patricia Yancy. 2001. "'Mobilizing Masculinities': Women's Experiences of Men at Work." *Organization* 8:587–618.

Mathias, Regina. 1993. "Female Labor in the Japanese Coal-Mining Industry." Pp. 98–121 in *Japanese Women Working,* edited by J. Hunter. New York: Routledge.

Matthaei, Julie A. 1982. *An Economic History of Women in America: Women's Work, the Sexual Division of Labor, and the Development of Capitalism.* New York: Schocken.

Maume, David J., Jr. 1999. "Glass Ceilings and Glass Escalators: Occupational Segregation and Race and Sex Differences in Managerial Promotions." *Work and Occupations* 26:483–509.

May, Martha. 1982. "The Historical Problem of the Family Wage: The Ford Motor Company and the Five Dollar Day." *Feminist Studies* 8:399–419.

McGeehan, Patrick. 1998. "Travelers Seeks to Fix Damage After Smith Barney Sex Case." *Wall Street Journal,* April 10, p. C1.

McGinley, Ann C. 1997. "The Emerging Cronyism Defense and Affirmative Action: A Critical Perspective on the Distinction Between Color Blind and Race-Conscious Decision Making Under Title VII." *Arizona Law Review* 39:1004–59.

McGuire, Gail M. 2000. "Gender, Race, Ethnicity, and Networks: The Factors Affecting the Status of Employees' Network Members." *Work and Occupations* 27:500–523.

McNeil, John. 1992. *Workers With Low Earnings: 1964–1990.* U.S. Bureau of the Census Current Population Reports, Consumer Income, Series P-60, No. 178. Washington, DC: U.S. Government Printing Office.

Merton, Robert K. 1972. "Insiders and Outsiders." *American Journal of Sociology* 78:9–47.

Messner, Michael A. 2000. "Barbie Girls and Sea Monsters: Children Constructing Gender." *Gender & Society* 14:765–84.

Meyerson, Deborah and Joyce Fletcher. 1999. "A Modest Manifesto for Shattering the Glass Ceiling." *Harvard Business Review,* Jan-Feb: 127–36 (reprint R00107).

Mies, Maria. 1998. *Patriarchy and Accumulation on a World Scale: Women in the International Division of Labor.* New York: Zed.

Milkman, Ruth. 1987. *Gender at Work.* Urbana: University of Illinois Press.

———. 1997. *Farewell to the Factory: Auto Workers in the Late Twentieth Century.* Berkeley: University of California Press.

Miller, Shazia R. and James E. Rosenbaum. 1997. "Hiring in a Hobbesian World." *Work and Occupations* 24:498–523.

Moen, Phyllis and Yan Yu. 1999. "Having It All: Overall Work/Life Success in Two-Earner Families." *Research in the Sociology of Work* 7:109–139.

————. 2000. "Effective Work/Life Strategies: Working Couples, Work Conditions, Gender, and Life Quality." *Social Problems* 47:291–326.

Moody, Kim. 2000. "Telephone Strikers Curb Verizon's Culture of Stress." *Labor Notes*, No. 259, Oct., pp. 1, 14.

Moore, Dorothy P. 1999. "Women Entrepreneurs: Approaching a New Millennium" Pp. 371–90 in *Handbook of Gender and Work*, edited by G. N. Powell. Thousand Oaks, CA: Sage.

Moore, Dorothy P. and E. H. Buttner. 1997. *Women Entrepreneurs: Moving Beyond the Glass Ceiling*. Thousand Oaks, CA: Sage.

Moore, Joan and Raquel Pinderhughes. 2001. "The Latino Population: The Importance of Economic Restructuring." Pp. 251–59 in *Race, Class and Gender*, 4th ed., edited by M. L. Andersen and P. H. Collins. Belmont, CA: Wadsworth.

Morgan, Frank. 1999. *Degrees and Other Awards Conferred by Title IV Eligible, Degree-Granting Institutions: 1996–1997*. Table E. National Center for Education Statistics. U.S. Department of Education. Washington, DC: U.S. Government Printing Office.

Morris, Betsy. 1997. "Is Your Family Wrecking Your Career?" *Fortune*, May 17, pp. 70–80.

Moss, Phillip and Chris Tilly. 2001. *Stories Employers Tell: Race, Skill, and Hiring in America*. New York: Russell Sage.

National Committee on Pay Equity. 1991. "After 28 Years, Equal Pay for Equal Work Still Not Achieved." *Newsnotes* 12(1):3.

National Council for Research on Women. 1995. *Sexual Harassment: Research and Resources*, 3d ed. New York: National Council for Research on Women.

————. 2001. *Balancing the Equation: Where Women Are in Science, Engineering, and Technology*. www.ncrw.org.

National Economic Council Interagency Working Group on Social Security. 1998.(Oct. 27). *Women and Retirement Security*. Washington, DC: Social Security Administration. www.ssa.gov/policy/pubs/womenrs.html.

NBC News/*Wall Street Journal*. 2000. Conducted by Hart & Teeter Research Companies. June 14–18.

Nelson, Robert L. and William P. Bridges. 1999. *Legalizing Gender Inequality: Courts, Markets, and Unequal Pay for Women in America*. New York: Cambridge University Press.

Neumark, David. 1996. "Sex Discrimination in the Restaurant Industry: An Audit Study." *Quarterly Journal of Economics* 111:915-41.

New York Times. 1999. "Race and Gender in the Military." November 25, p. A 36.

Nock, Steven L. 1998. *Marriage in Men's Lives*. New York: Oxford University Press.

Nyberg, Anita. 2000. "From Foster Mothers to Child Care Centers: A History of Working Mothers and Child Care in Sweden." *Feminist Economics* 6:5–20.

Oishi, Nana. 2001. *Women on the Move: Globalization, State Policies, and Labor Migration in Asia*. Cambridge, MA: Unpublished doctoral dissertation, Harvard University.

O'Neill, June and Solomon Polachek. 1993. "Why the Gender Gap in Wages Narrowed in the 1980s." *Journal of Labor Economics* 11:205–28.

Oppenheimer, Valerie Kincade. 1968. "The Sex-Labeling of Jobs." *Industrial Relations* 7:219–34.

Orbuch, Terri L. and Sandra L. Eyster. 1997. Division of Household Labor Among Black Couples and White Couples." *Social Forces* 76: 301–332.

Padavic, Irene. 1991. "The Re-Creation of Gender in a Male Workplace." *Symbolic Interaction* 14:279–94.

Padavic, Irene and James D. Orcutt. 1997. "Perceptions of Sexual Harassment in the Florida Legal System: A Comparison of Dominance and Spillover Explanations." *Gender & Society* 11:682–98.

Padavic, Irene and Barbara F. Reskin. 1990. "Men's Behavior and Women's Interest in Blue-Collar Jobs." *Social Problems* 37:613–28.

Parker-Pope, Tara. 1998. "Inside P&G, a Pitch to Keep Women Employees." *Wall Street Journal*, September 9, pp. B1, B6.

Perlow, Leslie. 2000. *Finding Time: How Corporations, Individuals, and Families Can Benefit From New Work Practices.* Ithaca, NY: ILR Press.

Perry, Elissa L., Alison Davis-Blake, and Carol T. Kulik. 1994. "Explaining Gender-Based Selection Decisions: A Synthesis of Contextual and Cognitive Approaches." *Academy of Management Review* 19:786–820.

Petersen, Trond and Laurie A. Morgan. 1995. "Separate and Unequal: Occupation-Establishment Sex Segregation and the Gender Wage Gap." *American Journal of Sociology* 101:329–65.

Pierce, Jennifer. 1995. *Gender Trials: Emotional Lives in Contemporary Law Firms.* Berkeley: University of California Press.

Pinchbeck, Ivy. 1930. *Women Workers and the Industrial Revolution, 1750–1850.* London: Virago.

Polachek, Solomon William. 1981. "Occupational Self-Selection: A Human Capital Approach to Sex Differences in Occupational Structure." *Review of Economics and Statistics* 63:60–69.

Polatnick, M. Rivka. 2000. "Working Parents: Issues for the Next Decades." *National Forum* 80:1–4. http://workingfamilies.berkeley.edu/papers. polatnick.pdf.

Powell, Gary N. 1999. "Reflections on the Glass Ceiling: Recent Trends and Future Prospects." Pp. 325–46 in *Handbook of Gender and Work*, edited by G. N. Powell. Thousand Oaks, CA: Sage.

Presser, Harriet B. 1994. "Employment Schedules Among Dual-Earner Spouses and the Division of Household Labor by Gender." *American Sociological Review* 59:348–64.

———. 2000. "Nonstandard Work Schedules and Marital Instability." *Journal of Marriage and the Family* 62:93–110.

Prokos, Anastasia and Irene Padavic. 2002. "'There Oughtta Be a Law Against Bitches': Masculinity Lessons in Police Academy Training." *Gender, Work, and Organization* 9(4):438–58.

Prugl, Elisabeth and Eileen Boris. 1996. *Homeworkers in Global Perspective: Invisible No More.* New York: Routledge.

Pyle, Jean L. 1999. "Third World Women and Global Restructuring." Pp. 81–104 in *Handbook of the Sociology of Gender*, edited by J. Chafetz. New York: Kluwer Academic/Plenum.

Pyle, Jean L. 2001. "Sex, Maids, and Export Processing: Risks and Reasons for Gendered Global Production Networks." *International Journal of Politics, Culture, and Society* 15:55–76.

Quadagno, Jill and Catherine Fobes. 1995. "The Welfare-State and the Cultural Reproduction of Gender: Making Good Girls and Boys in the Job Corps." *Social Problems* 42:171–90.

Rab, Sara. 2001. *Sex Discrimination in Restaurant Hiring Practices.* Philadelphia: Unpublished master's thesis: University of Pennsylvania.

Radcliffe Public Policy Center. 2000. "Work-Life Survey Results Released." *Perspectives.* Cambridge, MA: Radcliffe Public Policy Center. Spring.

Ragins, Belle R. 1999. "Gender and Mentoring Relationships: A Review and Research Agenda for the Next Decade." Pp. 347–70 in *Handbook of Gender and Work,* edited by G. N. Powell, Thousand Oaks, CA: Sage.

Ramamurthy, Priti. 1996. "Women, Work, Patriarchy, and Development in India." Pp. 471–74 in *Woman and Work: A Handbook,* edited by P. J. Dubeck and D. Borman. New York: Garland.

Reid, Lori L. 1998. "Devaluing Women and Minorities: The Effects of Race/Ethnic and Sex Composition of Occupations on Wage Levels." *Work and Occupations* 25:511–36.

Reid-Keene, Jennifer. 2001. *Beyond Role Models: Workers' Family-Work Adjustments and Perceptions of Work-Family Balance.* Tallahassee, FL: Unpublished doctoral dissertation, The Florida State University.

Reskin, Barbara F. 1988. "Bringing the Men Back In: Sex Differentiation and the Devaluation of Women's Work." *Gender & Society* 2:58–81.

———. 1998. *The Realities of Affirmative Action in Employment.* Washington, DC: American Sociological Association.

———. 2000. "The Proximate Causes of Discrimination: Research Agenda for the Twenty-First Century." *Contemporary Sociology* 29:319–29.

———. 2001. "Employment Discrimination and Its Remedies." Pp. 567–99 in *Sourcebook of Labor Markets: Evolving Structures and Processes,* edited by I. Berg and A. L. Kalleberg. New York: Plenum.

———. 2002. "Retheorizing Employment Discrimination and Its Remedies." Pp. 218–244 in *New Directions in Economic Sociology,* edited by M. F. Guillen, R. Collins, P. England, and M. Meyer. New York: Russell Sage.

Reskin, Barbara F., Lowell L. Hargens, and Deborah J. Merritt. 2001. "Explaining Sex Differences in the Labor Market for Legal Academe." Presented at the Annual Meeting of the American Sociological Association, Anaheim, CA.

Reskin, Barbara F. and Heidi Hartmann. 1986. *Women's Work, Men's Work: Sex Segregation on the Job.* Washington, DC: National Academy.

Reskin, Barbara F. and Debra McBrier. 2000. "Why Not Ascription? Organizations' Employment of Male and Female Managers." *American Sociological Review* 25:335–61.

Reskin, Barbara F. and Irene Padavic. 1999. "Sex, Race, and Ethnic Inequality in U.S. Workplaces." Pp. 343–74 in *Handbook of the Sociology of Gender,* edited by J. S. Chafetz. New York: Plenum.

Reskin, Barbara F. and Patricia A. Roos. 1990. *Job Queues, Gender Queues: Explaining Women's Inroads Into Male Occupations.* Philadelphia: Temple University Press.

Reskin, Barbara F. and Catherine E. Ross. 1992. "Jobs, Authority, and Earnings Among Managers: The Continuing Significance of Sex." *Work and Occupations* 19:342–65.

Rhode, Deborah L. 2001. *Unfinished Agenda: Women and the Legal Profession.* Chicago, IL: American Bar Association, Commission on Women in the Profession.

Ricks, Thomas E. 1998. "Defense Chief Won't Segregate Sexes in Basic Training, Despite Proposals." *Wall Street Journal*, March 17.

Ridgeway, Cecilia and Shelley J. Correll. 2000. "Limiting Inequality Through Interaction: The End(s) of Gender." *Contemporary Sociology* 29:110–20.

Ridgeway, Cecilia L. and Lynn Smith-Lovin. 1999. "Gender and Interaction." Pp. 247–74 in *Handbook of the Sociology of Gender*, edited by J. Chafetz. New York: Kluwer Academic/Plenum.

Risman, Barbara J. 1998. *Gender Vertigo: American Families in Transition.* New Haven, CT: Yale University Press.

Robertson, Nan. 1992. *The Girls in the Balcony.* New York: Random House.

Robinson, John P. and G. Godbey. 1999. *Time for Life: The Surprising Ways Americans Use Their Time.* University Park, PA: Pennsylvania State University Press.

Robinson, John P. and Melissa A. Milkie, 1997. "Dances with Dust Bunnies: Housecleaning in America." *American Demographics* 59:37–40.

Rogers, Jackie Krasas. 2000. *Temps: The Many Faces of the Changing Workplace.* Ithaca, NY: Cornell/ILR.

Roos, Patricia A. and Mary L. Gatta. 1999. "The Gender Gap in Earnings." Pp. 95—123 in *Handbook of Gender and Work*, edited by G. N. Powell. Thousand Oaks, CA: Sage.

Rosenfeld, Rachel A. and Arne L. Kalleberg. 1991. "A Cross-National Comparison of the Gender Gap in Income." *American Journal of Sociology* 96:69–106.

Roush, Chris. 1997. "Lawyer's Skill a Major Tool in Home Depot Settlement." *The Atlanta Journal and Constitution*, September 23.

Rubin, Gayle. 1975. "The Traffic in Women: Notes on the 'Political Economy' of Sex." Pp. 157–209 in *Toward an Anthropology of Women*, edited by R. Reiter. New York: Monthly Review.

Ruggles, Steven and Matthew Sobek. 1997. *Integrated Public Use Microdata Series: Version 2.0.* Minneapolis, MN: Historical Census Projects, University of Minnesota. www.ipums.umn.edu.

Ruhm, Christopher and Jacqueline L. Teague. 1997. "Parental Leave Policies in Europe and North America." Pp. 133–56 in *Gender and Family Issues in the Work Place*, edited by F. D. Blau and R. G. Ehrenberg. New York: Russell Sage.

Ryan, Mary P. 1983. *Womanhood in America*, 3d ed. New York: Franklin Watts.

Safilios-Rothschild, Constantina. 1990. "Socio-Economic Determinants of the Outcomes of Women's Income-Generation in Developing Countries."

Pp. 221–28 in *Women, Employment, and the Family in the International Division of Labour*, edited by S. Stichter and J. L. Parpart. Philadelphia: Temple University Press.

Salancik, Gerald R., and Jeffrey Pfeffer. 1978. "Uncertainty, Secrecy, and the Choice of Similar Others." *Social Psychology* 41:246–55.

Sanchez, Laura and Elizabeth Thomson. 1997. "Becoming Mothers and Fathers: Parenthood, Gender, and the Division of Labor." *Gender & Society* 11:747–72.

Sanders, L. H. 1943. "Efficiency of Women Employees." *Mass Transportation: City Transit's Industry-Wide Magazine*. 39(7) (July): 244, 257.

Saso, Mary. 1990. *Women in the Japanese Workplace*. London: Hilary Shipman.

Schafer, Sarah. 2000. "Many Workers Say Timeout to Overtime." *Washington Post*, Sept. 4.

Schmitt, Frederika and Patricia Y. Martin. 1999. "Unobtrusive Mobilization by an Institutionalized Rape Crisis Center: All We Do Comes From the Victims." *Gender & Society* 13:364–84.

Schultz, Vicki. 1998. "Reconceptualizing Sexual Harassment." *The Yale Law Journal* 107(6):1682–1805.

Scott, Joan Wallach and Louise A. Tilly. 1975. "Women's Work and the Family in Nineteenth Century Europe." *Comparative Studies in Society and History* 17:36–64.

Seager, Joni. 1997. *The State of Women in the World Atlas*. New York: Penguin.

Segal, Mady W. 1995. "Women's Military Roles Cross-Nationally: Past, Present, and Future." *Gender & Society* 9:757–75.

Sen, Gita. 2000. "Gender Mainstreaming in Finance Ministries." *World Development* 28(7).

Sessa, Valerie I. 1992. "Managing Diversity at the Xerox Corporation: Balanced Workforce Goals and Caucus Groups." Pp. 37–64 in *Diversity in the Workplace*, edited by S. E. Jackson and Associates. New York: Guilford.

Shelton, Beth Ann. 1999. "Gender and Unpaid Work." Pp. 375–89 in *Handbook of the Sociology of Gender*, edited by J. S. Chafetz. New York: Kluwer Academic/Plenum.

Shorter, Edward. 1975. *The Making of the Modern Family*. New York: Basic Books.

Skolnick, Arlene. 1991. *Embattled Paradise: The American Family in an Age of Uncertainty*. New York: Basic Books.

Smith, Dan. 1999. *The State of the World Atlas*. New York: Penguin Putnam.

Smith, Jane I. 1994. "Women in Islam." Pp. 303–325 in *Today's Woman in World Religions*, edited by A. Sharma. Albany: SUNY Press.

Smith, Randall. 1999. "Study Finds Diversity Is Lacking at Top Levels of Securities Firms." *Wall Street Journal*, April 20.

Smith, Ryan and James R. Elliott. 2002. "Does Ethnic Concentration Influence Employees' Access to Authority? An Examination of Contemporary Urban Labor Markets." *Social Forces* 81:255–280.

Smith, Shirley J. 1985. "Revised Worklife Tables Reflect 1979–80 Experience." *Monthly Labor Review* 108:23–30.

Sorensen, Annemette. 2001. "Gender Equality in Earnings at Work and at Home." Pp. 98–115 in *Nordic Welfare States in the European Context*, edited by M. Kautto, J. Fritzell, B. Hvinden, J. Kvist, and H. Uusitalo. New York: Routledge.

Sorensen, Elaine. 1989. "Measuring the Effect of Occupational Sex and Race Composition on Earnings." Pp. 49–69 in *Pay Equity: Empirical Inquiries*, edited by R. T. Michael, H. I. Hartmann, and B. O'Farrell. Washington, DC: National Academy.

Spaeth, Joe L. 1989. *Determinants of Promotion in Different Types of Organizations*. Unpublished manuscript. Urbana: University of Illinois.

Steinberg, Ronnie J. 1990. "The Social Construction of Skill." *Work and Occupations* 17:449–82.

Stender et al. v. Lucky. 1992. "Findings of Fact and Conclusion of Law," *Federal Reporter*, vol. 803, Fed. Supplement, p. 259.

Stockard, Jean. 1999. "Gender Socialization." Pp. 215–28 in *Handbook of the Sociology of Gender*, edited by J. S. Chafetz. New York: Kluwer Academic/Plenum.

Stombler, Mindy and Irene Padavic. 1999. "Sister Acts: Accommodation and Resistance to Men's Domination in Fraternity Little Sister Programs." *Social Problems* 44:257–75.

Sturm, Susan. 2001. "Second Generation Employment Discrimination: A Structural Approach." *Columbia Law Review* 101:458–568.

Sullins, Paul. 2000. "The Stained Glass Ceiling: Career Attainment for Women Clergy." *Sociology of Religion* 61:243–266

Swerdlow, Marian. 1989. "Men's Accommodations to Women Entering a Nontraditional Occupation: A Case of Rapid Transit Operatives." *Gender & Society* 3:373–87.

Swoboda, Frank. 1998. "US Airways Settles 'Glass Ceiling' Case." *Washington Post*, December, p. E2.

Tallichet, Suzanne E. 2000. "Barriers to Women's Advancement in Underground Coal Mining." *Rural Sociology* 65: 234–52.

Tentler, Leslie Woodcock. 1979. *Wage-Earning Women: Industrial Work and Family Life in the United States, 1900–1930*. New York: Oxford University Press.

Tetlock, Philip M. 1992. "The Impact of Accountability on Judgment and Choice: Towards a Social Contingency Model." Pp. 331–76 in *Advances in Experimental Social Psychology 23*, edited by M. P. Zanna. San Diego: Academic Press.

Thomas, David A. and Robin J. Ely. 1996. "Making Differences Matter: A New Paradigm for Managing Diversity." *Harvard Business Review*, September-October, pp. 79–90.

Thomas, Paulette. 2000. "At 'Camp,' Women Learn to Pitch Deals to Investors." *Wall Street Journal*, July 18.

Tiano, Susan. 1994. *Patriarchy on the Line: Labor, Gender, and Ideology in the Mexican Maquila Industry*. Philadelphia: Temple University Press.

Tomaskovic-Devey, Donald and Sheryl Skaggs. 1999. "Degendered Jobs? Organizational Processes and Gender Segregated Employment." *Research in Social Stratification and Mobility* 17:139–172.

Treiman, Donald J. and Heidi I. Hartmann. 1981. *Women, Work, and Wages*. Washington, DC: National Academy.

Trentham, Susan and Laurie Larwood. 1998. "Gender Discrimination and the Workplace: An Examination of Rational Bias Theory." *Sex Roles* 38:1–28.

United Nations. 1999. *1999 World Survey on the Role of Women in Development: Globalization, Gender and Work.* New York: UN Division for the Advancement of Women.

———. 2000. *The World's Women 2000: Trends and Statistics.* New York: United Nations.

United Nations Population Fund. 2000. "The State of World Population 2000." www.unfpa.org/swp2000/english/index.htm.

University of California at Los Angeles/Korn-Ferry International. 1993. *Decade of the Executive Woman.* Los Angeles: University of California at Los Angeles.

U.S. Bureau of Labor Statistics. 1998. "Issues in Labor Statistics: Employer-Sponsored Childcare Benefits." Summary 98-9, August. Washington, DC: U.S. Government Printing Office.

———. 1999a. "Fatal Occupational Injuries by Worker Characteristics and Event or Exposure, 1999." Census of Fatal Occupational Injuries. August 2000. Table A-6. http://stats.bls.gov/special.requests/ocwc/oshwc/cfoi/cftb0127.pdf

———. 1999b. "National Longitudinal Survey of Youth 1979 Cohort, 1979-1998 (rounds 1-18)" [computer file]. Columbus, OH: Center for Human Resource Research, the Ohio State University.

———. 1999c. "Employee Benefits in Small Private Establishments, 1996." Bulletin 2507. Washington, DC: U.S. Government Printing Office.

———. 1999d. "Employee Benefits in Medium and Large Private Establishments, 1996." Bulletin 2517. Washington, DC: U.S. Government Printing Office.

U.S. Census Bureau. 1972. "U.S. Census of Population, 1970." Subject Reports, 7C, Occupational Characteristics. Washington, DC: Census Bureau.

———. 1975. "Historical Statistics of the United States: Colonial Times to 1970." Part I. Washington, DC: U.S. Government Printing Office.

———. 1982a. "Census of Population and Housing, 1980: Public Use Microdata Samples U.S." [machine-readable data files, prepared by the Bureau of the Census.] Washington, DC: Census Bureau.

———. 1982b. Current Population Reports. Series P-60, No. 132. "Money Income of Households, Families, and Persons in the United States: 1980." Washington, DC: U.S. Government Printing Office.

———. 1983. Current Population Reports. Series P-60, No. 137. "Money Income of Households, Families, and Persons in the United States: 1981." Washington, DC: U.S. Government Printing Office.

———. 1988. Current Population Reports. Series P-60, No. 159. "Money Income of Households, Families, and Persons in the United States: 1986." Washington, DC: U.S. Government Printing Office.

———. 1991. Current Population Reports. Series P-60, No. 174. "Money Income of Households, Families, and Persons in the United States: 1990." Washington, DC: U.S. Government Printing Office.

———. 1996. Current Population Reports P60-193. "Money Income in the United States: 1995." Washington, DC: U.S. Government Printing Office.

———. 1998. Microdata from the Annual Demographic Survey of the March 1998 Current Population Surveys.

———. 1999. Microdata from the Annual Demographic Survey of the March 1998 Current Population Surveys.

———. 2000a. Microdata from the Annual Demographic Survey of the March 1998 Current Population Surveys.

———. 2000b. Current Population Reports, P60-209. "Money Income in the United States 1999." Washington, DC: U.S. Government Printing Office. www.census.gov/prod/2000pubs/p60-209.pdf.

———. 2000c. *Statistical Abstract of the United States.* Washington, DC: U.S. Government Printing Office.

———. 2000d. "PPL Table 11B: Average Weekly Child Care Expenditures by Employed Mothers of Children Under 5, Fall 1995." Survey of Income and Program Participation.

———. 2001. "1997 Revenues for Women-Owned Businesses Show Continued Growth, Census Bureau Reports." www.census.gov/press-release/www/2001/cb01-61.html.

U.S. Department of Defense. 1999. "Selected Manpower Statistics Fiscal Year 1999." Washington, DC: DOD Washington Headquarters Service, Directorate for Information, Operations, and Reports. http://web1.whs.osd.mil/mmid/m01/fy99/m01fy99.pdf.

U.S. Employment Standards Administration. 1997. "OFCCP Glass Ceiling Initiative: Are There Cracks in the Ceiling?" June. Office of Federal Contract Compliance Programs. www.dol.gov/dol/esa/public/media/reports/ofccp/gccover.htm.

———. 2000. "Birmingham, Alabama Bank Enters into EEO Settlement with U.S. Labor Department." Office of Federal Contract Compliance Programs. www/dol.gov/dol/esa/public/media/press/ofccp/of00314.htm

U.S. Equal Employment Opportunity Commission. 1999. "Charge Statistics FY 1992 through FY 1998." www.eeoc.gov/stats/charges.html.

———. 2000a. "EEOC Settles Pay Discrimination Suit for $450,000 Against Nationwide Trucking Company." www.eeoc.gov/press/12-7-00.html.

———. 2000b. "EEOC and George Junior Republic Settle Sex-Based Wage Discrimination Lawsuit." www.eeoc.gov/press/7-26-00.html.

———. 2001a. "Sexual Harassment Charges EEOC and FEPAs Combined: FY 1999–FY 2000." www.eeoc.gov/stats/ harass.html.

———. 2001b. "Job Patterns for Minorities and Women in Private Industry (EEO1)." www.eeoc.gov/stats.

U.S. Government Accounting Office. 1995. "Progress of Women and Minority Criminal Investigators at Selected Agencies." April. Washington, DC: U.S. GAO.

———. 2002. "A New Look Through the Glass Ceiling: Where Are the Women?" January. Washington, DC: U.S. GAO.

U.S. Merit Systems Protection Board. 1996. "Fair and Equitable Treatment: A Progress Report on Minority Employment in the Federal Government." Washington, DC: U.S. Merit Systems Protection Board.

U.S. Office of Personnel Management. 1999. "Women in the Federal Government: A Statistical Profile." apps.opm.gov/publications/pages/default_search.htm.

U.S. Office of Personnel Management. 2001. "Demographic Profile of the Federal Workforce, 2000 edition." Sept. 7. ww.opm.gov/feddata/demograph/ demograph.htm.

U.S. Women's Bureau. 1993. "Facts on Working Women." Report No. 93-2. Washington, DC: U.S. Government Printing Office.

———. 1998. "Facts on Working Women. Work and Elder Care: Facts for Caregivers and Their Employers." No. 98-1. May. www.dol.gov/dol/wb/ public/wb_pubs/elderc.htm.

———. 2000. "Earnings Differences Between Women and Men." www.dol.gov/dol/wb/public/wb_pubs/wagegap2000.htm.

Valenze, Deborah. 1995. *The First Industrial Woman*. New York: Oxford University Press.

Waldfogel, Jane. 1999a. "Family Leave Coverage in the 1990s." *Monthly Labor Review* 122:13–21.

———. 1999b. "The Impact of the Family and Medical Leave Act." *Journal of Policy Analysis and Management* 18:281–302.

Walsh, Mary Williams. 2000. "Where G.E. Falls Short: Diversity at the Top." *New York Times*, Sept. 3, p. C1.

West, Candace and Don H. Zimmerman. 1987. "Doing Gender." *Gender & Society* 1:125–51.

Weston, Kath. 1990. "Production as Means, Production as Metaphor: Women's Struggle to Enter the Trades." Pp. 137–51 in *Uncertain Terms: Negotiating Gender in American Culture*, edited by F. Ginsburg and A. L. Tsing. Boston: Beacon.

Westover, Belinda. 1986. "'To Fill the Kids' Tummies': The Lives and Work of Colchester Tailoresses, 1880–1918." Pp. 54–75 in *Our Work, Our Lives, Our Words*, edited by L. Davidoff and B. Westover. London: Macmillan.

White, Jane. 1992. *A Few Good Women: Breaking the Barriers to Top Management*. Englewood Cliffs, NJ: Prentice Hall.

Wilkinson, R. Keith. 1998. "Employment of Scientists and Engineers Reaches 3.2 Million in 1995." Data Brief NSF 98-325. Washington, DC: National Science Foundation. www.nsf.gov/srs/databrf/sdb98325.pdf.

Wilkinson-Weber, Clare M. 1999. *Embroidering Lives: Women's Work and Skill in the Lucknow Embroidery Industry*. Albany: SUNY Press.

Williams, Christine L. 1995. *Still a Man's World: Men Who Do "Women's Work."* Berkeley, CA: University of California Press.

Williams, Joan. 2000. *Unbending Gender: Why Family and Work Conflict and What to Do About It*. New York: Oxford University Press.

Wilson, Franklin D. and Lawrence L. Wu. 1993. "A Comparative Analysis of Labor Force Activities of Ethnic Populations." Center for Demography and Ecology Working Paper No. 93-01. Madison: University of Wisconsin.

Working Women. 1981. *In Defense of Affirmative Action: Taking the Profit Out of Discrimination*. Cleveland.

World Bank. 2000. World Development Indicators, 2000. www.worldbank.org/ data/wdi2000/pdfs/tab1_3.pdf.

Yarrow, Michael. 1987. "Class and Gender in the Developing Consciousness of Appalachian Coal Miners." Presented to the fifth UMIST-ASTON Annual Conference on Organization and Control of the Labor Process, April 22–24, Manchester, England.

Glossary/Index

A

Academia, sex gap in authority in, 108-109

Accountability, for employment decisions, 82-83

Accounting profession
  sex gap in authority in, 116-117, 118-119
  sex segregation in, 67, 76

Acker, Joan, 6, 7, 11, 14, 152

Affirmative action requirement that employers make special efforts to recruit, hire, and promote groups that have been victims of past discrimination, 80
  employers' implementation of, 81
  enforcement of, 80-81, 144
  judicial decisions on, 119
  and personnel practices, 80
  reducing sex segregation, 91

Africa
  labor force participation rate in, 32
  occupational sex segregation in, 71
  sexual division of labor in, 8-9

African Americans
  in agricultural work, 25
  in clerical work, 63, 68
  domestic division of labor among, 160
  in domestic service, x, 74
  labor force participation of, 27-28
  men's labor force participation among, 28
  occupational segregation by race and sex, 62, 68, 69(table), 73-74
  pay gap, 123-125, 135, 141
  promotion and authority, compared to other groups, 98, 99, 102-103, 105, 113
  sex stereotypes about, 42-43

sexual division of labor in sharecropping, 25
sexual division of labor under slavery, 8, 60
wartime employment opportunities, 62-63, 68
women's labor force participation among, 24, 27, 25, 36(n4)

Agricultural work
  effect of mechanization on women's work, 39
  Mexican immigrants in, 25, 63
  pay gap in, 122
  sexual division of labor among minority women in, 25
  sexual division of labor in colonial U.S. in, 60
  sexual division of labor in preindustrial Europe in, 17-18

Airline industry, 137, 155
  male flight attendants, 50

Albanese, Patricia, 50, 79

America, North
  occupational sex segregation in, 71
  sex difference in labor force participation rate, 32
  sex gap in authority in, 102

American Indians, women's labor force participation among, 28

Amott, Teresa L., 24, 25, 28, 36(n4), 61, 68, 69, 94(n2), 124

Anker, Richard, 7-8, 57, 59, 70, 95(n5), 128

Antidiscrimination laws, enforcement of, 13, 48, 63-64, 76, 80

Apprenticeship programs, 52
  unions' exclusion of women from, 45, 52

Artisan craft worker who produces a variety of products from scratch, 19

CPSIA information can be obtained
at www.ICGtesting.com
Printed in the USA
FFOW03n1627200116
20604FF